W9-BKU-998

MURDEROUS MINDS

MURDEROUS MINDS

Exploring the Criminal Psychopathic Brain: Neurological Imaging and the Manifestation of Evil

Dean A. Haycock, Ph.D.

PEGASUS BOOKS
NEW YORK LONDON

MURDEROUS MINDS

Pegasus Books LLC
80 Broad Street, 5th Floor
New York, NY 10004

First Pegasus Books cloth edition March 2014

Interior design by Maria Fernandez

Library of Congress Cataloging-in-Publication Data is available.

ISBN: 978-1-60598-498-8

10 9 8 7 6 5 4 3 2 1

Printed in the United States of America
Distributed by W. W. Norton & Company

For Marie E. Culver

CONTENTS

Preface

The neuroscientists and psychologists who are leading the way in the study of psychopathic personalities describe their fascinating research subjects by referring to the traits that distinguish them from 99 percent of the population. Some of these traits are related to emotional deficits such as lack of deep emotional attachments to other people and lack of empathy and guilt. Some traits like narcissism and superficial charm are related to how psychopaths interact with others. Their dishonesty, manipulativeness, recklessness and risk-taking activities are representative of their impulsive and antisocial behaviors.

The members of the Society for the Scientific Study of Psychopathy caution that "Although psychopathy is a risk factor for physical aggression, it is by no means synonymous with it. In contrast to individuals with psychotic disorders, most psychopaths are in touch with reality and seemingly rational. Psychopathic individuals are found at elevated rates in prisons and jails, but can be found in community settings as well."[1] The Society makes it clear that psychopathy is not the same thing as violence, serial killing, psychosis, mental illness, or what the American Psychiatric Association calls antisocial personality disorder.

Murderous Minds is about a subgroup of psychopaths called criminal psychopaths. They share traits with non-criminal psychopaths, but they should not be equated with them. "Criminal psychopathy refers instead to a meaner, more aggressively disinhibited conception of psychopathy that explicitly entails persistent and sometimes serious criminal behavior," psychologist Jennifer Skeem, Ph.D., and her co-authors declared in 2011.[2]

Criminal psychopaths are the only subgroup of psychopath for which there exists enough reproducible neurobiological data to begin to get a preliminary idea of how their brain structure and function relates to their antisocial behavior. This is in large part because many criminal psychopaths are currently in prison and thus researchers have had better access to this captive subgroup of the psychopathic population compared to non-criminal psychopaths, who are not incarcerated and therefore free citizens. Spread out geographically, many in this subgroup are more difficult to identify, test, and recruit or have no interest or desire to submit their brains to study. But when the brains of functional or successful psychopaths have been studied as extensively as the brains of their criminal counterparts, they, too, will deserve a book devoted to them.

Foreword

The world of the criminal psychopath is at once creepy and fascinating. You read about criminal psychopaths in the news, you see them portrayed in movies, you read about them in books. They do terrible things, horrific things. They are capable of murder, robbery, torture, and rape and they can do it all without a hint of remorse or a touch of empathy. And you wonder: how can these people be so evil?

You hope you do not run across them, but could you recognize a psychopath if you met one? Given that an estimated 1 out of 100 adults is a psychopath, the chances are in fact quite good that you have met some of them without realizing who or what they were. You may even have married one (psychopaths can be incredibly charming when they want or need to be). Have you joked at work that your boss is a psychopath? That could actually be the case—many non-criminal psychopaths are not violent. They can control their antisocial impulses and even attain mixed success as business executives. They do not fret over making difficult decisions that have a severe negative impact on their employees. They simply do what is best for themselves.

Does someone become a psychopath, or is one born a psychopath? Can psychopathy be treated or cured? Are the brains of psychopaths physically different from "normal" brains? If so, can society hold psychopaths to be morally responsible for what they have done? Can modern neuroscience identify psychopathic brains early on, before a psychopath has a chance to commit a crime? If so, should those thus identified be incarcerated before they have a chance to do something terrible?

Neuroscientists can, in fact, use brain-imaging techniques to identify physical differences in the brains of psychopaths vs. "normal" people. Further, structural abnormalities seen in specific brain regions in psychopaths are thought to underlie the striking emotional abnormalities that can be measured by psychological testing.

At first glance, the task—of understanding how abnormalities in specific brain areas arise, and how these abnormalities account for psychopathic behavior—is daunting. In this book, however, Dr. Dean Haycock has taken extremely complex material and rendered it readily digestible. One does not have to be a psychologist or a neuroscientist to understand this book. At the same time, the science has not been made more simple than necessary, and the topics covered have such breadth and depth that the book is also appropriate for professionals in the field. The information presented is evidence-based, and one cannot find a single example of information that is simply hearsay or otherwise unsubstantiated; the book is thoroughly documented with complete reference lists for each chapter. Moreover, Dr. Haycock has taken the extra steps of interviewing several of the major players in the field and accurately presenting their viewpoints. Finally, Dr. Haycock is a master at writing exciting prose to create a science-based book that is actually a "page-turner." From psychopathic Eskimos to mass-murdering high school students, the true nature of the criminal psychopath is explored here. And that exploration is such that it leads us not only to a better understanding of the criminal psychopath, but to a better understanding of ourselves.

—Charles C. Ouimet, Ph.D.,
Professor and Faculty Scholar in Neuroscience,
Florida State University College of Medicine,
Tallahassee, Florida

Introduction

Having a murderous mind is not always the same thing as being a murderer or even having the intention of killing. A glance into the Merriam-Webster dictionary confirms it. The primary definition of *murderous* is indeed "having the purpose or capability of murder" and "characterized by or causing murder or bloodshed." This accurately describes the psychopaths who fill the pages of true-crime books and are featured in news or infotainment stories. Criminals who lack a conscience, the sadistic psychopathic serial killers like Ted Bundy and John Wayne Gacy, the unfeeling psychopaths like Richard Kuklinsky who kill for personal gain, the school shooter Eric Harris, the rapist and murderer Brian Dugan, and the armed robber who kills without remorse to keep from being captured and then blames the victim, all have the *purpose* of murder.

The secondary and, in this context, more relevant definition of *murderous* is "having the ability or power to overwhelm: devastating." Without a conscience, and with a strong impulse to dominate and victimize, criminal psychopaths and some psychopaths who have avoided encounters with the law routinely leave their victims feeling overwhelmed and devastated. Consider the following synonyms of murderous. After marrying or being conned by a psychopath, many victims have gained firsthand experience with most of them: brutal, cruel, hard, harsh, oppressive, rough, searing, and, most intriguingly, inhuman. These offenses may involve more psychological than physical abuse, but by the dictionary definition they are murderous nonetheless. As victims know painfully well, their tormentors have the ability or power to overwhelm and devastate.

The odds are that any encounter you have with a psychopath will not result in a murder. For every psychopathic serial killer, there are literally millions of psychopaths who don't kill. It is certain, however, that any encounter you have with a criminal psychopath will be an encounter with a potentially murderous mind, in the sense of being capable, or having the ability or the power to overwhelm and devastate. The con man who serially seduces women and depletes their bank accounts, and the businessman who disappears with his partner's assets and destroys their company, use their power to overwhelm and devastate their victims. If these individuals, it is important to stress, are *strongly* psychopathic, then they are still distinct from individuals who have *some* psychopathic traits. This is a distinction that confuses many readers and even some psychologists. It stems from the use and misuse of the word "psychopath" to describe everyone from the rare psychopathic serial killer to the ambitious co-worker who will befriend you and undermine you to get ahead at work. There is a range of psychopathy and psychopathic behavior.

Some psychologists point out that many psychopaths or people with significant psychopathic features do not victimize others. "Most psychopaths are not violent, and most violent people are not psychopaths," Scott Lilienfeld, Ph.D., and Hal Arkowitz, Ph.D., said in their 2007 essay "What 'Psychopath' Means."[1] Yet, in 2011, neuroscientist Kent Kiehl, Ph.D., and Judge Morris Hoffman estimated that "approximately 93% of adult male psychopaths in the United States are in prison, jail, parole, or probation."[2] Then, also in 2011, Lilienfeld and his co-authors stated that criminal psychopaths are widely regarded as meaner and "more aggressively disinhibited" than other psychopaths.[3] It is hard to reconcile these claims. They stem, in large part, from the use of different tools used to measure psychopathy. Some researchers rely on newer self-report tests to identify psychopaths, while others rely on the Hare Psychopathy Checklist. This is a naming problem, and it is a serious one. Imagine using two pieces of string of slightly different lengths to measure out two standard units, each based on the length of one of the bits of string. Now call both standard units "inches." You can see the problem. Two people using different "inches" will get different true lengths when measuring something. Until problems like this are resolved, the public will continue to be misinformed and confused by discussions of "psychopaths." I have seen some scientists roll their eyes when the Press is mentioned because they are unimpressed with the sloppiness in some science-related stories. But sometimes members of the Press might be forgiven for rolling their eyes a bit when they discover that "inches" don't measure up.

In any case, we know even less about non-violent psychopaths than we know about criminal psychopaths. The only reason this book does not discuss non-criminal or "successful" psychopaths more than it does is because criminal psychopaths have provided the vast majority of data about the psychopathic brain, which, preliminary findings suggest, may be different in criminal and non-criminal psychopaths.

The phenomenon of psychopathy is multifaceted and complex. It consists of a variety of personality and behavioral traits that vary in degree in different individuals. The frequency of the presence of these traits in individuals is normally distributed throughout members of our society. Some people score very low in psychopathic traits, some score in the middle, and some score very high. The chance that an abnormality in one part of the brain accounts for the presence of very high-scoring psychopaths is small. So too are the chances that psychopathic behavior can be traced to one or a few genes. Thinning of the brain's cerebral cortex, sluggish amygdala, silent frontal lobes, or inheritance of genes linked to violent behavior by themselves are still not enough to explain in detail the presence of this fascinating subpopulation of humans who live among us.

People have been proposing biological causes of criminality for over a century, often citing physical features such as the shape of the skull, size of the ears and jaw, and other unsubstantiated "signs" and "evidence" that leaves us shaking our heads today. One of the remarkable achievements of modern neuroscience is its ability to routinely show us living brains at work. Functional magnetic resonance imaging, or fMRI, allows us to see the flow of blood to large clusters of brain cells as they deal with an increased workload in response to a specific mental challenge. The purpose of neuronal activity is to support communication between brain cells—which occurs at points of contact called synapses—and to establish neuronal circuits that underlie our behavior, both good and bad. "Neurological and mental disorders are going to be about synaptic function. We know this. They're going to be about failure of communications between brain cells,"[4] Baylor College of Medicine professor of neurology, molecular and human genetics, and pediatrics Huda Zoghbi, M.D., told Kayt Sukel of the Dana Foundation in 2013.

Unfortunately, telling someone that their occipital frontal cortex or amygdala is sluggish compared to others when performing certain tasks does not yet provide an explanation of why someone has no conscience or otherwise behaves in an antisocial manner. We now know that personalities and personality disorders, like the majority of mental disorders, cannot be traced to one cause or factor, to bumps on the skull or to poor parenting. They are the result of complex processes that include genetics, brain development, and neurobiology, which are then influenced by experience and the environment. A person with brain-activity patterns identical to those seen in the brains of psychopaths may not be a psychopath. A person with genetic traits associated with violent behavior may not be a psychopath. A person who was abused as a child, or who was exposed to violence, may not turn into a psychopath. But when these factors are combined in one person, watch out. All the ingredients for creating a psychopath are then present.

A secondary goal of this book is to provide readers with some background so they might answer a few questions they have about the psychopathic brain. But its major purpose is to prepare readers to be more critical of news stories and even scientific claims about psychopathy[5] and other intriguing topics in neuroscience. Ideally, it will be a starting point for further exploration into neuroscience and the brain using a fascinating subject—people who lack a conscience and empathy—as an introduction.

We are far from having a complete picture of how the brain works, or even how its parts are connected. "Most people really want to understand the mind, not the brain," Allison Gopnik, Ph.D., pointed out in a *Wall Street Journal* column.[6] The brain is the physical organ and the center of the nervous system, whereas the mind is the sum total of the brain's product: awareness, perception, emotion, memory, reasoning, thought, and imagination. The University of California at Berkeley psychology professor describes the last twenty years of brain imaging studies as "an important first step." But it is safe to add that this first step has brought the study of the brain and the study of the mind closer together than ever before, and nowhere is this truer than in the study of criminal psychopaths.

Chapter One

Who Would Do Something Like This?

It's close to two o'clock in the morning on Saturday, January 8, 2011. In Tucson, Arizona, twenty-two-year-old Jared Lee Loughner calls Bryce Tierney, a friend he has known since middle school. Bryce doesn't answer, so Jared leaves a message: "Hey, man, it's Jared. Me and you had good times. Peace out. Later."[1]

At six A.M., Jared leaves his parents' home, driving his father's green 1969 Chevrolet Nova. He returns in an hour, but minutes later he heads out again. He may be in a hurry because he has something important to do today. Perhaps thoughts are rushing through his head. Perhaps he is distracted by voices only he hears. He is under stress.

Around 7:30 A.M., Alen Edward Forney, an officer with the Arizona Game and Fish Department, sees Jared run a red light.[2] Lights flash and spin on Forney's patrol vehicle. Jared pulls over. His license and registration are up-to-date and legal. Officer Forney admonishes him for speeding: "It's bad for your health. You're gonna kill somebody. You're gonna kill yourself." Jared gets off with a warning. And he starts to cry.

"Are you okay?" Forney asks him.

"Yeah," Jared replies. "I'm okay, I've just had a rough time and I really thought I was gonna get a ticket and I'm really glad that you're not [going to give me one]."

Forney asks him again if he is okay.

"I'm fine. I'm just heading home," Jared answers. "It isn't too far, and I'll be okay."[3]

By the time he returns to his parents' house at 8:30 A.M., he has visited two Walmart stores to buy ammunition for his 9-millimeter Glock semiautomatic handgun. He had legally purchased the pistol from a local gun shop 39 days ago. The sporting-goods associate in the first Walmart Jared visits is wary. The associate finds Jared rude and impatient. Without thoroughly checking the inventory, he tells Jared the store is out of 9-millimeter ammunition.[4]

An associate at a second Walmart has no problem with Jared. Jared acts friendly as he asks if there is a limit on how many rounds of 9-millimeter cartridges he can buy. The sales associate checks Jared's ID and finds nothing wrong. He double-bags six or seven boxes of ammunition for Jared.[5]

Around 8:30 A.M. at his parent's home, Jared removes a backpack from the trunk of the car before he enters the house. His mother and father are concerned about their son's behavior. They try to confront him. They want to know what's in the backpack. What's he going to do with it? Jared says nothing and flees, running down the street. His father drops his coffee and tries to catch up with him. But Jared is gone. His father goes back inside.[6]

By around 9:20 A.M., Jared is in a convenience store. His final destination is too far to walk in the Sketchers shoes he's wearing today. He needs a ride to reach the site of a "Congress on Your Corner" event being held in the parking lot of the Safeway supermarket. He asks the clerk to call a cab company for him. Nervously waiting for his ride to arrive, Jared looks at the wall clock.

"9:25," he says, "I still got time."[7]

He means he still has time to see United States Congresswoman Gabrielle Giffords in the parking lot in front of the supermarket where she is hosting the meet-and-greet event for her constituents.

It's been three to four years since Loughner fixated on Giffords. During one of the Congresswoman's public appearances back then, he asked her a question. He was seriously, bitterly disappointed when he didn't get an answer. He felt insulted by her lack of response. He had asked her: "What is government if words have no meaning?"[8]

Jared will see Giffords again soon. He gets into the cab and tells the driver to take him to the Safeway in Tucson. Like Jared's parents, the cab driver has no idea Jared is carrying his 9-millimeter Glock. He drops Jared off in the parking lot in front of the supermarket. It is the most important address on Jared's schedule today. For scores of people, it will be the most traumatic day of their lives. They have no idea Jared is coming, no hint of what he is about to do.

Jared joins the people who have gathered near Giffords. Among them are U.S. District Court Chief Judge John M. Roll, Giffords's aide Gabriel M. Zimmerman, her constituents Dorothy J. Morris, Phyllis C. Schneck, and Dorwan C. Stoddard, and nine-year-old Christina-Taylor Green.

It's close to 10:10 A.M. Jared has inserted peach-colored earplugs into his ears.[9] Constituents write their names on a sign-up sheet offered by Giffords's intern, Daniel Hernandez. Hernandez offers the sheet to a man wearing a black beanie and a black hooded sweatshirt. It's Jared.

"Gun!" someone yells.[10]

In an instant, Jared's pistol changes from a concealed weapon into a murder weapon.

He pulls the trigger of the sleek black pistol again and again. The semi-automatic handgun fires with each pull of the trigger—33 times. Bullet after bullet after bullet slide up the long ammunition clip into the pistol's chamber and out the barrel. In twenty seconds, the gun is empty.[11]

People scream. And run. Jared tries to reload. He has two more ammo clips stuffed into the left front pocket of his khaki pants.[12] He's made sure he has plenty of bullets. Altogether, he has two long ammo clips and two short ones, plus a folded pocket knife.

Congresswoman Giffords lies on the ground with a bullet in her brain. Her intern reassures her and tries to keep her from slipping into unconsciousness. Her eyes closed, she mumbles. Her breathing becomes shallow, but she survives with brain damage.[13] She faces a long rehabilitation.

Judge John Roll, Gabriel Zimmerman, Dorwan Stoddard, Dorothy Morris, Phyllis Schneck, and Christina-Taylor Green do not survive. They are now mortally wounded or already dead. A dozen others, in addition to Giffords, are injured.[14]

As Jared tries to reload, bystanders tackle and disarm him. They undoubtedly save many lives and prevent many injuries. Jared wants more victims, but the angry and brave bystanders hold him down until police arrive and arrest him.

Now wearing handcuffs, Jared is driven away in a police car, accompanied by two deputies.[15]

"I just want you to know that I'm the only person that knew about this," Loughner tells the police after his arrest.

He leaves behind six dead, thirteen wounded, a bloody parking lot, and many questions. Most of the questions begin with "Why" or "How."

Before we look inside Jared's brain to try to answer some of these questions, it will be useful to contrast Jared's horrendous actions with those of a very different murderer, Eric Harris.

Jared and Eric are both young, white males who carry guns to crowded places to shoot people they know and people they don't. They both see their acts as nihilistic, but meaningful, while most people see them as deranged and pointless.

Although Jared acts alone and Eric has a weak, depressed, and impressionable accomplice, both Jared and Eric are the driving forces behind their murderous plans. They both leave behind dead and wounded victims, confusion, blood—and the same questions.

This Is Not Awesome

Eric Harris doesn't care that he is late for class today. He's more concerned about falling behind his own schedule on this Tuesday morning, April 20, 1999.[16] He and his friend Dylan Klebold have plans for their fellow students and for the teachers at Columbine High School in Littleton, Colorado.[17] Today, just eleven days before Eric's eighteenth birthday, his day planner reads:

> 10:30 set up 4 things
> 11: go to school
> 11:10 set up duffel bags
> 11:12 wait near cars, gear up
> 11:16 HAHAHA[18]

Sometime after 10:30 A.M., he drives to a spot near the intersection of Chatfield Avenue and Wadsworth Boulevard, three miles southwest of the high school. He drops off a couple of backpacks stuffed with propane tanks, aerosol containers, and pipe bombs. When they go off, he figures, local police and rescue services will be distracted by the size and surprise of the explosions. They will rush to this intersection far from the school, slowing their response to the awesome end-of-the-high-school-world apocalypse he has planned for over a year.

At 11:10 A.M. Eric pulls his thirteen-year-old light gray Honda Civic into a parking space in the school's south parking lot. His fellow high school senior and co-conspirator, 17½-year-old Dylan, drives his black 1982 BMW into the west parking lot across from, but within sight of, Eric's parking spot.

Dylan has coordinated his agenda with Eric's. His "to do" list for this morning includes:

> Walk in, set bombs at 11:09, for 11:17
> Leave,
> Drive to Clemete Park. Gear up.
> Get back by 11:15
> Park cars. set car bombs for 11:18
> get out, go to outside hill, wait.
> When first bombs go off, attack.
> have fun![19]

Soon after Eric arrives, his off-and-on-again friend and fellow high school student Brooks Brown approaches him in the parking lot. Brooks excitedly tells Eric that he has missed a psychology test. Eric says it doesn't matter now.

"Brooks, I like you now. Get out of here. Go home," Eric tells him.[20] Of the 1,945 registered students and approximately 140 teachers and administrative staff at the school,[21] Brooks will be the only one to get a warning and a break like this today.

Eric and Dylan pull out duffel bags—one orange and one blue—from their cars and carry them into the cafeteria. Unnoticed, they set them on the floor near some tables in the crowded cafeteria before returning to their cars. The bags conceal homemade bombs amateurishly constructed with 20-pound propane tanks, flammable liquid, timers, and detonators. The homemade devices are set to explode at 11:17 A.M. But it is already 11:14 A.M. Eric and Dylan are leaving themselves dangerously little time to drop off the bombs and get out. They needn't worry.

They sit in their cars now, waiting for the explosions. They expect the twin blasts to bring part of the second floor crashing down into the cafeteria, killing hundreds. When the propane tanks explode, the blasts alone could directly kill many of the estimated 500 students in the dining area. When the survivors flee from the cafeteria, Eric and Dylan plan on gunning them down. This is the goal, and it makes sense only to them.

Fortunately, they are incompetent bomb makers. Neither knows how to wire these compound bombs or set their fuses properly.[22] The duffel bags lie, unexploded and unnoticed, among hundreds of other backpacks and bags belonging to students filling the cafeteria.

With no explosion in the cafeteria, Eric and Dylan's master plan has begun to falter. They continue with the next stage of their attack by setting the timers on two additional bombs in their cars. The car bombs are timed to go off after the police cars, fire trucks, ambulances and journalists arrive. They are meant to boost the body count.

Just before 11:20 A.M., road crew workers toss aside the bags which Eric left as a diversion miles from the school. Some pipe bombs and an aerosol container explode. But like those now in the cafeteria and in their cars, these devices are poorly constructed; the propane tanks included to make the explosion really noticeable remain intact. Some grass catches fire. Appropriately, the local Littleton Fire Department and the Sheriff's office are alerted, but there is no mass response by area police racing to the grass fire.

Now the two young men are on the move. They claim the campus's high ground. They stand atop the west stairs outside the school. They are armed with sawed-off shotguns, a 9-mm rifle, and a TEC-9 semi-automatic handgun. This weapon is a civilian version of a military submachine gun. It is sometimes referred to as the cheap man's Uzi, a submachine gun once used by Israel's military.

Realizing their big bombs have fizzled, their supplementary shooting plan becomes their only option for creating mayhem. As journalist Dave Cullen writes in his excellent account of the attack, *Columbine*, for Eric and Dylan "There was no Plan B."[23]

The two are wearing long black coats called dusters,[24] which are often associated with cowboys and horseback riding. On this and subsequent days, the coats are frequently misidentified as trench coats. Both are good for hiding long-barreled rifles and shotguns. Trench coats, once associated with spies, private eyes, and investigative journalists, soon will become linked to murderous, socially outcast students who kill to avenge the ill treatment they receive from their peers. But as Cullen points out in his account of the massacre, and as forensic psychiatrists and psychologists later conclude after studying the writings and videotapes left behind by Eric, this motivation does not apply to, or explain, the actions of these two murderous friends, as we will discover.

"Go! Go!" one of the soon-to-be killers shouts.[25] It is probably Eric, the dominant member of the lethal team.

Eric and Dylan pull out their shotguns and 9-mm weapons and begin by firing at students who are seated on the grass, eating lunch. They wound Richard Castaldo and shoot Rachel Scott in the head and chest, killing her.

Three more students are moving up the stairs toward them. Eric fires his carbine again and again, killing Danny Rohrbough instantly and wounding Lance Kirkland in four places from his chest down to his foot. Sean Graves runs but falls wounded before he can get away from the shooters.

From time to time throughout the massacre, the attackers pause to light pipe bombs, the most reliable of their homemade explosives. Now they are throwing them high onto the roof and down onto the lawn. Later they will throw them, to their amusement, throughout the school.

More students run across the grass, trying to get away. One, Mark Taylor, falls seriously wounded. Although shot, Michael Johnson manages to reach a storage shed and joins several others already using it for cover.[26]

The gunmen are moving again. One reaches Lance, who lies wounded on the ground. Lance, weak and disoriented from his wounds, grabs a pant leg of the figure standing over him and asks for help.

"Sure, I'll help," the owner of the pant leg says, and shoots Lance in the face.[27] Lance, despite multiple wounds, survives.

Eric, the leader and by far the more murderous of the two killers, climbs the stairs. He laughs. From his elevated vantage point, he sees Anne Marie Hochhalter running. He fires. She falls, shot multiple times.

It's been less than five minutes since the carnage began.

"This is what we always wanted to do. This is awesome!" one of the killers yells.[28]

Seeing hall monitor Patti Nielson and student Brian Anderson inside the school behind a westward-facing exit, one of the shooters fires. The bullets drive metal and glass shrapnel into Patti's arm, shoulder and knee, and into Brian's chest.

Eric looks toward the south parking lot. He easily spots Sheriff's Deputy Neil Gardner. The deputy is wearing a hard-to-miss bright yellow School Community Service Officer's shirt. Deputy Gardner is getting out of his patrol car about 180 feet away. Eric shoots at him repeatedly. Bullets fly into parked cars behind Deputy Gardner. None of the ten or so shots he manages to get off hits the deputy. Then Eric's rifle jams.

As Eric tries to clear his weapon, Gardner fires four shots at him, but misses. Eric clears his jammed weapon. He fires and misses the deputy again before he retreats into the school through the shattered west doors.

It's now around 11:26 A.M. From inside the entrance, Eric exchanges more fire with Gardner and another deputy, who has joined the shootout. The gunmen disappear into the school. The deputies, following orders, do not go after the gunmen.

Together, Eric and Dylan walk back and forth along the library hallway, throwing pipe bombs, shooting at nothing in particular, and laughing.

A couple of minutes later, they enter the library where 56 classmates hide or cower. Immediately, Eric points his shotgun at the top of the front counter and pulls the trigger. Wood splinters fly into the air and into a student crouched behind a copying machine at the end of the counter. As they move across the room toward the library windows, the coldblooded pair nonchalantly shoot and kill another student. Windows shatter as they fire outside at students fleeing the killing field Eric and Dylan have created out of the once-familiar campus. Police and deputies fire back through the windows at the killers.

Before retreating across the library, away from the windows, the killers shoot eight more students. Four of them die.

They walk back toward the library entrance, where Dylan blasts a display case. Then they shoot eight more kids. Three of them die.

Surrounded by dead, dying, wounded, and cowering victims—one of the killers shouts "Yahoo!"

Eric and Dylan move to the center of the large room. It's approximately 11:34 A.M. They reload their weapons and turn them on nearby students. Four are hit. Two of them die.

In just seven minutes and thirty seconds, Eric and Dylan execute ten people and wound half a dozen others in the library.

A few minutes later, they leave the library and walk through the halls near the science classrooms and laboratories. They look through the windows of locked classroom doors. They see students hiding inside, but they pass by. Like medieval figures of Death, carrying firearms instead of scythes, they randomly and opportunistically choose their victims. They shoot up the school, even firing into empty rooms. And they throw some more pipe bombs, creating several explosions.

About twelve minutes before noon, they wander down to the cafeteria. Eric kneels on the stairs. He raises his carbine and fires repeatedly at one of the duffel bags containing one of the homemade, 20-pound propane bombs he and Dylan had left there before the shooting began. The gas tank does not explode.

Eric and Dylan look at the abandoned lunch tables. They grab a couple of abandoned bottles of water, raise them to their lips, and drink.

"Today," one of them announces grandly at some point during this visit to the cafeteria, "the world's going to come to an end. Today is the day we die."[29]

The pair succeeds in setting off an explosion in the cafeteria that ignites a container of flammable liquid. The fire sprinklers in the ceiling spray water. The large propane bombs never explode.

Eric and Dylan go back to wandering the hallways, briefly visiting the office area and the kitchen before ending up back in the library on the second floor.

Now they have killed all they are going to kill: thirteen students and one teacher. Twenty-one others are wounded. It is far fewer than they had hoped to slaughter; they wanted to kill hundreds. Had either of them known how to connect a fuse, had either understood bomb construction, their homemade propane bombs could have killed most of the 500 students eating lunch on this day.

Eric and Dylan walk back to the library for the last time. Around 12:08 P.M., they take some final shots at paramedics and law-enforcement officers from the windows on the library's second floor. They move toward the end bookshelves in the southwest corner of the library. One of them lights a cloth stuck into a glass bottle filled with flammable liquid and sets it on a library table. This becomes their next-to-last violent act.

Their final violent act is suicide. They shoot themselves. Each dies from a single self-inflicted gunshot wound to the head. The Molotov cocktail starts a small fire on the tabletop. The fire alarm is screaming so loudly, it drowns out speech.

"Not Used Technically"

Despite the similarities of the atrocities Jared and Eric committed, the brains of these two particular killers most certainly malfunctioned in very different ways. Their murderous intentions differed, as did their mental states before and during their crimes.

One had lost touch with reality. The other had no delusions and clearly understood the difference between right and wrong. One suffers from a mental illness; the other has what the American Psychiatric Association calls a "personality disorder." Most neuroscientists and research psychologists call it psychopathy.

Eric left behind very convincing evidence that he had highly psychopathic traits. Although he understood the difference between right and wrong, he appeared to lack a conscience. Combined with a disdain for nearly everyone, a lack of conscience can be a very dangerous thing, as we have seen. Jared was legally insane when he killed. Eric was legally sane when he committed the same acts.

But sane and insane are legal, not scientific or medical, definitions. As neuroscientists find more indications that the brains of killers differ from those of non-killers, some scientists are joining defense attorneys in claiming that the violence committed by legally sane killers, like psychopaths, can be traced to their abnormal brain structure and function.

In fact, the editors of the magazine *Scientific American Mind* prefaced a 2010 article titled "Inside the Mind of a Psychopath" with the teaser "Neuroscientists are discovering that some of the most cold-blooded killers aren't *bad*"[30] [emphasis added].

Aren't bad?

"They suffer," the preview continues, "from a brain abnormality that sets them adrift in an emotionless world."

"Poor babies," some cynics might comment on reading this.

Skeptics might wonder if this means we will see descriptions of the not-bad serial killer Ted Bundy, the not-bad serial killer John Wayne Gacy, the not-bad killer Richard Kuklinski, and the not-bad mass murderer Eric Harris—all of whom displayed traits strongly indicative of psychopathy—in future accounts of their crimes.

The provocative lead-in to Kent A. Kiehl's and Joshua W. Buckholtz's article *Inside the Mind of a Psychopath* succeeds in drawing the reader's attention with what many would consider an outrageous statement. But in their defense, scientists are reporting more and more evidence that points to links between brain abnormalities and violent behavior. But does it make them evil? And what is the correlation between such abnormalities and violent behavior? Do certain brain abnormalities guarantee violent behavior? Can understanding what is going on in the brains of psychopaths and cold-blooded killers really justify a claim that they are "not bad?" Goodness and badness are moral judgments with sometimes tenuous links to the law. The debate about whether or not someone is bad or evil is not a scientific one. But the scientific findings, if they hold up, have serious legal implications.

Some people might shake their heads and dismiss murderous behavior as incomprehensible. And they may be content to look no further for explanations or for greater understanding. Others, when they hear about Jared, Eric, Sandy Hook Elementary School gunman Adam Lanza, and other mass murderers, quickly dismiss them as "psychos" or, more descriptively, "psycho killers."

A "psycho" is a person "who behaves in a frightening or violent way," according to the primary definition offered by the Macmillan Dictionary. That could be a useful definition if it were limited to that meaning. In the minds of many, however, it merges with the second definition: "an offensive word for someone who has a mental illness."

For readers of the Merriam-Webster Dictionary, a psycho is "a deranged or psychopathic person—not used technically." With a popular diagnosis like this brought out every time there is a mass shooting or other despicable act of violence, it's not surprising the media asks over and over again in the wake of violent attacks: "How and why does this happen?" "Who's responsible?" And it's no wonder many people have little or no understanding of what motivates or drives the killers. The senselessness of such acts is so great, and so defies the logic of most people, that clumping them all together and dismissing them as the acts of "psychos" seems to make sense. In an easy way, it helps the public to make some sense of seemingly senseless crimes.

A major problem is that people frequently confuse psychotic with psychopathic. Psychopathic and psychotic are two different terms used by professionals to describe people with very different mentalities.

Psychotic refers to psychosis, a key feature of serious mental illnesses like the one that afflicts Jared Loughner: schizophrenia. During and before his shooting spree, he displayed classic symptoms of psychosis. They included mental derangement with a loss of contact with reality, hallucinations, delusions, and disorganized thought, speech, and behavior.

In popular culture, the word "psycho" is thus an inaccurate and confusing mixture of an offensive word for someone with a mental illness and/or someone who is a psychopath. Psychopathy is not madness. People with undeniable and striking psychopathic traits, people like Eric Harris, remain sane in the eyes of the law. They appear quite sane too, even to experts who know they are different from you and me, because of their complete lack of empathy and conscience. They can easily fool family, friends, court officials, strangers, and even mental health professionals who haven't had a chance to examine them closely.

Part of the confusion stems from the fact that, as we have seen in the cases of Jared and Eric, people with psychosis sometimes commit the same kinds of crimes that some criminal psychopaths commit. The difference is that a psychopath on a killing spree knows what he (the killer is usually a male) is doing and he knows it is wrong. He is in touch with reality and very likely enjoying what he is doing. Witnesses heard Eric laughing during his shooting spree and appearing to have a great time.

A psychotic person, by contrast, acts in response to delusional, often paranoid thoughts, as when Jared became obsessed with Giffords because he perceived a personal slight after she failed to respond to his question: "What is government if words have no meaning?" A psychotic person is out of touch with reality. He or she cannot distinguish between what is going on in the outside world and what is going on inside their heads. Theoretically, in a legal sense, psychotic individuals should not be held accountable for their actions. Medically, they are mentally ill and suffering from a brain disorder. In the real world, violent psychotic individuals are often convicted as if they were in touch with reality and aware they were committing crimes society agrees are abhorrent. In courtrooms in the real world, mentally ill killers are often treated like psychopaths, who actually know better but don't care.

If we ever hope to prevent such tragedies in the future, we will have to intercept the Erics and Jareds and Adam Lanzas of the world before they make their murderous plans. To do that, educators and mental health professionals will have to make better use of mental-illness screening programs. And neuroscientists will have to find out more about brain abnormalities that are present before the killing starts if they are to make a contribution to deterring criminal behavior in society.

Jared's violent behavior started with his pulling out a 9-mm pistol and emptying its ammunition clip into a group of people gathered in front of a grocery store in Tucson, Arizona. The reason he did it lies somewhere in, or perhaps throughout much of, his brain, which was deranged by paranoid schizophrenia.

We know where and when Loughner obtained his murder weapon. He legally purchased it from a gun store near Tucson on Tuesday, November 30, 2010. We are not so sure where or how he acquired his mental illness. We do know it developed long before the day he used his semiautomatic handgun to shoot nineteen people, killing six of them.

Jared's mental disorder may have developed more than twenty-two years earlier as his fetal brain grew and developed. By the time he was in his late teens and early twenties, the overt symptoms of paranoid schizophrenia began to become obvious.

However the disorder developed in his brain, it was there long before he became violent. In the months before the attack, his behavior and thought processes became erratic, his anger troubling.

"My concern was like, meth or something . . . because his behavior and his, was, um, odd," his mother said later.[31] He was disruptive in his college classes and eventually expelled. His behavior led his father to confiscate his shotgun and at times to prevent him from using the family car. But when he tried to talk to Jared on the day of the attack, his son walked out.

"Sometimes you'd hear him in his room, like, having conversations," his mother recalled. "And sometimes he would look like he was having a conversation with someone right there, be talking to someone. I don't know how to explain it."[32]

The explanation is, of course, that Jared was hallucinating because he had a brain disease. The illness that twisted Loughner's thought processes is a very familiar, poorly understood, complex disease which typically begins to show in the late teens or young adulthood. His illness was there that Tuesday in 2010 when he purchased his Glock handgun. It was certainly there a little over a year and a month later, on January 8, 2011, when he took a cab to the parking lot in front of the Safeway grocery store in Tucson. It was there when he inserted earplugs, to protect his ears from what he was about to do. It was there at 10:10 A.M. that Saturday when he opened fire, shooting U.S. Representative Gabrielle Giffords in the head before turning the gun on the crowd.

It is possible that it had been developing a long time before it became apparent to his friends and family. Many things Jared and his mother possibly were exposed to—for example, flus and other viruses—could have interacted with the genes he inherited to result in paranoid schizophrenia. The possible factors that might have transformed Jared's predisposition to schizophrenia into the tragic, crippling reality of severe mental illness range from exposure to maternal infections and stress before birth to exposure to stress during childhood.

While the cause of schizophrenia is unknown, many researchers believe it is a neurodevelopmental disorder, which could be one reason its symptoms become apparent in late adolescence or young adulthood. Interactions between some of the genes people like Jared are born with and things they are exposed to in the environment are suspected of producing abnormalities in brain function and structure.

For example, in 2013 when Jong H. Yoon and his colleagues at the University of California-Davis used functional magnetic resonance imaging (fMRI) to measure activity in the brains of 18 individuals with, and 19 without, schizophrenia, they saw *decreased* activity in the prefrontal cortices of those with the mental disease.[33]

The cells in this part of the brain, located behind the forehead, are closely associated with higher mental functions. They influence your ability to set priorities, make plans, figure out strategies, and predict the consequences of your actions. Brain scientists call these "executive functions." It is a part of the brain, as we will see, that is also implicated in psychopathy and other disorders.

At the same time that the prefrontal cortices of people with schizophrenia appear to have *decreased* activity, another part of the brain appears to have *increased* activity. This is the substantia nigra and it is located deep in the brain, in a subdivision called the midbrain. The researchers found that communication between the prefrontal cortex and the substantia nigra was weaker in the group of people with schizophrenia.

Latin speakers can readily figure out that brain cells in the substantia nigra are pigmented; the translation is "black substance" or "black body." The color comes from melanin, a pigment produced when the neurons make dopamine, a neurotransmitter closely associated with schizophrenia. Antipsychotic medications prescribed to treat schizophrenia interact with dopamine-signaling mechanisms in the brain.

Another condition linked to the substantia nigra is Parkinson's disease, in which these pigmented neurons are lost. The loss of dopamine-producing neurons in the substantia nigra affects a neighboring part of the brain called the striatum, whose cells depend on dopamine to function properly.

The connection between the striatum and the substantia nigra may also play a role in schizophrenia. The results suggest that communication between these regions is "out of sync"[34] in the people with schizophrenia.

Furthermore, the research turned up evidence of a correlation between how psychotic a person was and how closely connected his or her substantia nigra was to the nearby striatum.

The study needs to be reproduced with more subjects before we can be sure the results represent a general finding in schizophrenia. But they raise the possibility that the communication pathway, or neuronal circuit, that connects the prefrontal cortex with the basal ganglia may be a route through which psychoses are linked to the disordered thought patterns that characterize schizophrenia. Distinct pathways that connect the same brain structures but which follow different routes are being implicated in other mental illnesses and with personality disorders like psychopathy.

Our society's routine failure to examine people like Jared is a wasted opportunity to increase our insights into abnormal behavior. No one knows if Jared's prefrontal cortex would have looked less active while his basal ganglia looked more active compared to healthy individuals. We don't know if, like some people with schizophrenia, he has slightly less gray matter in parts of his cerebral cortex or if he has slightly larger-than-normal, fluid-filled spaces called ventricles in the middle of his brain, as some people with schizophrenia do. He and other prisoners can't be forced to volunteer for scientific study.

At first thought, you might suppose that smaller brain volume must be due to loss of brain cells. But it might be due to neurons being smaller in these brains. Decreased volume in the cerebral cortex also might be due to decreased density in the mass of intertwined contacts and connections among brain cells.[35] The projections of neurons, which receive and send signals to other brain cells, are called axons and dendrites. Together with a second type of brain cell called neuroglial cells or glia, these projections form an intricate and very complex network of interwoven processes in your brain called the neuropil. It is in this meshwork that much of the cell-to-cell communication that underlies thinking and feeling is somehow realized. It's easy to imagine how reducing this crucial area of brain cell interaction and communication could severely compromise thought processes.

Jared had never been treated with antipsychotic medications before he attacked. One caveat of research on people with schizophrenia is that many of them, unlike Jared, have received antipsychotic drugs before and during the time they are examined by scientists. Could long or short-term exposure to these powerful medications be responsible for the brain changes we see in people with schizophrenia? Researchers in this field, like Yoon and his collaborators, acknowledge the possibility that such drugs could make a difference and that their work should be extended to include people who have not yet received medication.

Yet we also know that in the past four decades, more than 120 studies have reported neurobiological abnormalities in the brains of people with schizophrenia who have never received a single dose of antipsychotic medication.[36] There seems, therefore, to be strong evidence that the brains of people with schizophrenia are physically different from the brains of people without schizophrenia. But it's not quite that simple.

It turns out that the brain abnormalities associated with schizophrenia are not really limited to schizophrenia. We are more likely to find them in people with schizophrenia, but you can also find them in people with other brain diseases, such as Parkinson's disease, and even in people with no brain disease at all.[37] Later we will see that some of the differences associated with the brains of psychopaths can sometimes be found in the brains of people with few psychopathic traits. Biological results often fall short of being completely black or white.

However Jared's brain differs from that of an average healthy person, we do know that it does respond to antipsychotic medication, the only means we now have for treating the delusional thought processes that led to six deaths, thirteen disrupted lives and intense suffering for family and friends of the victims. Jared's apprehension eventually led to his being forced, under court order, to take antipsychotic medication. Only under its influence would he begin to get a sense of the horror he had perpetrated.

Jared was charged with murder, attempted murder, and the attempted assassination of a member of Congress. A psychiatrist and a psychologist diagnosed paranoid schizophrenia following a total of sixteen hours of interviews. Loughner, they reported, was delusional and hallucinated. His thoughts were disorganized, random and bizarre. In August 2012, he pled guilty to nineteen charges to avoid the death penalty. Given a life sentence, he is now receiving court-ordered antipsychotic medication at the U.S. Medical Center for Federal Prisoners in Springfield, Missouri.[38]

Forensic psychologist J. Reid Meloy has studied the crimes of people like Jared and other mass murderers, both adolescents and adults, which have occurred over the past half-century. "The majority of adult mass murderers typically are individuals who have a psychiatric history and typically a majority is psychotic at the time that they're actually carrying out the killing," Meloy said in a 2007 interview on NPR.[39] The minority who are not psychotic include rare depressive individuals like Dylan Klebold who want to take others with them on their suicidal journey. Another minority are individuals with many psychopathic traits, like Eric.

It is commonly assumed that people with schizophrenia like Jared are more likely to be violent than people without schizophrenia. Criminologist Adrian Raine, for example, cites studies from around the world showing that people with schizophrenia are more likely to have a criminal and violent history than healthy people.[40]

He concludes in his book, *The Anatomy of Violence*, that the "relationship between violence and schizophrenia is not weak." Later he softens his assertion by noting that "It's true that most schizophrenics are not dangerous, and neither kill nor perpetuate violence."

It is true that studies show that only a small number of people with mental illnesses do become violent. The threat in the public's imagination, however, is exaggerated by the publicity that acts such as Jared's receive and by the public's general lack of understanding of the disease schizophrenia.

"The challenge for medical practitioners is to remain aware that some of their psychiatric patients do in fact pose a small risk of violence, while not losing sight of the larger perspective—that most people who are violent are not mentally ill, and most people who are mentally ill are not violent," Richard A. Friedman, M.D., wrote in *The New England Journal of Medicine*.[41] It is worth reiterating that most violent people are not mentally ill—as countless acts of violence are committed every day by sane people with decidedly obvious motives: frustration, desperation, jealousy, greed, or anger.

Crimes like Jared's are "extraordinarily rare events," according to Meloy. And that, the clinical professor of psychiatry at the University of California in San Diego says, is the reason they get so much publicity. The media coverage of such events skews the public perception of the threat posed by the mentally ill.

A look back at nearly thirty years of research reveals that there is indeed an association between schizophrenia and violence—homicide, in particular. But most of this violence can be attributed to drug and alcohol abuse. In fact, people *with* schizophrenia who abuse drugs are about as violent as people *without* schizophrenia who abuse drugs,[42] so the corollary to violence could arguably be the drug use versus the schizophrenia itself. Jared's friends reported that he had used drugs extensively in the years before he was arrested, although he had reportedly stopped using them in the last few months before he was arrested. His past history included abuse of alcohol, marijuana, and hallucinogens.[43]

The confounding issue of drug abuse and violence illustrates the difficulty of sorting out a complex issue like violence and its multiple causes. Robert Hare and his co-workers, for example, suggested in 1994 that drug use by psychopaths, which is hardly rare, could probably be linked more to their unstable and antisocial lifestyles than to the characteristic features of psychopathy.[44]

There are superficial similarities between brain abnormalities reported in schizophrenia and abnormalities found in psychopaths. For example, they both are believed to involve dysfunction in the frontal lobes. But schizophrenia and psychopathy are distinct disorders. The uninformed diagnosis of "psycho killer" doesn't begin to capture the mysteries behind either condition. Of the two, psychopathy may be the more puzzling, and even the scarier, because when it involves violence, the violence springs from someone who on the surface appears as normal as the rest of us.

"No I Am Not Crazy . . ."

—Eric Harris[45]

Eric Harris left us thousands of words in his notebooks and on his web pages, words that tell us a lot about him: "My belief is that if I say something, it goes," he ranted. "I am the law, and if you don't like it, you die. If I don't like you or I don't like what you want me to do, you die. . . . I'll just go to some downtown area in some big ass city and blow up and shoot everything I can. Feel no remorse, no sense of shame."[46]

There are indeed no indications of remorse or shame in Eric's personal manifestos and ranting announcements. But he had no problem feigning those feelings when it would help him, as Dave Cullen pointed out in his 2004 *Slate* article, "The Depressive and the Psychopath: At Last We Know Why the Columbine Killers Did It."

Frank Ochberg, M.D., a Clinical Professor of Psychiatry at Michigan State University, said he believes Eric lacked a conscience.[47] Based on his history and writings, Eric impressed Ochberg and other experts as someone who was good at reading and manipulating people and ingratiating himself to them when it would benefit him.[48]

For example, the FBI agent perhaps most familiar with the motivations of the Columbine killers, clinical psychologist Dr. Dwayne Fuselier, told Cullen that Eric wrote "an ingratiating letter" to a person he had robbed.[49] Eric wrote it when he was participating in a community service program that allowed him to avoid prosecution for breaking into a man's van. The letter offered not just apologies, but went so far as to express empathy. Fuselier said Eric's letter "was packed with statements like *Jeez, I understand now how you feel and I understand what this did to you.*"[50]

Eric added: "My parents and everyone else that knew me was shocked that I did something like that. My parents lost almost all their trust in me and I was grounded for two months . . . I am truly sorry for what I have done."[51]

That is the mask of contrition and human decency Eric brought out and wore when it suited him. Eric and other criminal psychopaths may be able to express empathy, but it is not part of their emotional repertoire. Behind the mask, in private, he revealed how he really felt: "Isn't America supposed to be the land of the free? How come, if I'm free, I can't deprive a stupid fucking dumbshit from his possessions if he leaves them sitting in the front seat of his fucking van out in plain sight and in the middle of fucking nowhere on a Frifuckingday night. NATURAL SELECTION. Fucker should be shot."[52]

This is the type of rationalization for immoral, unethical, or criminal behavior typical of many criminals whose psychopathy has been established by psychological testing: if someone is dumb enough to become a victim, they deserve it.

"I'll never forget talking to the head counselor, who counseled both boys before all this [the shooting] happened. He described how different they were. Harris would just tell you what you needed to know to satisfy your needs so he could get what he wanted," psychiatrist Ochberg remembered fourteen years after the events at Columbine. Dylan, on the other hand, was depressive and emotional, Ochberg recalls.

Eric's writings provide a fascinating and revealing look into the mind of a non-psychotic person who would not just dream about—but actually take the extraordinary step of—planning and executing a cold-blooded massacre.

There is no record that a formal "psychological autopsy" had been performed on either Eric or Dylan, and no evidence of an official document describing their psychological state. Former FBI Special Agent and criminal profiler Mary Ellen O'Toole, Ph.D., an expert on psychopathy with firsthand knowledge of the behavior of the Columbine shooters, confirms that no formal evaluation analysis was issued.

Cullen's *Slate* magazine article describing the opinions of Drs. Ochberg and Fuselier is still the main source of information for most people about the killers' psychological states.

O'Toole, who worked for over fourteen years as a profiler in the FBI's Behavioral Analysis Unit, recalled the crime scene this way: "Based on the behavior at the crime scene: it was predatory, it was preplanned, and it was extremely callous." As the killers moved through the school picking out victims and shooting them, they displayed a calm cold-bloodedness, according to O'Toole. Experts call this eerily calm style of execution hypo-emotionality, and it is characteristic of other campus and school shooters. They moved through the school, O'Toole said, "in a very tempered and controlled way. When I saw his [Eric's] videotapes in which he talked about his plans, there was a sense of thrill and excitement. It was [a] very risk-taking kind of behavior. I would say, based on the behavior at the crime scene, that would be a manifestation of some of the traits of psychopathy."[53]

O'Toole's FBI colleague Fuselier and Ochberg, a former Associate Director of the National Institute of Mental Health, go a bit further in discussing Eric's psychopathic traits. Fuselier, a clinical psychologist, spent months studying Eric and Dylan before he arrived at his opinion. In the summer of 1999, according to Cullen's book *Columbine*, Fuselier was in

Leesburg, Virginia attending a meeting organized by the FBI to discuss school shootings.[54] He reviewed his findings about Eric's personality by concluding that Eric was a "budding young psychopath."

A prominent psychiatrist at the meeting, however, disagreed with Fuselier, according to Cullen's account:

"'I don't think he was a budding young psychopath,' the psychiatrist said.

"'What's your objection?'

"'I think he was a full-blown psychopath.'

"His colleagues agreed. Eric Harris was textbook."[55]

Like Fuselier, Ochberg saw a budding psychopath in Eric. Ochberg traveled to Columbine repeatedly in the year following the tragedy to help victims and members of the community recover from the trauma. And he read Eric's writings and reviewed his history.

"I did reach a conclusion that Eric Harris appeared on his way to becoming psychopathic, that he was very good at imitating caring," Ochberg recalled in an interview for this book.

Few mental health professionals are willing to call someone a psychopath before they reach the age of eighteen. Eric would have been eighteen years old a mere eleven days after he calmly shot his classmates and teachers.

"You don't call someone a psychopath until they have given a lot of evidence and they have grown up. . . . After age eighteen and in the adult range, they have a series of behaviors that can be observed," Ochberg said in a short film produced by Joyce Boaz, *What Is a Psychopath?*[56] While Eric's crimes prevented him from graduating from high school, they were also evidence that he appeared to have graduated into adult psychopathy before his eighteenth birthday.

"Some psychopaths become sadists," Ochberg continued. "Being sadistic means you enjoy hurting another person. Not every psychopath becomes a sadist but if they stumble into sadism, they have absolutely no regret, no empathy, no remorse as a product of their being a psychopath. And they practice and they get better.

"The worst are the serial killers who are not only psychopaths and sadists, but they have learned to enjoy their own grandiosity. They're narcissist. They care about themselves. They want to outwit the police. They want to humiliate logical, decent people. They hold us in contempt.

They are 'the worst of bad.'" Eric was not a serial killer, but his personal history and his status as a mass murderer suggest he had the traits Ochberg describes. Mass murderers kill multiple people during a single violent event, while serial killers commit a series of murders over an extended period of time. Between murders, they often do not attract attention. Spree killers murder multiple people in a series of violent, related events.

Eric's parents have since come to accept that their son was a psychopath. He had fooled them, as he had fooled a psychiatrist he had once been sent to visit.[57] But being fooled by a psychopath is nothing to be ashamed of. Experts who have spent their careers working with psychopaths, experts like Dr. Robert Hare, attest to the fact that even they, for a time anyway, have been fooled by the appearance of normality that psychopaths can convincingly present.[58] It can take time to see behind what psychiatrist Hervey Cleckley referred to as "the mask of sanity."

It is fair to document a person's psychopathic characteristics or traits, but it is up to the reader to realize that psychopathy requires documentation of more than a few such traits before the label "psychopath" can be authoritatively applied to an individual. One nasty comment, spiteful act, fist fight, theft, lawsuit, or self-serving action doesn't amount to psychopathy. A lifetime pattern of antisocial behavior, such as Eric was well on his way to establishing just before his eighteenth birthday, may—providing the determination is made by a professional trained to evaluate a person's behavior as well as his or her legal and medical history.

Eric's personal history, his journals and videos, combined with his many traits characteristic of psychopathy, convinced the experts who examined his writings and life that he was either well on his way to being a psychopath or had already become one, a "textbook psychopath."

"I am higher than you people," he announced. "If you disagree I would shoot you . . . some people go through life begging to be shot."

And some people go through life without a conscience. Scientists are accepting the difficult challenge of trying to figure out why an estimated one out of every hundred adults share this deficit with Eric. Not all of them are killers, but so many are criminals that they make up an estimated 15 to 25 percent of the prison population in the United States. And criminal psychopaths, by one estimate, commit half again as many crimes as non-psychopathic criminals.[59] Criminal or unsuccessful psychopaths may be a subgroup in the heterogeneous population of all psychopaths that includes non-criminal or successful psychopaths. It is the record they leave and often their confinement that make criminal psychopaths the best scientific subjects for anyone who wants to see into the psychopathic brain.

If you hope to come away with useful insights by studying human beings, you have to know what kind of human beings you are studying. We have already seen that similar violent actions do not reflect the functioning of similar brains. You have to know who you have invited into your laboratory and who you have slid into your brain-imaging machine as you watch their brains in action. It's important to know their background, gender, age, weight, medical history, ethnicity, and drinking and drug use habits, for a start, because many factors can influence behavior, behavioral responses, and even the structure of the brain. And it is most important that you have a way to identify who is a psychopath and who is not. You have to know, as best as you can determine, where on the spectrum of psychopathy the person you are studying lies.

Chapter Two

Kunlangeta, Psychopaths, and Sociopaths: Does the Label Matter?

> "... the definition of psychopathy itself—what it is, what it is not—is one of the most fundamental questions for psychological science."
>
> —Jennifer Skeem, et al.[1]

There is no record of his real name, but we do know he was a Siberian Yup'ik Eskimo[2] who lived on the remote island of Seevookuk between 1940 and 1955. We'll call him Kopanuk. An Eskimo elder who was familiar with nearly five hundred of his fellow Eskimo said Kopanuk's behavior made him stand out.[3]

Seevookuk is only about fifty miles from Siberia, so it is not surprising that one of the first Europeans to reach it was a Russian explorer. Vitus Bering stepped onto the island in 1728. He called it St. Lawrence Island, and that is how it is labeled on maps showing its location near the Bering Strait in the Bering Sea.

In isolated lands with long winters, cutting wind chill, and subzero temperatures, cooperation in traditional, self-sufficient Eskimo and Inuit societies was valued and essential for survival. Meat was shared in Kopanuk's day, as it is today. Laws were not codified. Instead, responses to social transgressions were adjusted by members of the tribe and, for more serious offenses by tribal leaders, to suit the individual circumstances of the offense.[4] The communities, ranging in population from twenty to two hundred people, depended on social pressure to guide the behavior of their members.[5]

Kopanuk's personality was clearly different from others in his group of self-sufficient hunters and gatherers. He didn't seem to feel social pressure or worry about social guidelines. He knew what was expected of him as a member of a tight-knit community living in a very harsh environment, but he didn't seem to care. Even as an adolescent, he stole, lied, and cheated. He avoided the work of fishing for salmon, a mainstay of the Yup'ik diet. He made excuses to avoid hunting the caribou, whale, seal, walrus, and polar bear that his people needed to survive. If he came across birds' eggs, he rarely shared them, or anything else he found. When he did share, he usually wanted something in return. This was unusual behavior in the typically cooperative community, which had had limited exposure to outsiders who had little opportunity to introduce Kopanuk to a more selfish outlook. His antisocial behavior persisted into adulthood, despite all the times his peers dragged Kopanuk to stand before the elders. The elders spoke to him. They reprimanded him. They told him to make amends to those he had taken advantage of and harmed. But none of it changed his behavior for long. He always returned to being Kopanuk.

Some of the Eskimo asked their shaman if he could help, if he could influence or change Kopanuk's behavior. But, as they feared, the shaman said he had no power to help. There was nothing he could do, because Kopanuk was not the victim of a harmful spirit, or anything else the shaman could influence. Rather, Kopanuk was a *kunlangeta*, a person whose "mind knows what to do but he does not do it."[6]

As in modern North America, being a *kunlangeta* among the Eskimo was not the same as being psychotic, or *nuthkavihak* in the Yup'ik language. The Yup'ik translation of *nuthkavihak* is "being crazy."[7] Kopanuk, his fellow Eskimo agreed, was not *nuthkavihak,* so they didn't think his behavior could be excused when he did things like taking advantage of women.

The traditional Eskimo and Inuit had a lenient attitude about sexual activity among adults, but Kopanuk's behavior went too far. Avoiding another challenging hunting and fishing expedition, Kopanuk stayed behind with the women and children. When the hunters returned, they learned that Kopanuk had visited most of the Yup'ik dwellings, half a dozen or so, and had sex with most of the women.

What happened to people like Kopanuk before Eskimo and Inuit societies were transformed by Western culture, technology, and law? During the first field trip of her career in 1954–55, a young anthropologist named Jane M. Murphy visited Seevookuk to conduct a pilot study. She wanted to learn how people on the island viewed physical and mental illness.[8] When she asked her source, an elder, how people like Kopanuk were dealt with in traditional Yup'ik society, he told her that someone like Kopanuk probably would have been taken on a hunting trip. Then, she learned, "somebody would have pushed him off the ice when nobody else was looking."[9] It's possible the interviewee gave the young anthropologist a flippant answer. But in a challenging environment like Seevookuk where cooperation and sharing is essential for survival, it would not be surprising if the anthropologist got a straight answer.

If Kopanuk avoided the fateful hunting trip that may have awaited other *kunlangeta*, he would have had more time to observe Yup'ik girls play with *yaaruin*, story knives. They used them like pencils to draw in the snow or sand as they told stories. Sometimes the stories were told for fun. Sometimes they were about their families. And sometimes the stories had a moral message. It would be interesting to know if Kopanuk was ever featured in the girls' illustrated stories, if his lack of conscience and empathy was ever explained with an image in the sand.

Traditional Eskimo experiences with, and treatments of, extremely antisocial individuals have parallels to modern North American experiences with such people. According to Murphy, who went on to become the Director of Massachusetts General Hospital's Psychiatric Epidemiology Unit, professor of psychiatry at the Harvard Medical School, and professor of epidemiology at the Harvard School of Public Health, the *kunlangeta* parallel our concept of the psychopath. It's easy to compare the Eskimo elders with our court system, and their shaman with our psychologists and psychiatrists. A socially tolerated act like pushing a *kunlangeta* "off the ice" could be seen as a vigilante version of pushing a psychopath into the execution chamber or, for less severe crimes, pushing one into a prison cell or forensic psychiatric hospital.

People like Kopanuk turn up in cultures all over the world. Murphy reports that the Yoruba people of West Africa, whom she studied during field trips in 1961 and 1963, describe them as *arankan*. *Arankan* refers to "a person who always goes his own way regardless of others, who is uncooperative, full of malice, and bullheaded."[10] Interestingly, Murphy reported that the Yoruba do not consider an *arankan* to be ill. Just as psychopaths are not considered insane in modern Western society and *kunlangeta* are not regarded as insane in Yup'ik Eskimo society, *arankan* are not considered insane in Yoruba society, but they are considered uniquely different.

Today, while many people would refer to Kopanuk as a psychopath, others would call him a sociopath. And there are those, particularly psychiatrists and psychologists who follow the lead of the American Psychiatric Association, who would say he suffered from antisocial personality disorder. But what exactly do those labels mean for the individuals encountering such people and the societies they live in?

No Matter What You Call It, Something Is Not Right

The labeling situation sounds confusing because it *is* confusing. Over time, the labels have accumulated. Sociopathy, psychopathy, antisocial personality disorder, and dyssocial personality disorder are sometimes confused and often used synonymously. Experts and amateurs declare with conviction that a sociopath differs from, or is identical to, a psychopath who is essentially the same as, or different in significant ways from, someone with antisocial personality disorder.

Psychiatrists, psychologists, and neuroscientists have yet to agree on the nature of this disorder—or, it may be more accurate to say, on the nature of the subtypes of personalities with psychopathic traits. Until there is an agreed-upon common language to describe the spectrum of antisocial behavior identified by these different labels, it is unlikely we will be able to claim we have a good understanding of behavior included under the heading "psychopathy." In part because we lack so much information about this type of human behavior, academic researchers are engaged in a sometimes bitter controversy concerning the nature of psychopathy and how it should be measured and defined. It is not unusual for a researcher submitting a paper to a peer-reviewed scientific journal to ask the editor to avoid sending the manuscript to certain competing or antagonistic fellow scientists. This happens in other fields of research as well. Sometimes this request is made to prevent a competing research group from rushing their own findings into print and "scooping" their competitors. Sometimes it is made to prevent competitors from using the reported data to correct or further their own research and so gain an advantage. But another reason such requests are made can be traced to ill feelings between researchers. Competition can be vicious in scientific research. Egos can be strong. Feelings are hurt. On occasion, sending your paper for review to a competitor, someone who dislikes you or whom you may have slighted, can result in rejection or delay, no matter how good your data is. Such pettiness seems at odds with the ideals of Science, but scientific research is a career, a competitive one, which at times is heavily influenced by ambitions and emotions that in some cases would be interesting subjects for research in themselves.

There is nothing unique about the field of psychopathy research in this regard; the same thing has happened in various departments of prestigious universities around the country. The co-discoverer of the chemical structure of DNA, Nobel laureate James D. Watson, once said that scientists are not like many people think they are. In his view "a lot of us are more like Michael Douglas—slightly evil, highly competitive [in his movie roles]."[11] But anyone on the receiving end of an unfair review or an inexplicably rejected grant application might wonder if it was Gordon Gekko, Douglas's character in the movie *Wall Street*, writing the evaluation.

Woodrow Wilson observed that the ferociousness of the academic infighting he witnessed while he was president of Princeton University was related to the triviality of the issues at stake.[12] Over time, the quote has become a version of "academic politics are so vicious because the stakes are so small." Many people who have spent a few semesters among the faculty in an academic setting can relate to this sentiment. Positions at universities open up rarely, while many people in the same field are competing for a portion of a limited supply of grant money.

In the case of the controversy surrounding the definition of psychopathy, however, the stakes are by no means small. The magnitude of the problem posed by psychopathic behavior is at least as great as that posed by schizophrenia. The National Institute of Mental Health estimates that around 2.4 million American adults 18 years of age or older have schizophrenia.[13] That is approximately 1 in 100 people in this age group. Experts generally believe that around 1 in 100 non-institutionalized adult males 18 years and older are psychopaths, meaning there could be between 2 and 3 million psychopaths in North America alone. Approximately 1 million psychopaths are locked up, on parole, or on probation.[14] These people may be responsible for half of all serious crime.[15] Their crimes, trials, and confinement have been estimated to cost between $250 and $400 billion each year.[16] In 2002, the cost of schizophrenia in the United States was an estimated $63 billion.[17] Furthermore, one out of two serial rapists may be psychopaths.[18]

Classifying someone as a psychopath, even as an adult, is a very serious step that can follow a person for life and play an important role in determining how he or she is treated by the courts. This issue clearly troubled NPR correspondent Alix Spiegel when she prepared a piece called "Can a Test Really Tell Who's a Psychopath?" in May 2011. Her subject was Robert Dixon, a convicted felon coming up for parole.[19]

Thirty years ago, a surprised Dixon asked "What happened?" when he saw the dead body of the robbery victim his accomplice had shot. Because he acted as the lookout for the robbery-turned-murder, Dixon was sentenced to 15 years to life with the possibility of parole. Coming up for parole after 26 years of confinement, Dixon agreed to be evaluated using the Psychopathy Checklist–Revised (PCL–R), which has repeatedly been called the "Gold Standard" of psychopathy measures.[20] Versions of the Checklist have dominated psychopathy research since it was first developed by Canadian psychologist and psychopathy expert Dr. Robert Hare in the 1970s. Even some academics who are highly critical of this method for measuring psychopathy and how it has come to be associated with the definition of the disorder consider it "the most widely used and extensively validated measure of psychopathy."[21] The PCL–R rates each of 20 antisocial behaviors and emotional and interpersonal traits on a three-point scale. The criteria range from need for stimulation and proneness to boredom to sexual promiscuity, from glibness and superficial charm to callousness and lack of empathy.

Among academics, a big part of the controversy surrounding psychopathy centers on the influence this test still has on researchers' views about the nature of psychopathy and the influence it has on the fate of criminal psychopaths.

As Spiegel reported it: "And so Dixon found himself sitting across a table from a no-nonsense female psychologist, answering a series of questions about his family and troubled youth.

"The woman, Dixon says, didn't look at him. Instead, she stared at the computer, methodically entering his answers, her face dimly lit by the screen.

"They talked for over an hour. Then the psychologist thanked him, closed her computer and went away."

The report doesn't mention that the evaluation, to be valid, should have included a review of his criminal record and past history. Diagnosing someone as a psychopath using the full PCL–R requires more than a pencil (or a computer) and a list of 20 items. (Some writers like Jon Ronson, the author of *The Psychopath Test*, journalists, and bloggers oversimplify the process of identifying a psychopath to a misleading degree when they lightheartedly, and at times without a clue, do exactly this and with far fewer than 20 items.) Competent, qualified professionals are trained to administer the PCL–R interview and taught to observe the subject. They should review court and other institutional records as well. Ideally, they should interview people who know the subject and can provide evidence of his or her behavior. In addition, the subject's home life and upbringing, as well as behavior during childhood, adolescence, and adulthood, in school, at work, and toward friends and lovers, should be considered. Even someone's hobbies and how they spend their "off" time may factor into the final diagnosis. All this information should then be integrated into the total psychological assessment before assigning a score.[22] More than one interview may be necessary to accumulate all the information, and the process may take as little as two hours or as many as six to complete.[23] But this, of course, is the ideal. It takes time and costs money to conduct a series of interviews, if that is required. There is always concern that unqualified examiners might cut corners.

Although it would be unconscionable to skimp when administering a test that has such significant implications for a person facing sentencing or parole, the quality control lies with the test administrator, who should be certified. While this tool for measuring psychopathy was developed for research purposes, it has become highly influential in court systems in many parts of the world, including North America and Europe. Incompetent administration of the PCL–R or other tests of psychopathy is as serious as incompetent medical care or failure to follow legal due process.

Improper application or administration of the test by unqualified personnel has raised concerns, like those expressed in Spiegel's report, that the test could be used improperly. "I feel ambivalent about it," Hare told Spiegel on air, referring to how the test may be used in the judicial system.[24]

Spiegel may have wanted more from Hare. He formed the impression over the two days Spiegel interviewed him that the NPR correspondent had an agenda to get him to repudiate the use of the test in the judicial system.

Spiegel denied she had an agenda but, according to Hare, "It turns out she was trying to get me to say that I was really concerned about how the PCL–R is being used and misused in criminal justice. Now, I am; I'm very concerned about it. But the way it was presented somehow indicated that it should not be used at all, which is clearly inappropriate. The real gist of the program was to take up the case of the California lifers [prisoners serving life terms in California prisons]. These are people who are very unlikely to get out for a very long period of time. They are in for murder and other serious crimes."[25] Hare concluded that Spiegel was trying to make the point that these convicts are never going to get out of prison because of their high PCL–R test results.

"Well, in fact, the PCL–R is never, ever the sole instrument used for parole purposes," Hare said. "In fact, it is not a risk assessment tool at all. It just measures a personality condition or disorder, as most people would say, although I don't think it is a disorder." (Hare later explained that "Disorder in psychiatry has several meanings, and does not necessarily imply deficit or malfunction."[26] After more than half a century studying psychopaths, he believes that they "have an intellectual understanding of the rules of society and the conventional meanings of right and wrong, and know enough about what they are doing to be held accountable for their actions.")[27]

Forensic psychologist Stephen Porter, Ph.D., of the University of British Columbia also questions the widely held view that high PCL–R scores routinely condemn criminals to serve their prison time with little chance of parole.

Porter and his collaborator found "that when given the opportunity to speak to a parole board, high PCL–R scores were associated with likelihood of release.[28] I think the finding relates specifically to this context in which an offender has been granted the opportunity to speak (and perhaps put on an acting job) in front of observers. Yes, the [Canadian] parole board would have been fully aware of the offenders' PCL–R scores prior to the hearing. In a more recent study we found that psychopathy was associated with the ability to effectively simulate/fake facial expressions."[29]

"I wonder," Porter continued, "if there is good evidence that high PCL–Rs actually keep people in prison longer in the U.S. It is possible that U.S. courts are more punitive and/or their parole boards are less liberal, such that people get longer sentences and then have stricter criteria to be eligible for parole in the U.S. than Canada."[30]

"Because high PCL–R scorers are such effective actors and manipulators," he added, "I would predict you'd find the same pattern in the U.S., such that IF provided the opportunity to speak to a parole board and express remorse, high PCL–R scorers would have an advantage over low scorers."

Dixon's lawyer, Charles Carbone, doesn't agree. After reading the psychologist's conclusion that "Mr. Dixon obtained a total score on the PCL–R which placed him in the high range of the clinical construct of psychopathy," he told Spiegel, "I remember reading the report and feeling heartbroken because I knew no matter how hard I worked from that day forward, that when I brought him back to the board, we were going to get denied."

One example of the fallout following Spiegel's broadcast was that psychologists in California became concerned that the report gave the impression that the PCL–R is unfairly keeping people in prison.

Hare's concern is that unqualified people may be administering and interpreting the test results. Anytime a tool or instrument is misused, whether it is a screwdriver or a test of personality traits, damage can occur. The rhetoric surrounding the use of the test can become strong inside, and outside, academia.

"One of my former students, Stephen Hart, said the PCL–R *kills* people," Hare recalled with traces of disappointment, resentment, and pain in his voice. Hart is the lead author of the short version of the PCL–R, *The Hare Psychopathy Checklist: Screening Version (PCL: SV).*[31] "Well, I don't know where it kills people," Hare said. "I don't know of anyone who's ever been condemned to death because of the PCL–R."

The short version of the test, which Hart developed with David Cox and Hare, takes about half as much time to complete as the full version. It allows a screener to determine if someone has a score high enough to justify spending the time and money to administer the full version.

If Dixon was evaluated by a qualified examiner using the most recent, full version of the PCL–R, he would have provided information concerning 20 different items, each rated 0, 1, or 2 during a semi-structured interview. The evaluation also would have included a review of his written records. He would have received a rating of "0" for any trait he lacked, a "1" when there was some indication he had the trait, and a "2" if there was abundant evidence he had it. His potential maximum score was thus 40, but a score of 30 and above in North America was sufficient to get him a diagnosis of psychopathy. In Europe, a score of 25 or higher would have secured him the same diagnosis.[32]

Most of the items—18 out of the 20—included among the PCL–R measures fall into one of four related categories or clusters.[33] Psychologists often refer to them as Factors.

It is not possible to measure a concept like psychopathy directly any more than it is possible to measure directly a concept such as intelligence. You can't heft it in your hand, weigh it on a scale, or set it next to a ruler. One of the reasons psychology is such a challenging field is because it deals with intangibles, concepts like personality, emotions, mental states, etc. We know they are real because we experience them and observe their effects, but they are impossible to measure physically. This is why some scientists in fields like physics and chemistry, and later biology, once referred to psychology and social science as "soft sciences" while they, with a bit of snobbishness and feeling of superiority, regarded their fields of study as "hard sciences."

Psychopathy research has entered the interesting in-between realm of social psychology and neuroscience. Neuroscience is bringing aspects of "hard science" to the field—for example, as we'll see, measurement of brain activity, volume, and structure—but at the same time psychologists are still arguing over what psychopathy is, who is a psychopath, and—as one can see with the debate surrounding the PCL–R—how this knowledge should be used in our society. Many researchers devoted to studying the neurobiological basis—the "hard science" aspect—of psychopathy still rely on the PCL–R, as they have for decades. It is a proven, reliable indicator of something that distinguishes the criminal psychopath who lacks a conscience from a person who has a conscience.

Because they can't measure psychopathy directly, psychologists use a statistical method called factor analysis to evaluate the features of psychopathy. It indicates to them whether or not a collection of variables, such as the behaviors or traits we associate with psychopathy, are in fact actually related to a smaller number of unknown factors. Smaller is better; it gets you closer to the source and eliminates false leads. Factor analysis in the past has yielded two-factor, three-factor, and four-factor models of psychopathy based on PCL scores.

Some statisticians are fans of factor analysis, and others think it can be used to show whatever a user wants it to show. The generally accepted view is that, like many statistical techniques, it can be used or misused. Used properly, it can identify useful patterns hidden in large, messy piles of data. Used properly, it can reduce the number of variables researchers have to deal with as they struggle to better understand complicated human behaviors. Used improperly, it could mislead.

Questions in the PCL–R[34] designed to detect Glibness and Superficial Charm, Grandiose Sense of Self-Worth, Pathological Lying, and Conning/Manipulative Behavior fall into the category of Interpersonal factors. Some people with considerable psychopathic traits are good at manipulating others with smooth talk. They often are good at persuading others and talking their way out of trouble, as Eric Harris did on many occasions while growing up. The glibness and confidence make these people effective persuaders and sometimes come across as overconfidence or arrogance. As with the other factors or dimensions of psychopathy, these traits are not obvious or apparent in all psychopaths all the time. Some show stronger traits in some of these areas than in others. It's possible these differences may reflect different subtypes of psychopaths, although that remains unresolved.

A second category of factors, Affective, includes features related to feelings or emotions: Lack of Remorse or Guilt, Shallow Affect, and Callous Lack of Empathy. Psychopaths do not feel the way other people do, and these differences show up in the laboratory. They do not respond physiologically to images that make most people cringe, even other criminals. Show most folks a picture of someone crushing their fingers in a car door, for example, and they will react almost as if they feel the pain. This is not so with psychopaths. They also differ in the way they process and use language. For example, words that have emotional connotations for most people—slaughter, rape, death—subtly grab people's attentions more than neutral words—air, float, walk. Robert Hare and his colleagues saw this back in 1991 when they compared the time it took psychopaths and non-psychopaths to decide if a group of letters represented a word or not.[35] They also used EEG (electroencephalography) to measure the subjects' brain waves (called event-related potentials) during the task. They found that non-psychopaths identified emotion-laden words faster than psychopaths and they showed greater brain wave changes while doing so. People with high psychopathy scores respond to the two sets of words as if they were the same. These deficits may be related to the inability of people who score high on the psychopathy checklist to relate to, care about, or appreciate others' emotions.

A third category on the PCL–R concerns the psychopathic lifestyle: Parasitic Lifestyle, Lack of Realistic Long-Term Goals, Impulsivity, and Irresponsibility. Many criminal psychopaths have trouble sticking with long-term projects or commitments, including jobs and relationships. Perhaps because they lack much of the ability to feel the way others do, they seek stimulation by dropping what is boring and looking for new experiences. Sometimes this means a regular job is too boring and they may find someone to exploit instead, a strategy that evokes no feelings of guilt; it is simply a means to an end.

The fourth category concerns Antisocial factors: Poor Behavioral Controls, Early Behavioral Problems, Juvenile Delinquency, Revocation of Conditional Release, and Criminal Versatility. This dimension,

David Kosson and Robert Hare maintain, "is associated not with criminal behavior per se, but with early, versatile, and persistent antisocial behavior that often is extremely distressing and frustrating for others."[36]

The final two topics look like they should fall into one or more of the above categories, but statistical analysis doesn't support this: Failure to Accept Responsibility and Many Marital Relationships.

Dixon scored high enough on the test of the above items to be considered a psychopath in the eyes of the legal system. Spiegel's NPR piece made it clear she believed Dixon's test result would condemn him, perhaps unfairly, to prison for life despite the change for the better his family and friends had seen in him in recent years. His evaluation should have considered the fact that as a youth he had threatened to kill his father and commit suicide, and that he had been convicted of assaulting a woman and raping another during a date. It's not unusual for people with high psychopathy scores to mellow with age, to turn down the antisocial behavior, if not the attitudes associated with it. It's also not unusual for them to manipulate the system and act however they need to act to get what they want. In some cases, it is possible that the perception of "mellowing with age" is simply an act.

From 1956 to 1957, Peter Woodcock, for example, killed three children in Toronto, Canada. He was seventeen years old at the time and had endured a tragic childhood, although he impressed his high school teachers as being intelligent and charming. After thirty-four years of treatment in a psychiatric institution, and now aged fifty-one, he managed to convince the staff that he should receive his first day pass. Within hours, he killed a fellow inmate, twenty-seven-year-old Dennis Kerr, on the perimeter of the hospital grounds by beating him with a pipe wrench. He said he would have killed another man too, but was too tired.[37]

There is no scientific way to balance forgiveness and wariness. Many researchers remain convinced that high-scoring individuals can never be treated, trusted, or changed, while others say that change is possible. But no parole board or judge wants to risk taking the blame if someone they release commits a heinous crime. They don't want to have critics point at them and say "You released a psychopath?! What were you thinking?"

When Hare, a pioneer of modern psychopathy research, began to study psychopathy in the late 1960s, there was no reliable—or even generally accepted—way to measure the degree of psychopathy in a person. The best measurement systems then available were "inventories" like the Minnesota Multiphasic Personality Inventory, which had been developed in the 1930s. These have the drawback of depending on the word of the subject; that is, they are self-report inventories. Needless to say, people with strong psychopathic traits are not the most reliable sources of insight into their thoughts and motivations, since deception and lying are often prominent features of psychopathy. Many people with this type of personality—or, in the opinion of some, personality disorder—can and have figured out what is being tested and adjusted their answers to sway the results.[38] A better way to measure a person's degree of psychopathic traits was necessary if scientists were ever going to understand the subjects they wanted to study.

During the development of his groundbreaking measurement instrument, Hare was influenced[39] by psychiatrist Hervey Cleckley's 1941 book, *The Mask of Sanity: An Attempt to Clarify Some Issues About the So-Called Psychopathic Personality.*[40] The anonymous, mostly favorable review of the book in the *Journal of the American Medical Association* (JAMA) began: "As a psychiatrist in the United States Veterans Administration, the author became interested in that nosological [disease classification] *wastebasket* known as 'psychopathic inferiority' and its diagnostic variations [emphasis added]."[41] Now a classic in the field, the book included 15 detailed case histories and descriptions of patients with psychopathic traits, whom Cleckley—then a professor of neuropsychiatry at the University of Georgia School of Medicine—had encountered during his career.

In gathering together these case histories and describing the personality disorder of psychopathy in 1941, Cleckley took a fresh look at a subject to which scattered references had been made for hundreds of years, and which had been described in various ways since the end of the 19th century.[42]

French physician Philippe Pinel, a key figure in the history of psychiatry, used the phrase *manie sans délire* in 1801 to describe people he recognized as having "insanity without delirium." People lacking consciences came to the attention of at least one eminent physician in North America too: just a year before he died in 1813, Dr. Benjamin Rush, a pioneer of American psychiatry and signer of the Declaration of Independence, described them as people with a "moral derangement."

You can spot familiar aspects of the psychopathic personality in people who were later described as suffering from "psychopathic inferiority," "psychopathic personality," and one now-quaint but descriptive phrase: "moral insanity."[43]

English psychiatrist James Pritchard introduced the term in 1835 to describe individuals whose moral judgment was absent or flawed but whose intellectual judgment was intact. Moral insanity captures the unique and troubling blend of seemingly rational thought processes—free of hallucinations and thought disorder—and the depravity of criminal psychopathic crimes.

It is the kind of murderous depravity that makes the morally sane mutter "Whoever did that *has* to be insane." But it would be more accurate to mutter, much less succinctly, "Whoever did that has to be insane, or has to have a personality disorder referred to as criminal psychopathy." Both Pinel and Pritchard warned their readers that people with insanity without delirium or moral insanity were next to impossible to treat, a belief that would be shared by many mental health professionals into this century.

The 19th-century psychiatrist and "criminal anthropologist" Cesare Lombroso liked the phrase *moral insanity* too. As far back as 1876, Lombroso tried to convince the world that criminal behavior had its roots in biology. Here's how his adoring daughter Gina summarized his description of one type of criminal in Lombroso's files:

"No one, before my father, had ever recognized in the criminal an abnormal being driven by an irresistible atavistic impulse to commit anti-social acts, but many had observed (cases of the kind were too frequent to escape notice) the existence of certain individuals, nearly always members of degenerate families, who seemed from their earliest infancy to be prompted by some fatal impulse to do evil to their fellow-men. They differed from ordinary people, because they hated the very persons who to normal beings are the nearest and dearest, parents, husbands, wives, and children, and because their inhuman deeds seemed to cause them no remorse. These individuals, who were sometimes treated as lunatics, sometimes as diseased persons, and sometimes as criminals, were said by the earliest observers to be afflicted with moral insanity."[44]

Lombroso insisted that criminals had distinguishing, often inherited, physical and mental abnormalities. Today, scientists are comfortable entertaining the possibility of mental anomalies and genetic influences. They long ago discounted Lombroso's suggestion that born criminals could be distinguished from decent folk by the shape of their skulls, facial bones, projecting ears, receding foreheads, badly shaped teeth, and other physical markers he called "stigmata." An intriguing and complex character, the Father of Criminal Anthropology was typically racist for his time but also supported more humane treatment for criminals, whom he saw as primitive evolutionary throwbacks.

Lombroso was only ten years old in 1845 (a decade after Pritchard described moral insanity), when the word *psychopathy*, used in the modern sense, first appeared in print. It showed up in *The Principles of Medical Psychology, Being the Outlines of a Course of Lectures by Baron Ernst von Feuchtersleben*, by whom else but Baron Ernst von Feuchtersleben.[45] After this work was translated four decades later, von Feuchtersleben's label became more common in English speaking countries. The concept of psychopathy, however, would remain a wastebasket diagnosis in the U.S. until Cleckley wrote his classic.

"With a flair for the literary," the JAMA reviewer noted, Cleckley presented key behavioral patterns and personality traits characteristic of psychopathic personalities to his fellow psychiatrists. He provided evidence that psychopathy was worthy of more serious study than it had received.

The Gold Standard or the 800-Pound Gorilla

Unfortunately, fellow psychiatrists failed to follow up on the insights into psychopathy that Cleckley offered. Psychologist Hare recognized the value of Cleckley's work and used it as the basis for the earliest versions of what was to become the Psychopathy Checklist, which he introduced in 1980. He issued a revised version, the Psychopathy Checklist–Revised (PCL–R), in 1991. The second edition of the PCL–R was published in 2003.[46]

Some researchers aren't happy with the status of the Antisocial factors in the PCL–R. David Cooke, Professor of Forensic Clinical Psychology, and his colleagues at the Glasgow Caledonian University, for example, conclude that "antisocial behavior is best viewed as a secondary symptom or consequence of psychopathy."[47] Hare and his colleagues disagree. They point out that a psychopathic offender's tendency to botch the opportunities afforded by parole and probation—like "LTK," a prototypical criminal psychopath we'll meet in Chapter 7 and rapist/murdered Brian Dugan, whom we'll meet in the last chapter—as well as his tendency to get into trouble when behind bars and to engage in criminal activity, "appear quite useful in identifying psychopaths within offender samples." They also acknowledge that not enough studies examining the importance of antisocial features in non-offenders have been done, but they add "the available research is consistent with clinical lore about individuals with psychopathic personalities who do not break the law."[48]

Hare also notes that critics ignore the fact that the shorter screening version of the PCL–R is a parallel instrument that is designed for use in people who are not criminals, and yet, research results show, that it does exactly the same thing PCL–R does.

This and other criticisms surrounding the use of the PCL–R inspired Adrian Raine, a professor of criminology, psychiatry, and psychology at the University of Pennsylvania, to mischievously ask a provocative question at the 5th Biennial Meeting of the Society for the Scientific Study of Psychopathy. It was, he said, a question that many psychopathy researchers were gossiping about. "Does the psychopathy checklist have too much of a stranglehold on research in psychopathy?" he asked the two hundred or so psychologists, neuroscientists, psychiatrists, students, and journalists gathered in the grand ballroom of the L'Enfant Plaza Hotel in Washington, D.C., on June 6, 2013.

Was the PCL–R, he continued, "the 800-pound gorilla" in this field?[49] An important inspiration behind his controversy-spurring challenge to the attendees was a 2011 paper by Jennifer Skeem of the University of California, Irvine and her colleagues.[50] That monograph, Raine said, implied that the checklist has done a wonderful job in the past twenty or thirty years of promoting progress in the field, but there is a "worry that psychopathy, the construct, is getting equated with a measurement instrument."

Raine here indeed touched on a sensitive issue in the field: when many people say PCL–R, they mean psychopathy. "And that really rankles a lot of people," according to Hare.

Perhaps, the review suggested to Raine, other ways of measuring and rating psychopathy should be more widely tested and used. To Raine, it seemed like a call to "not get ourselves blinded by always using the psychopathy checklist."

Many psychologists might not agree, but it might be useful to compare the concern—that a measure of psychopathy is being confused with psychopathy itself (or the construct of psychopathy, as psychologists would put it)—to the study of another controversial topic: intelligence. Early tests of intelligence were once confused with the nature of intelligence itself—that is, the construct of intelligence.

Psychologists continue to refine intelligence tests and develop new theories of intelligence. For example Howard Gardner's IQ test measures what he refers to as "multiple intelligences." In addition to verbal and mathematical skills, he tests mechanical, physical, musical, and social skills. The cognitive psychologist Robert Sternberg suggests that intelligence involves three components. His triarchic (a fancy word for three-component) model includes creative, analytical, and practical or common-sense intelligence.[51]

Everyone has an intuitive sense of what intelligence is, but measuring it clearly is not a simple matter. Different measures of intelligence seem to bring us closer to different aspects of the essence or the construct of intelligence.

"We will always need some way of making intelligent decisions about people," psychologist and former president of the American Psychological Association Diane F. Halpern told a reporter for *Monitor on Psychology* in 2003. "We're not all the same; we have different skills and abilities. What's wrong is thinking of intelligence as a fixed, innate ability, instead of something that develops in a context."[52]

The study of psychopathy today presents problems just as challenging. While criminal psychopaths often share a remarkably similar constellation of traits, some appear to have more characteristics described in some categories or factors of the PCL–R than others. Non-criminal psychopaths may have their own distinguishing profile of psychological traits.

A few researchers are developing new theories of psychopathy and now the field of psychopathy research has its own Triarchic model developed by Christopher Patrick, of Florida State University, and his colleagues.[53]

Early in his career, Patrick had done research on pain and lie detection and got interested in psychopathy, a subject he thought "was kind of cool" when he was a graduate student. He said he was "lucky enough to be at the University of British Columbia, where Bob Hare, the top expert in the world, was studying the topic with a number of students. I really benefited a lot from that."[54]

Patrick's theoretical model attempts to reorganize, or make better sense of, various descriptions of psychopathy that emphasize different core features of the disorder. Psychopathy, according to this model, includes three distinct components: disinhibition, boldness, and meanness. Disinhibition covers a person's inability to control their impulses. Pierre, an intelligent college student and a patient of Hervey Cleckley, for example, forged signatures on checks for small amounts of money he did not need. He could have walked a short way to other businesses where he would have been unfamiliar to his victim. Instead, he cashed one forged check in a nearby tavern owned by his girlfriend's father, making it easy to identify him. His teachers, parents, and authorities were baffled by his behavior. "I just don't know why I did it," he first told Cleckley. Later he said he was "impelled by desire for money." On another day Pierre explained that "It seems there was some sort of an impulse I can't account for." A couple of days later he said "I just didn't think [about] what I was doing."[55]

Boldness covers the traits of "social dominance, emotional resiliency, and venturesomeness." And "meanness" refers to aggressive behavior used to obtain benefits without concern for anyone else. For the term "anyone else," in many cases you might substitute the word "victims." The Triarchic model of psychopathy is an effort to reconcile different views of psychopathy. It has already been credited with advancing the assessment of the condition and providing insights into its nature. Future research will reveal whether it can succeed in further clarifying the concept while providing practical guidelines for psychologists and psychiatrists to use in the clinic.

Whether the Triarchic or another model someday provides the best insight and description of the phenomenon of psychopathy, researchers like Adrian Raine acknowledge that there is a counterpoint to the criticism of the suggestion that the PCL–R is not the "Gold Standard" of psychopathy testing, that it is just one way of testing and examining a complex condition: "My perspective is: it's not 24-karat gold, but it's 18-karat gold. And for better or worse, we still have the '800-pound gorilla' to contend with."

Near the end of the discussion he led on the question of the dominance of the PCL–R psychopathy measure, Raine saw Robert Hare raise his hand. He turned the floor over to the researcher who had pioneered much of the scientific study of psychopathy in the second half of the 20th century, and who had developed (depending on your viewpoint) the Gold Standard and/or the 800-pound gorilla of psychopathy research.

"The question sounds interesting," Hare said in a soft Canadian accent. "'Has the PCL–R strangled research?' Hardly. As a matter of fact, I would argue that the PCL–R has fomented research in psychopathy with different forms, different approaches, and different instruments. In fact, if you look at the program for this particular meeting, more than half of the presentations have nothing to do with the PCL–R; they have to do with other measuring tools. So I think the question is a mock question, and it is also a red herring."

Hare went on to mention the problems of using self-report inventories when measuring psychopathy. Their use has serious implications for scientific research, potential new treatments, and, perhaps one day, sentencing. He acknowledged that many of them have very good predictive power, but posed the question: "What is going to happen to the self-report inventories when an offender knows that how he or she fills out the inventory is going to have a direct impact upon what is going to happen to him or her in subsequent hearings? In all of the research we do [in the laboratory], the responses are anonymous, but that is not how it works in the real world."

Next, Hare addressed the criticism that everything relates back to the cluster of psychopathic traits examined in the PCL–R under the heading Antisocial Behavior, Factor 4. "That is simply not true," Hare asserted. He explained that results depend on how the data is analyzed, whether various correlations are simplified and what the outcome measure is.

The PCL–R is criticized by Skeem and others because they claim it over-emphasizes criminality in the construct of psychopathy. "Technically it does," Hare said later, "there are some items that involve criminality, but if you take the screening version—the 12-item version—there's no criminality at all and it is highly correlated with the PCL–R. Whenever anyone criticizes the PCL–R for criminal behavior, they ignore the fact that we have a parallel instrument that has no criminality in it, and yet does exactly the same thing."

This issue is so contentious that it almost came to legal blows when Jennifer Skeem of the University of California, Irvine and David Cooke of the Glasgow Caledonian University wrote an opinion piece in 2010 for the journal *Psychological Assessment*. This controversial article criticized what they saw as confusion between the measurement of psychopathic traits using the PCL–R and the very nature or construct of psychopathy. They accused Hare of overemphasizing criminal behavior in the analysis of psychopathic behavior. They concluded: "Failure to distinguish between personality pathology and criminal behavior can only serve to confuse the field."[56]

Although the paper had been approved for publication in 2007, Hare obtained a copy before it was published. He felt the opinion piece misquoted his publications and misrepresented his views by using fabrications and straw man arguments. Hare persuaded the senior editor of *Psychological Assessment* to request that the authors reconsider portions of their manuscript that he claimed misquoted and misrepresented his published statements. Skeem and Cooke made some changes, but they were insufficient in Hare's view. Having exhausted his options for getting the corrections he sought, Hare threatened to sue for defamation if the corrections were not made. "The main issue here is that these authors misrepresented my views by distorting things I said," he told a *New York Times* reporter in 2010. "I have been doing this work for 40 years and never seen anything like it."[57]

Skeem told the reporter: "When we first wrote the paper, we saw it simply as a call to the field to recognize we were going down a path where we were equating an abstract concept with a checklist, and it was preventing us from looking at the concept more closely."

Publication of the paper was delayed by three years, although it circulated widely among psychologists in the field. It was finally published in June 2010 with changes by the authors. It was accompanied by a response by Hare and a response to his response by Skeem and Cooke. The paper leaves no doubt about how the authors feel about Hare's body of work relating to the PCL–R and his influence on the field. It makes the point that a test of psychopathy should not be confused with the construct of psychopathy.

Many fellow researchers felt that Hare, for his part, was mistaken to threaten a lawsuit, no matter how personal an attack he perceived it to be and no matter how misrepresented he felt his work to be. As unpleasant and at times nasty these controversies can be, many believed the battle should have been fought in the journals and not in the courtroom.

Hare, however, has documented several examples where his published statements were changed in the original version of the article by Skeem and Cooke. These mis-quotes were eventually corrected but only, Hare maintains, after he threatened legal action.[58]

As he summed up his response to Adrian Raine's question, "Does the psychopathy checklist have too much of a stranglehold on research in psychopathy?" Hare told the audience that:

The development of new measures is a terrific idea. It's how science progresses. And if the PCL–R is proven to be inferior to other measures, that's fine. So far, he noted, "it has been shown to be different, as opposed to inferior." He continued on to say that it makes sense for researchers to look at psychopathy from different perspectives while trying to focus in on the same construct. (He later described Patrick's Triarchic model of psychopathy as brilliant but difficult for many people to follow because of the complex detail behind its formulation.)

"On the other hand, I do worry that new tests are being developed so frequently that I think we are in danger of maybe going back to where we were 25 or 30 years ago when we were all talking about the same construct, but were actually measuring many different things or constructs."

The Sociopath Next Door to the Psychopath

In addition to the dangers of measuring many different things or constructs when trying to understand psychopathy, something the Triarchic model hopes to avoid, people are still struggling with imprecise terminology. Today many people, including many mental health professionals, equate psychopaths with sociopaths. The American Psychiatric Association, and many psychiatrists like Frank Ochberg and psychologists like Martha Stout, the author of *The Sociopath Next Door*, consider a sociopath and a psychopath to be, if not exactly, then practically the same thing. For most clinicians, the differences don't matter in their work. Frequently, the two terms also are used interchangeably by many members of the public. The problem with this viewpoint is that some people have assigned different meanings to the word sociopath that, in their minds, distinguish it from psychopath.

There are a couple of reasons the label sociopath gained a foothold firm enough to create confusion in the field of abnormal psychology which is still struggling for agreed upon definitions. In the early part of the 20th century, the word psychopath described not only individuals who lacked a conscience but included others who had additional mental or personality disorders such as weak-mindedness and depression. The term sociopath became popular starting in the 1930s in part because it conveys the impression that the antisocial symptoms can be traced to social influences rather than to biological ones. In the past, social influences in criminal behavior were considered more important than biological influences. Today, the most popular explanation is that both influences contribute to criminal behavior and, very likely, to the development of psychopathic behavior.

As already noted, some people differentiate between sociopaths and psychopaths as if well–understood and well–documented nuances separate the terms. The inclusion of "socio" in the term sociopath may still appeal to people who believe that the origin of the pathology can be traced more to the influences of society than to biology. For them, a sociopath is created but a psychopath is born. Also, use of the word sociopath would be one way to avoid the confusion between psychotic and psychopathic. Sadly, there is no general agreement that the label sociopath reflects these distinctions, and academic researchers favor the term psychopath.

The definition of terms, the popular philosopher and history explainer Will Durant wrote, "is difficult, and ruthlessly tests the mind; but once done it is half of any task."[59] Psychologists do not appear to have reached the halfway point in their task of reaching a reasonable understanding of psychopathy, but there are at least plenty of terms from which they have to choose.

The Word of "The Bible"

The word "sociopath" has multiple definitions and yet is still a byword in popular culture. One of the reasons it persists despite its vagueness is because the American Psychiatric Association (APA) used the diagnosis *Sociopathic* Personality Disturbance between 1952 and 1968. As a result, *sociopath* has lingered ever since as a synonym for someone who has antisocial personality disorder or is a psychopath.

Today, the APA uses the diagnosis Antisocial Personality Disorder in the most recent edition of the Diagnostic and Statistical Manual of Mental Disorders, DSM-5. This is the encyclopedia-like guide most clinicians and insurance companies use to diagnose and classify mental and personality disorders. It is frequently referred to as "The Bible" of psychiatry because it plays such a central role in the field. Consequently, with so little still understood about the nature and causes of mental disorders, it has been a focus of controversy since it was first published in 1952. But, if someone has a mental disorder, that person can almost certainly find its symptoms listed neatly somewhere in the 947 pages of the DSM-5.

Critics suggest that it is even possible to read up on some mental disorders that aren't really mental disorders within the volume. They say these are more like traits, eccentricities, or even perhaps extreme, but nevertheless normal, examples of human behavior. They cite Hoarding Disorder, Oppositional Defiant Disorder ("A pattern of angry/irritable mood, argumentative/defiant behavior, or vindictiveness . . ."), Binge-eating Disorder, and Disruptive Mood Dysregulation Disorder ("chronic, severe persistent irritability . . . frequent temper outbursts") as examples.

The same critics often fail to mention that any behavior or syndrome that causes pain and suffering, or that interferes with or prevents someone from living a satisfying and productive life, is a legitimate subject for psychiatric or medical care, and thus worthy of inclusion in the manual. The problem may affect only the person diagnosed with the disorder, or it may extend to others, including family members and society itself, as is the case with antisocial personality disorder.

Another criticism is that the American Psychiatric Association is too heavily influenced by pharmaceutical companies who stand to benefit if more pills are prescribed for more disorders. One study concluded that 56% of the 170 mental health professionals contributing to the DSM–IV, which was published in 1994 and revised in 2000, received money from the pharmaceutical industry in the form of research funding, consultancies, or speaking fees.[60] Reportedly, 70% of the contributors to the DSM-5, which appeared in 2013, have such ties.[61] The description of antisocial personality disorder in various editions of the DSM and its relationship to psychopathy has been just as great a source of controversy over the years.

You might think that the term "sociopath" would be a good label for people with antisocial personality disorder (ASPD), the closest diagnosis to psychopathy the American Psychiatric Association recognizes. In fact, the organization considers sociopathy, psychopathy, and the World Health Organization's version, dyssocial or dissocial personality disorder, to be the same thing as ASPD.

The criteria for antisocial personality disorder and other personality disorders, including borderline, paranoid, narcissistic, obsessive-compulsive, etc., listed in the previous edition of the standard manual for classifying mental disorders, the DSM-IV, have not changed in the most recent edition. In fact, it hasn't changed much since the DSM-III came out in 1980. Does this mean psychiatrists have made no progress in recent decades in understanding personality disorders, including the one it says is the same thing as psychopathy?

It depends, of course, on whom you ask. Not surprisingly, some psychiatrists see encouraging progress. In 2012, for example, Jerold Heisman and Hal Strauss, authors of *I Hate You, Don't Leave Me: Understanding the Borderline Personality,* recognized enough progress in understanding this disorder to release an updated edition of their classic 1991 book. For over twenty years, their book was one of the most popular sources of information for the general public about people burdened with a poor sense of identity who often are self-destructive, are afraid of being abandoned, and experience rapid mood swings. And psychiatrist David Kupfer, M.D., the chair of APA's DSM-5 Task Force, sees progress in our understanding of schizophrenia, bipolar disorder, and autism spectrum disorder based on the experiences psychiatrists have gained studying and treating these disorders, despite the inability of neuroscientists so far to identify the neural basis of 97 percent of the mental disorders listed in the DSM-5.

Others, including the Director of the National Institute of Mental Health, Tom Insel, M.D., a former Professor of Psychiatry at Emory

University, are not impressed with recent psychiatric progress. Insel has largely given up on the DSM-5—and the approach it takes.

The DSM, Insel insists, lacks scientific validity. He sees it as a good dictionary, one that provides "reliability" [his use of quotes] since its common use ensures that mental healthcare providers are all talking about the same thing when they mention a diagnosis. The problem the Director sees is the lack of objective laboratory measurements for making the diagnoses in the first place. It still relies on lists or clusters of clinical symptoms to make diagnoses. "In the rest of medicine, this would be equivalent to creating diagnostic systems based on the nature of chest pain or the quality of fever," Insel blogged.[62]

He wants to spur psychiatric research into the 21st century by promoting research in genetics, brain imaging, and cognitive science to transform the way mental illnesses are diagnosed. The NIMH, which funded more than $912 million in research project grants in 2013, will no longer award grants based on DSM classifications. Instead they "will be supporting research projects that look across current categories—or sub-divide current categories—to begin to develop a better system."

It may take years, even decades, to come up with reliable clinical tests that will be able to accurately diagnose mental disorders from a neurological standpoint. Insel knows this and wants to get started finding better ways to diagnose mental disorders based on biological markers. Unfortunately, neuroscience, the basis of biological psychiatry, is way behind older fields of biology like physiology in understanding the fundamentals of its subject. Before progress is likely in mental health research, there will need to be considerable progress in understanding the brain itself. Despite a pop-neuroscience industry that today tacks "neuro" onto seemingly anything: economics, ethics, law, marketing, semantics, education, energetics, fitness, fuel, drinks, and more, the field is very young and researchers are still struggling to understand basic principles of brain organization and function and how it relates to behavior.

This is why psychiatrist Kupfer as chair of the DSM-5 Task Force responded to psychiatrist and NIMH Director Insel by noting that we have been waiting for biological and genetic markers of mental disorder for at least forty years and we are still waiting. Efforts to provide these markers are obviously important. "But they cannot serve us in the here and now, and they cannot supplant DSM-5," Kupfer wrote in an APA news release in response to Insel's broadside attack. "In the meantime," he concluded, "should we merely hand patients another promissory note that something may happen sometime? Every day, we are dealing with impairment or tangible suffering, and we must respond. Our patients deserve no less."

The field of psychopathy research is somewhat entangled in this complicated controversy. For the most part, academic researchers are convinced that antisocial personality disorder as defined in the DSM-5 does not fully capture all of the features and personality traits of psychopathy as they conceive of the concept. The majority of people diagnosed with antisocial personality disorder are given that diagnosis because they have displayed behaviors that are criminal, antisocial, and in some cases violent. But these behaviors, the criteria for diagnosing the disorder, don't address some of the core, defining features of psychopathy, such as lack of empathy, grandiose sense of self-worth, and emotional poverty (shallow affect). Measuring psychopathy, by contrast, involves determination of personality traits *based* on past and present behaviors, not on the behaviors by themselves. Consequently, you won't find any indication in the following diagnostic checklist that a prisoner with antisocial personality exhibits superficial charm, fearlessness, lack of empathy, lack of a conscience, or lack of emotional depth, for example.

The U.S. Justice Department's Bureau of Justice Statistics reported in July 2013 that there were around 1,571,013 inmates in federal or state prisons in 2012.[63] This is 27,770 fewer inmates than were locked up in 2011. The promising drop, the third in a three-year streak, unfortunately doesn't mean the incidence of criminal psychopathy or antisocial personality disorder is declining.

For every one of the million or more adult male criminal psychopaths you are liable to encounter behind bars, on probation, on parole, or on trial, you will meet two or three non-psychopaths with criminal records who have ASPD.[64] In other words, the six or seven million males in the U.S. judicial system include different types of people who commit crimes for different reasons. An estimated 16% of them are psychopaths,[65] but as many as 80% of them have antisocial personality disorder. These figures mean that around two or three million criminals eighteen years or older in the U.S have demonstrated three or more of the following behaviors:

- "Failure to conform to social norms with respect to lawful behaviors, as indicated by repeatedly performing acts that are grounds for arrest.
- "Deceitfulness, as indicated by repeated lying, use of aliases, or conning others for personal profit or pleasure.
- "Impulsivity or failure to plan ahead.
- "Irritability and aggressiveness, as indicated by repeated physical fights or assaults.
- "Reckless disregard for safety of self or others.
- "Consistent irresponsibility, as indicated by repeated failure to sustain consistent work behavior or honor financial obligations.
- "Lack of remorse, as indicated by being indifferent to or rationalizing having hurt, mistreated, or stolen from another."[66]

It turns out that most criminal psychopaths meet the criteria for ASPD listed above, "*but most individuals with ASPD are not psychopaths* [original emphasis]" according to Hare.[67]

When criminals with ASPD also have psychopathy in their personality profile, the results aren't good news for the rest of us. Summarizing their ongoing legacies, King's College London researcher Sarah Gregory and her collaborators note that such men "begin offending earlier, engage in a broader range and greater density of offending behaviors, and respond less well to treatment programs in childhood and adulthood compared with those with ASPD without psychopathy."[68]

The final requirement for a diagnosis of ASPD is evidence of conduct disorder before age 15. "Conduct disorder" is a diagnosis given mainly to children and teens whose antisocial behavior goes far beyond the typical behavioral problems that the parents of less troubled children have to deal with. It involves serious and troubling behaviors like:

- Aggression to people and animals. Examples include physical fighting, bullying, intimidation, threatening behavior, use of a weapon to harm another, and cruelty to people or animals.
- Destruction of property. Setting fires and/or otherwise destroying property.

- Deceitfulness or theft. Conning others, breaking into others' property, and stealing.
- Serious violation of rules. Running away from home, skipping school, often staying out at night after starting this behavior before age 13.

You don't need to go to prison to become familiar with ASPD. If you were to hang out with a gang in Great Britain, for instance, you would find that eight or nine out of every ten of your companions would have antisocial personality disorder.[69] All children with conduct disorder, of course, do not become psychopaths, but many criminal psychopaths show some of these behaviors growing up.

With the publication of the DSM-5, this subgroup may be recognized with a new addition to the psychiatric manual's description of conduct disorder. The latest version includes the characteristic "Callous—lack of empathy." Recognizing that a subgroup of children with conduct disorder have a cold, uncaring outlook and a nearly complete disregard for the feelings of others—including others they have harmed—is an important step toward someday including the core features of psychopathy in the descriptive entries of the standard psychiatric manual for diagnosing mental disorders.

Another indication that clinical psychiatry and academic research in time might better define the concept of psychopathy is found toward the back of the DSM-5 in Section III: Alternative DSM-5 Model for Personality Disorders. These descriptions are based on the assumption that personality traits are present in different degrees in different people. Instead of using an all-or-none approach by trying to nail down a diagnosis by determining whether a particular trait is present or not, this approach, which psychologists refer to as a dimensional approach, tries to determine how much of a personality trait is present in an individual. Among the alternative models of personality disorders in the DSM-5 you can find a description of antisocial personality disorder with psychopathic features.

Christopher Patrick, who served as a special advisor to the committee that wrote the personality-disorder section of the manual, says this specifier incorporates key features of his Triarchic model of psychopathy: boldness, meanness, and disinhibition. So why isn't this newer, dimensionally based model of psychopathy in the front section of the DSM-5, the section clinicians will refer to when they diagnose troublesome people seated across from them in the office or prison exam room?

The workgroup rewriting the personality section didn't spend any time revising the older version and ran out of time working on the revised version. "They ran out of time at the very last minute [and] had the rug pulled out from under them," Patrick said. The Trustees, who had overall responsibility for the rewrite, "were really nervous about this new system," he recalled. They didn't feel comfortable putting it into the main manual, so they relegated it to a back section.

Perhaps we shouldn't be surprised that progress in this field often appears to crawl. After all, it represents an attempt to understand what distinguishes a human being with a conscience from one without a conscience. Insights into the traits we have come to identify with psychopathy, and which appear in both older and emerging models of the disorder, can be traced in medical writings all the way back to Philippe Pinel around the turn of the 18th century. Progress building on Pinel's description of people with "insanity without delirium" was sluggish for hundreds of years. Jeff Feix, Ph.D., Director of Forensic and Juvenile Court Services at the Tennessee Department of Mental Health, estimated in 2006 that "the concept of psychopathy has undergone more study and refinement in the past 20 years than in the previous 200. . . ."[70]

In the lobby of the L'Enfant Plaza Hotel in Washington, D.C. on a Friday afternoon, Robert Hare wistfully mentioned that many of the young people attending the 2013 meeting of the Society for the Scientific Study of Psychopathy didn't know who he was. This was a day after Chris Patrick began his acceptance speech upon receiving the 2013 R. D. Hare Lifetime Achievement Award by saying to Hare, who was seated in the audience:

"I want to thank you for keeping the field alive for so many years. I can only imagine what it must've been like to be starting out with no one else working in the area in the same way, to do the kind of work you did for all those years. And I think through the 1960s and '70s and '80s, you made the field what it was and opened up the opportunities for a lot of us.

I really want to thank you. I'm proud to be a recipient of an award named for Robert D. Hare."

Hare's work in the 20th century is still exerting a significant influence in the 21st century. His development of the PCL–R marks the point when "the story of psychopathy becomes the science of psychopathy," according to Feix. The concept will continue to evolve, but "psychopath" as described by Hare remains the most useful, practical description of the criminals who are the subjects of much of the neurobiological research being conducted today. Future challenges will involve incorporating insights from social-cognitive and neurosciences into a cohesive picture of this intriguing version of human nature in which empathy and conscience are absent.

On February 6, 1940, poet Ezra Pound wrote a letter to philosopher George Santayana in which he proposed they co-author, with poet T. S. Eliot, a book on education. In his attempt to persuade the philosopher, the poet included what he thought was a quote by Santayana: "It doesn't matter what so long as they all read the same things."[71]

The quote may not accurately reflect Santayana's views, but it nevertheless makes some sense when adapted for any group that wants to educate itself. For mental health researchers who want to learn about a specific population, it doesn't matter which population they study, so long as everyone in the field studies the same population.

Once they agree on what a psychopath is, they can begin gathering meaningful and interpretable information about whatever it is that makes a morally insane brain physically different from a morally sane one. The most direct way to do that is to look at living, functional brains using one of the neurosciences' most popular tools: functional magnetic resonance imaging.

Chapter Three

What Does Brain Imaging See?

To the unaided eye, most brains look alike. Even brains that lack some of the honorable traits of humanity—a conscience and a sense of empathy—appear deceptively normal at first glance. Scientists have reported subtle differences in structure and function in the brains of psychopaths compared to the brains of psychologically healthy individuals, but detecting these differences requires millions of dollars' worth of equipment, years of training, and months or years of work. Besides the basic cost of one to three million dollars for an fMRI machine, you can add on the expense of building special housing for the device as well as maintenance fees. The total can easily surpass five million dollars.

Researchers have turned to this expensive tool, however, because it allows them to see activity in living, working brains whose functioning results in what we call the mind and whose products include, if we are lucky, empathy, altruism, and a conscience. Brain scans, of course, cannot see human emotions or traits. There is a difference between what technology reveals in a brain scan and what we infer is taking place in the thought processes of the person being scanned. This chapter will review the technology behind fMRI brain scans, but it is still up to readers to ask themselves how much the technology does—and could—reveal about psychopathic or other behavior and how this technology can complement insights from psychological tests and assessments.

Despite the general similarities between the brains of psychopaths and non-psychopaths, hints of differences may show up during a chat with a criminal psychopath, before the fMRI is turned on. These suggestions of abnormalities don't require the multimillion-dollar equipment that is being used in the search for biological influences on psychopathic behavior. They do, however, partially explain why many researchers are willing to devote their careers and raise millions of dollars in research grants in the hope of tracking down the source of psychopathic behavior.

For example, some of the core emotional and interpersonal traits of psychopathy are suggested in an interview with "Brad," as Joshua Buckholtz, Ph.D., refers to the criminal psychopath in an article he co-authored with Kent Kiehl for *Scientific American Mind*.[1] During the exchange, Brad's conversation suggested some of the textbook features of psychopathy: lack of empathy, lack of remorse, lack of guilt, impulsiveness, callousness, and superficial charm.

According to Buckholtz, who is now an Assistant Professor of Psychology at Harvard University, Brad recalled abducting a young woman and rendering her defenseless by tying her to a tree. He calmly told of sexually assaulting her over the course of two days. Then he described how he finally killed her by cutting her throat.

Without pausing, the kidnapper, rapist, torturer, and murderer finished his account by asking the interviewer: "Do you have a girl? Because I think it's really important to practice the three C's—caring, communication, and compassion. That's the secret to a good relationship. I tried to practice the three C's in all my relationships."[2]

Surreal conversational twists that reveal a disconnection between empathy and action are not unusual in interviews with criminal psychopaths like Brad. Any brain incapable of grasping the incongruity of admitting to a heinous crime an instant before asserting a personal commitment to practicing "caring, communication, and compassion" in all relationships must, common sense would suggest, be very different on a fundamental level from most brains.

Robert Hare provides multiple examples in his book *Without Conscience*. In one, an armed robber counters a witness's testimony placing him at the scene of a crime by saying "He's lying. I wasn't there. I should have blown his fucking head off."[3]

"Jack," a petty thief and con man who scored the maximum 40 on the PCL–R, told an interviewer that his start in crime had to do with his mother: ". . . the most beautiful person in the world. She was strong, she worked hard to take care of four kids. A beautiful person. I started stealing her jewelry when I was in the fifth grade. You know, I never really knew the bitch—we went our separate ways."[4]

"Willem Boerema" displayed slightly less odd contradictory speech when he expressed his opinion of the value of a brain-imaging study he took part in. "It was stupid, boring," he told *Nature* magazine's Senior European Correspondent Alison Abbott in 2007 before adding "if they say the study can help people then it's good."[5] Abbott assigned Willem his pseudonym in 2001[6] when she first encountered him in the course of her work. She later described him as "smart, articulate and multilingual."[7]

Unlike Brad and Jack, Willem didn't want to talk about his crimes. In return for not having to discuss his past history, Willem agreed to be featured in Abbott's *Nature* articles as he took part in experiments in the Netherlands. He was part of a study comparing brain responses in people with empathy to those without. The latter group includes people with autism and, in Willem's case, psychopathy.

Willem's criminal history was less important than his rating of 35 out of 40 on the PCL–R. In North America, a score of 30 generally is the cutoff for a diagnosis of psychopathy. In much of Europe, it is 25. With a score of 35, Willem readily exceeded the entry requirements. His high score was more than enough to earn him a break from his daily routine so he could enjoy the novelty of taking part in a neuroscience experiment. It was also a significant factor in his involuntary commitment to the high-security Dutch Forensic Psychiatric Clinic, where he had been confined since 1996.

The type of brain-scanning experiment Willem volunteered for depends on a relatively new technology. fMRI has only been around for a couple of decades, but it has quickly become a preeminent tool in cognitive neuroscience. Its popularity with neuroscientists can be traced directly to the conviction that mental phenomena such as a lack of empathy and other deficits that make up the defining personality traits of criminal psychopaths can be traced to the function of interacting clusters of brain cells. In other words, according to this point of view, products of the mind like empathy, remorse, compassion, cruelty, and violent tendencies are products of physical brain tissue.

Some fundamental questions—Is the mind a product of the brain? Is the mind distinct from the brain?—must be addressed because they linger in—or, in some cases, haunt the thoughts of—many people whenever scientists discuss or investigate mental activity. Unanswerable (and sometimes tedious) discussions of free will versus determinism have been known to crop up even when neuroscientists discuss psychopathy. The philosophical topic arose very briefly during Adrian Raine's audience-participation session at the 5th Biennial Meeting of the Society for the Scientific Study of Psychopathy.

Philosophizing Before Scanning

Many philosophers, theologians, and people of other walks of life insist that the mind is more than the brain. They rely largely on verbal arguments to defend this viewpoint. They may be correct; no one can say for sure. It is not possible to disprove the existence of an intangible entity that many people assume or believe exists. But their arguments lie outside the boundaries and limitations of science because they can't be tested convincingly and reproducibly in a laboratory. Consequently, many neuroscientists with a quantitative bent are not dualist: they don't recognize a separation between mind and brain.

Instead, they point to experimental results to support the argument that there is no reason or need to postulate a mind distinct from the brain. Changes in the brain are closely associated with changes in behavior, outlook, and emotional state. Drugs, surgery, injury, and stroke—all of which alter or change the structure and function of the brain, can also alter or change personality and behavior, two concepts closely associated with the mind. In the view of modern science, there is no reason to believe that the mind and brain exist or function separately. Mind and brain can be thought of as being on different levels of *analysis*, but not on different levels of *existence*.

Property dualism is the label philosophers use to describe the belief that mind and brain are separate properties of a single tangible substance:

for example, lots and lots of neurons and their complex interconnections. Property dualists, however, might not agree that the mind can be reduced to the brain, even though both owe their existence to the same substance.

That belief belongs to the opposing side in this age-old battle in the arena of the philosophy of mind. It is called monism. The subcategory of monism that comes closest to what neuroscientists are up to when they peek into the brains of psychopaths and other volunteers is called physicalism. Anyone who believes that the mind can be reduced to what happens in the brain is a physicalist in the eyes of philosophers. And anyone who believes that mental states and brain states are the same thing is a type physicalist.

If the physicalists are correct, then key underlying elements of psychopathy can be found ultimately somewhere in the structures that make up the brain and in the interconnections of its different regions. Somewhere in the neural circuits of the brains of psychopaths we'll discuss like Brad, Willem, and Jack are answers that explain their aberrant outlook, behavior, and crimes.

Their brains, like the brains of non-psychopaths, have billions of brain cells, although no one knows precisely how many lie beneath the glistening, pink-tinted surface of the neocortex. The cerebral cortex is divided into neocortex and allocortex. They differ based on their cellular organization and how they develop in a fetus. Neocortex represents about 85 percent of the cerebral cortex and is prominent in large areas of the brain implicated in psychopathy including the frontal and temporal lobes (Figures 8 and 9).

Some studies have found that the brains of psychopaths may be a little light in cortical density or thickness in these regions, but not so much that you could see the difference with your naked eye. The highlighted region in Figure 9, for example, marks one area which reportedly contains less gray matter in psychopaths than in non-psychopaths.[8] This part of the brain—it is the temporal pole in the temporal lobe—is involved, along with other brain regions, in processing and recognizing emotions.

Back in 2000, Adrian Raine and his co-workers reported an 11 percent decrease in prefrontal gray matter in the brains of 21 men with average Hare psychopathy scores of 29 (plus or minus 6) out of 40. In their view, the prefrontal lobe deficit they found with structural MRI imagining "may underlie the low arousal, poor fear conditioning, lack of conscience, and decision-making deficits" that characterize psychopathic behavior.[9]

Another region that may come up short in psychopaths is located at the tip of the front part of the brain (Figure 3).[10] Although sometimes called the anterior rostral prefrontal cortex, a more precise address is Brodmann area 10, a portion of the anteroventral prefrontal cortex. Brodmann areas are discrete regions of the cerebral cortex made up of neurons with similar features and organization. In the early 20th century, the German neurologist Korbinian Brodmann surveyed the brain's cortex on a microscopic level and divided it into 52 Brodmann areas. His impressive painstaking efforts of 115 years ago are still helping neuroanatomists, neuroscientists, and psychologists find their way around the cortex.

If the brain had a figurehead like a ship, Brodmann area 10 would be it, positioned at its foremost point. The contributions of this part of the brain are poorly understood. It, however, is known to have extensive connections to other regions implicated in psychopathy and higher mental functions. These include the temporal pole (Figure 9), the cingulate cortex (Figure 10), and other parts of the prefrontal cortex (Figure 8). Besides having a role in other executive functions, the neurons seated at the very front of the brain—along with other regions (Figure 7)—may play a role in moral decision-making.

A more recent study by Martina Ly, et al. reported that 21 psychopathic criminal inmates had thinner cerebral cortices in half a dozen or so different regions of the brain compared to incarcerated non-psychopaths.[11] These and other studies "strongly reinforce the suggestion that psychopathy is a neurobiological condition," according to psychopathy expert R. J. R. Blair of the National Institute of Mental Health in Bethesda, Maryland.[12] Cortical thinning reported in psychopathy and conditions such as schizophrenia, depression, posttraumatic stress disorder, attention-deficit/hyperactivity disorder, and autism could be due to fewer neurons, smaller neurons, fewer connections between neurons, abnormalities affecting glial cells, or some combination of these.

Estimates of the average number of neurons in a healthy person range from 10 to 200 billion. A recent study suggests that there are 86 billion neurons, and a similar number of brain cells called glia, neuroglia, or glial cells—give or take 8 or 10 billion.[13] Glia were once thought to serve as glue (glia in Greek) holding neurons in place. Now we know they are essential partners in nervous-system function because they modulate and support neuronal activity.[14] They have been neglected by researchers who, for most of the history of neuroscience, have concentrated their attention on neurons.

To add another level to the complexity of the central nervous system, there are many different types of glial cells and neurons. Neuroscientists aren't even sure how many different types of neurons there are in the mammalian brain, because they often have features that make it difficult to categorize them reliably and authoritatively.

However you want to categorize neurons, overall there probably are at least 100 trillion points of contact—communicating connections called synapses—between these cells. Again, no one knows exactly how many connections they make, but it's safe to say there are many more combinations of connections than there are stars in the Milky Way galaxy, a comparatively wimpy 400 billion. There may be one billion synapses in just one cubic millimeter of cerebral cortical brain tissue; that's how complex a marvel the human brain has evolved into. Even the computers at the National Security Agency are dullards compared to a moderately intelligent human brain. They, together with smart phones, tablets, and fMRI machines, are merely useful tools developed by more impressive human brains for their own purposes.

As staggering as brain-cell statistics are—and they are still staggering even for many scientists who have spent their careers studying the brain—it nevertheless is possible to observe thinking, feeling brains by sliding people into devices such as fMRI machines. This significant technical breakthrough in the field of neuroscience does not mean, however, that scientists can now identify locations in the brain where thoughts and feelings originate or are located. Although many press reports of brain imaging studies imply, outright suggest, or mistakenly assume that they can, the science behind brain scans is more subtle—and limited—than that.

The goal in studies such as the one for which Willem and others with high PCL–R scores volunteered is to compare activity and responses in the brains of psychopaths to activity in the brains of non-psychopaths. The comparisons are made when the subjects are presented with images and other stimuli designed by researchers to detect differences in brain function in the two groups. One group, the controls, knows what a conscience is. The other group of individuals knows as much about a conscience as a person born without sight knows about the color red.

In 2000, German scientists were the first to apply fMRI technology in the study of psychopathy.[15] Frank Schneider, M.D., Ph.D., at the University of Düsseldorf and his fellow researchers compared a dozen men between the ages of 18 and 45 years with an average PCL–R score of 29 to a dozen psychologically healthy men. They showed their 24 subjects pictures of faces with neutral expressions. They paired the faces with either a puff of room air (a neutral stimulus) or a puff of rotten yeast odor (an aversive stimulus). Neither group liked the rotten smell; they both learned to associate smells with the pictures of the faces. The difference between the two groups appeared in the fMRI images when they were learning to make these associations. The non-psychopaths showed decreased activity, while the psychopaths showed increased activity in regions of the brain closely involved in emotional responses: the dorsolateral prefrontal cortex and the amygdala. The authors suggest that the increased activity in these regions observed in psychopaths might reflect greater effort to make an emotional association between a bad smell and a particular face. It is as if the neuronal processing mechanism devoted to learning this task with an emotional component ("I hate that smell") is more efficient in non-psychopaths compared to psychopaths. Specific brain cells involved in emotional processing in psychopaths may have to work harder to make the association.

Since 2000, thousands of criminals—mostly in the United States, but also in Willem's home the Netherlands, the United Kingdom, Finland, Germany, and other nations—have volunteered to have their brains scanned. Once escorted from their cells to a lab equipped with a scanner, they lie flat on their backs on a slab, which is a couple of feet wide. For the experiment to produce usable information, they must be still; movement will blur the results, so their heads are held in cushioned restraints or headrests. After their upper bodies are slid into the long donut-hole opening in the center of the device, the noise starts. The banging, vibrating, magnet-bearing mechanism pounds out industrial-strength noise as the volunteers try to complete mental tasks devised by the investigators who study this subset of humanity in an attempt to find the source of their antisocial and—in the opinion of most people—evil behavior. The researchers believe their results reveal functional deficits in the brains of criminal psychopaths. These deficits and abnormalities are thought to mirror the emotional deficiencies that characterize people with this extreme type of personality—or, according to many, this type of personality *disorder.*

fMRI technology is complex and logistically cumbersome, yet the actual scan is the result of the exploitation of the simplest atom, hydrogen. This minimalist element has just one electron moving around one positively charged proton. Outside an MRI machine, protons in hydrogen atoms spin about randomly. That changes when they are inside a functioning MRI machine; this is where the magnetic part of magnetic resonance imaging becomes essential. The randomly spinning protons snap to attention in response to the powerful electromagnetic field generated by the MRI machine. Under the influences of this field, the protons flip en masse into an aligned state.

The MRI machine then sends a radio wave that snaps the protons back to their usual randomly oriented states. This sequence of events wouldn't be much help in providing a picture of the brain except for one thing: when the protons flip back to their usual state of randomness, they emit a kind of echo in the form of radio waves. These mini-broadcasts announce to a detector in the MRI precisely where the protons are located.

Thanks to the complex calculations of mathematicians and the efficient coding of computer programmers, the "echoes," or proton-generated signals, are turned into three-dimensional images of the brain. Denser brain matter has more hydrogen nuclei than less-dense material and will thus broadcast more signals. The contrast between dense and less-dense brain tissue, darker and lighter, produces MRI images such as those in Figures 3 (bottom), 5, 12, and 13.

The result is a potentially valuable collection of relatively detailed anatomical pictures that can show the brain from different angles. The noisy but painless process of having an MRI can reveal tumors and aneurisms and structural abnormalities of the brain. It can just as easily produce images of other organs and reveal the presence of cancer, blood-vessel anomalies, damaged nerves, shredded muscle, and other health problems. All the while, it avoids the health risks associated with radiation from X-rays or radioactive materials.

From Here to There and Back Again: DT-MRI

MRI technology isn't just for taking static, high-tech, 3-D X-ray-like pictures. It has been adapted to provide specialized tools for studying specialized structures in the brain. One, called Diffusion Tensor Magnetic Resonance Imaging, or DT-MRI, is useful for studying connections in the brain, the communication pathways that allow the brain to function.

Disconnecting your prefrontal lobes from the rest of your brain, for example, may disconnect you from your former joie de vivre and much of your personality. This consequence was established after Egas Moniz received the 1949 Nobel Prize for pioneering the use of frontal lobotomies. Physicians used the simple new surgical technique to treat people with schizophrenia and other then-untreatable mental disorders, as well as some individuals who simply displayed troubling behavior. The prize-winning psychosurgery, worked out and popularized shortly before the development of effective antipsychotic drugs, left thousands mentally maimed. This most tragic and embarrassing episode in neurology, however, at least revealed the essential role that the connections between the frontal lobes and other parts of the brain play in higher mental functioning.

A brain structure like the amygdala, for example, which figures prominently in neurobiological investigations of psychopathy, needs its connections to the frontal lobes to work effectively. The amygdala just isn't the amygdala unless it's part of a neural circuit. The same is true of other brain structures. The amygdala has mistakenly been portrayed in the news media as a "center" of fear, anger, or aggression, depending on the story of the day. In fact, it is a small but highly influential structure that is active when you experience something that is immediately interesting or important. Subtleties like this are not that difficult to convey in the media, but they aren't as catchy as erroneously portraying the structure as a key center that controls our basic instincts like aggression and sex.

DT-MRI provides a way to examine pathways in the brain such as the one linking the amygdala to the prefrontal cortex by taking advantage of the fact that water molecules jiggle. Pour a little milk into your tea or coffee and you can appreciate that the suspension spreads out or diffuses in your cup. Water molecules in cells, and in their extensions like the long projections of neurons called axons, diffuse. In something that is long and narrow like an axon, water molecules will diffuse more along the length of the structure than along its cross-section. Imagine a Ping-Pong ball in a pipe. If the ball moves steadily, you can bet it is likely to move along the length of the pipe and not bounce up and down in one place across its narrow width.

DT-MRI detects the motion of hydrogen in water molecules as they move along the length of the tract. Long structures like muscles, tendons, and ligaments are good subjects for DT-MRI. So are nerve fiber tracts in the brain. These extensions, axons, carry electrical signals to other neurons in other parts of the brain. The axons are surrounded by a fatty, white insulating substance called myelin, provided by glial cells. That's why fiber tracts in the brain are called white matter. Areas rich in neurons are called gray matter (although it actually looks more pink than gray). Processing the data produced by a DT-MRI scan can result in striking three-dimensional images of nerve pathways in the living brain. Take a look at Figure 6 to get an idea of the potential of this approach for illuminating brain structure.

If water in a structure such as a nerve fiber bundle moves about randomly—if it is as likely to go in one direction as another—the bundle gets a score of zero. If movement is highly directional, then the bundle gets a score of 1. Physicists call this score fractional anisotropy (FA). (The word anisotropy is used when something depends on direction. The opposite, isotropy, is used when something is independent of direction.) FA is influenced by the health of nerve fibers, their density, their size, and their insulation. FA provides an indirect indication of the health or structural integrity of a bundle of nerve fibers connecting one part of the brain to another.

A practical drawback of the MRI technology is posed by the powerful magnet encased in the MRI machine. It is so powerful that it will rip any metal object you take near it through whatever is holding it. Magnetic field strength is measured in units called Tesla. The 7-Tesla magnet in the MRI at the University of Oxford Centre for Functional Magnetic Resonance Imaging of the Brain could pick up a double-decker bus.[16] Magnets of *one* Tesla can pick up cars, and they do just that when used in junkyards. Most MRI scanners have 1- to 3-Tesla magnets. It's important, therefore, not to forget if you have had metal implanted anywhere in your body before you have an MRI. A pacemaker, a skull plate, or a pin holding together a fractured bone, for example, will disqualify you from the procedure and inconvenience you considerably if you were to forget. Other than that, the only potential drawbacks of the procedure are the expense ($500 or so for a session) and the patience a patient or subject must muster as the machine takes 20 to 45 minutes to scan the brain or most other parts of the body.

Hot Scans

Before fMRI scanning was developed in the 1990s, the brains of violent volunteers were imaged using a more invasive procedure: positron emission tomography or PET scanning. Unlike fMRI, PET scans are considered invasive because they require an intravenous injection of a radioactively labeled tracer just before the scan begins. When the radioactive tracer is attached to glucose, the brain's fuel, it travels to the brain and is preferentially taken up by active nerve cells. Less active cells don't require as much energy. As the radioactive material decays, it emits subatomic particles called positrons. When positrons are emitted, radiation in the form of gamma rays is released. The scanner detects these rays. A computer analyzes the pattern of gamma ray release and translates it into an image of the brain. The more radiation that is detected in a particular region, the brighter that region is in the image.

The radioactive tracer is short-lived. It quickly becomes nonradioactive and poses no significant health threat. But few folks are thrilled by the idea of receiving a radioactive IV, no matter how harmless it is. Also, it is more trouble for researchers to deal with short-lived radioisotopes on a routine basis than it is to get people ready for an fMRI scan. In the past, PET scanners produced images less sharp than modern MRI machines. That has changed as PET scanning technology has improved. The spatial resolution of brain scanners depends on the quality of the machine, imaging time, calibration, and other technical factors; but a regular PET scanner can now have twice the resolution of a typical fMRI machine.[17]

The advantages of PET include the fact that any molecule that can be radioactively tagged and introduced safely into the brain can be imaged. The resulting image reflects a straightforward physiological mechanism. Where a labeled molecule—whether a neurotransmitter, sugar, or drug—ends up in the brain is where you find it emitting its radioactive signal.

A functional MRI machine extends MRI technology almost like a video camera extends the capability of a still camera; like PET, it provides images of the brain in action. Despite what tabloid news sources claim, however, it cannot reveal what a brain is thinking, reasoning, or feeling. It cannot identify specific brain sites responsible for emotions, beliefs, or strong feelings such as love, hate, fear, anger, conservatism, liberalism, or other emotions. Those are interpretations applied by observers. The brain is far too dynamic, and its different subdivisions too interactive, to reduce higher cognitive functions or philosophical outlooks to individual central nervous system addresses. But the technology can show brain activity in the form of increased blood flow to specific brain regions. This method is known as BOLD (Blood Oxygenation Level Dependent) contrast imaging.

More-active brain cells use more energy, require more oxygen, and produce more byproducts, than less-active brain cells. The brain consumes an impressive 20 percent of the calories you eat and 20 percent of the oxygen you breathe. When neurons in a specific region of the brain become more active, they need more oxygen and more energy in the form of glucose.

Blood flow increases to meet these needs. Used blood has delivered its oxygen to nerve cells and is heading back to the heart and lungs to be refreshed, to pick up more oxygen. fMRI takes advantage of the fact that the molecule in red blood cells that carries oxygen, hemoglobin, has different effects on the magnetic resonance signal coming from hydrogen in nearby water molecules, depending on whether or not it is bound to oxygen. When hemoglobin has lost its oxygen and become deoxyhemoglobin, it dampens the signal. Hemoglobin that is carrying oxygen, oxyhemoglobin, does not dampen the signal.

When fresh blood transporting lots of oxyhemoglobin flows into a hard-working brain region, it becomes the major type of hemoglobin in that part of the brain. The presence of lots of oxyhemoglobin decreases the signal-dampening effect of deoxyhemoglobin. Decreasing a dampening effect is like decreasing pressure on a brake: when the brake is released by an influx of oxyhemoglobin into an active brain region, the fMRI picks up a greater signal from that region compared to other regions.

Researchers exploit the differing effects of fresh and used blood on the signal picked up by the MRI machine. But does the resulting image reflect nerve-cell activity merely *responding* to a direct stimulus, or does it reflect nerve-cell activity *processing* information? Neurons responding to something send nerve signals down long axons. Neurons processing information provided by stimuli generate a lot of local electrical signaling activity.

In 2001, scientists at the Max Planck Institute for Biological Cybernetics, Tübingen, Germany managed to get a more precise idea of what type of nerve-cell activity fMRI detects. They did it by simultaneously measuring neuronal electrical activity in monkeys undergoing brain scans. They found that fMRI detects increased activity due to neurons processing information rather than responding to it.[18] BOLD signals detected by fMRI, later research showed, indeed seem to be more closely associated with activity taking place in and around synapses than in spikes generated along long axons.[19]

This ongoing process which reflects the flow of blood to specific spots in the brain adds a dimension to the 3-D image produced by the MRI machine. The additional, fourth dimension allows the fMRI machine to produce images that show the relative metabolic activity of brain structures in time (a little bit delayed) as well as in space.

Researchers using fMRI create artificial color scales and assign different colors to brain regions depending on how much blood flows to them. The artificially colored results in fMRI images highlight parts of the brain that show more or less activity when performing a mental task or responding to a stimulus. The bright reds and yellows seen on fMRI images in news stories obviously do not depict what you would see if you could peer inside someone's skull to directly observe the brain surface or subsurface structures. It might be less flashy and even more accurate to Photoshop numbers indicating the amount of blood flow to brain regions of interest, but that would be more challenging to interpret. The technology's usefulness and popularity stems from its ability to provide images of brain anatomy coupled with function. The reliability, significance, and relevance of the resulting pictures are determined by the scientists who design and carry out the experiments and then subsequently by anyone who views and interprets the results.

A 2010 report by Carla Harenski, Ph.D., and her co-authors at the MIND Research Network in Albuquerque, N.M. illustrates a representative study made possible by fMRI technology.[20] Before considering this report, recall the last time you saw a picture in the news of someone attacking another person. If you were asked to decide how good or bad, right or wrong, justified or unjustified the assault was, then brain cells in some parts of your brain involved in making moral decisions (see Figure 7 for candidates) presumably increased their activity as you made your decision.

Harenski and colleagues scanned the brains of sixteen criminals with low psychopathic traits as they considered images with moral connotations. Examples of some images used to evoke moral judgments include depictions of a physical assault in which one person attacks another, or a crime such as a home break-in. The results showed that a part of the brain called the amygdala appeared to "light up" (that is, experienced increased blood flow) when these men looked at pictures that most people agree have moral implications. The same thing happened when twenty-eight non-criminals with no psychopathic traits evaluated the pictures.

When another group of sixteen incarcerated men with high levels of psychopathic traits considered the same pictures, however, the resulting images of their brain function differed considerably from the other two groups. A glance at Figure 13 indicates that criminals with high psychopathic traits appear to have *decreased* levels of activation in their amygdalae when looking at these images of moral violations.

The presence of psychopathic traits seems to affect the amygdala's response to other select stimuli in a similar way, even in the presence of a major psychiatric disorder such as schizophrenia. An fMRI study carried out in Australia, for example, looked at the effect of psychopathic traits on amygdala response to images of fearful faces. The researchers concluded that violent patients with schizophrenia and *high* psychopathy scores showed decreased amygdala responses compared to violent patients with schizophrenia and *low* psychopathy scores.[21]

It is important to remember that such changes detected in fMRI studies, although real, may sometimes represent small differences between groups. Also, individual variations in human brain activity may vary greatly from one person to another, and in one person from day to day, or even from hour to hour. Consequently, fMRI results are often shown as averaged changes displayed on a single representative brain image.

Limitations

An activated brain region—one involved in recognizing a potential threat raised by a disturbing photograph, for instance—may be marked by less than a five percent increase in blood flow compared to uninvolved brain regions. As mentioned, the brain uses a lot of energy even when it seems to be resting. This means it is a highly active organ metabolically. When it "goes to work" on a particular task, the increased flow of blood delivering oxygen and glucose to a particular area is not as large as you might predict. It is not easy to pick out small changes in such a complex and active structure, because the brain's background activity is like "noise" that can make it a challenge to pick out the particular signal you might be interested in. It is, after all, a system capable, in the best instances, of creating and appreciating great literature, art, and scientific insights, and, in the worst, of concocting and executing schemes to gain control, victimize, and even terrorize individuals or entire populations.

Craig M. Bennett, Ph.D., is a cognitive neuroscientist at the University of California, Santa Barbara with an interest in magnetic resonance imaging methods and a talent for explaining the complexity of his field to scientists and nonscientists alike. He and his colleagues, for example, used a memorable approach to emphasize the precautions and steps researchers must take to make sure they end up with valid brain images using fMRI. They produced an unusual abstract presentation entitled "Neural Correlates of Interspecies Perspective Taking In the Post-Mortem Atlantic Salmon: An Argument for Multiple Comparisons Correction."[22] The poster presentation included authentic fMRI images of a dead fish whose brain clearly shows activity in the form of a dab of overlaid red color.

The apparent mental activity coincided with the fish's participation in a brain-scanning experiment in which the subject was presented with a series of photographs of human faces and asked to identify the emotion expressed in each picture. To paraphrase John Cleese in *Monty Python's Flying Circus*'s famous Dead Parrot Sketch,[23] the piscine subject of this demonstration—it bears repeating—was no more, had ceased to be, expired, gone to meet its maker, was bereft of life, its metabolic process now history. If it had not been slid into an fMRI machine, it would have been pushing up the daisies or else been prepared for dinner.

This tongue-in-cheek experiment, of course, was conducted for a serious purpose. It was performed to emphasize to users of the increasingly popular fMRI technology that extreme care must be taken to avoid false positive results—that is, indications that something is happening when it is not. "Images of brain activity only have meaning when acquired using the correct experimental design and interpreted using the correct analyses," the authors of the one-time experiment noted.

"Not only are the steps not standardized, they are easily manipulated by a person with knowledge of the technology. Color coding, for example, can be arbitrary and may present the illusion of huge differences in some aspect of brain activity, when little actually exists," the authors warned back in 2009. But things have improved since then. "If I give you a dart and have you throw it at a dartboard [without aiming], there is a certain probability (let's say 1%) that you will get a bull's-eye," Bennett explained four years later.[24] "If I give you 30,000 darts, then you are going to get approximately 300 bull's-eye hits just because of random chance. The same is generally true in neuroimaging. We are testing for significant results across 30,000+ voxels [the 3-dimensional MRI equivalent of a flat screen's pixels], and some will be significant by chance. To really know the true probability of a false positive in our data, we need to do a statistical correction for this multiple testing problem. In 2008, 30–40% of papers did not utilize any form of correction. In 2010, it was less than 10%."

The field of psychopathy research using fMRI imaging is young, but it has made enough progress that its findings are clearly fitting into a pattern. They are being reproduced in different labs and so are laying the groundwork for one day developing a good understanding of how the brains of criminal psychopaths differ from the brains of non-psychopaths. As we will see, the evidence points to problems involving many parts of the brain that lie below its surface and with regions of the cerebral cortex directly connected to them. However, as always, consumers need to be aware of the limitations of the techniques used to gain these insights. In the future, the progress and the limitations of this research are likely to produce some interesting challenges for a society concerned about the personal cost of living with psychopaths—both criminal and those who never commit a crime.

By one estimate, criminal psychopaths cost the U.S. economy at least $460 billion per year (in 2009 dollars) in direct and indirect costs. This figure includes lost property and the expense of finding, arresting, charging, trying, defending, and incarcerating psychopathic offenders. The figure would be even higher if the costs of keeping psychopaths in psychiatric hospitals and treating victims of violent crime perpetrated by psychopaths were included in the estimate.[25] An unknown cost is the psychological damage both criminal and non-criminal psychopaths produce. Even if a psychopath does not break the law, he may break people's spirits. Psychological abuse of spouses and family members by psychopaths is a common topic in self-help groups and on several online forums. Some clinical psychologists like Martha Stout, Ph.D., author of *The Sociopath Next Door*, have acquired specialized experience treating patients who have been victimized by psychopaths.

Domestic psychological abuse is tragic enough. But for an estimated 1.3 million women who are victimized by current and former spouses or other intimate partners each year in the U.S., the abuse is both psychological and physical.[26] And an estimated 15 to 30 percent of the men responsible for this abuse are psychopaths.[27]

Chapter Four

A Problem Just Behind the Forehead

Burly, bearded James Fallon tells people he has the brain of a psychopathic killer.[1] And he has some brain scans he thinks back up his claim.

The PET scans behind his surprising claim—and which have provided entertaining material for his lectures—were taken where he works. He's Professor Emeritus of Anatomy & Neurobiology and Professor of Psychiatry & Human Behavior in the School of Medicine at the University of California, Irvine (UCI). There he studies higher brain functions at the Human Brain Imaging Lab. Fallon describes his interests as "the neural circuitry and genetics of creativity, artistic talent, psychopathology, criminal behavior, and levels of consciousness."

A neuroscientist with a forty-year-long, successful career, Fallon, now sixty-six, arranged to have his own brain scanned. He made the decision after his mother, Jenny, recalled some interesting family history during a family barbeque. She knew her son, the scientist, lectured about his research on violent offenders. His lectures covered what he saw in the brains of murderers and what the images revealed to him about the causes of violent behavior. That led Jenny, as she said on NPR, to challenge her son: "Jim, why don't you find out about your father's relatives? I think there were some cuckoos back there."[2]

She was right. There turned out to be numerous—and murderous—cuckoos back there, including Lizzy Borden and seven other alleged killers. They were all on his father's side, to his mother's amusement. Borden, the most infamous, was acquitted—quite controversially—of the axe murders of her father and stepmother in 1882. One of Fallon's male ancestors, Thomas Cornell, wasn't so lucky. He didn't beat the rap for the crime he was accused of committing: the murder of his mother. He hung for it in 1667.[3]

Brain scans and genetic tests of Jenny and of Fallon's wife, son, and daughters were normal. Fallon's family has nothing in common with psychopaths or murderers, in terms of their behavior or brain activity. Fallon's brain, on the other hand, shows the characteristic metabolic sluggishness in the frontal lobes first observed in violent and murderous individuals back in the late 1980s. And among the family members he's tested, only he has inherited some genes that show up frequently in violent individuals. In fact, his blood test shows he has genes linked to violent tendencies—five in all, including one called the "warrior gene" (although any gene linked to violence might deserve the same nickname).

No single gene makes someone violent or psychopathic. Even inheriting multiple genes can't do this. If they did, Jim Fallon might have spent more time before a judge's bench than before his lab bench. Besides the warrior gene, Jim says he inherited genes associated with antisocial behavior, low anxiety, and low empathy. Several encode instructions for making proteins involved in the function of neurotransmitters like serotonin and dopamine. But different versions of genes do influence behavior in some people, some of it unpleasant indeed. Differences in the effect of these genes on brain development, and on the way it receives, interprets, and responds to inputs influence how likely someone like Jim is to turn violent and/or show signs of psychopathy.

The discovery of the warrior gene-violence connection goes back to the late 1980s and early 1990s in the Netherlands. Hans Brunner, a geneticist at the University Hospital in Nijmegen, learned about a family that seemed to be full of men who easily lost their tempers, were aggressive, and, worse, were adding to their rap sheet with entries related to assault, arson, rape, and murder. The women in the family asked the geneticist if their men might be behaving badly because they had inherited something bad.

In 1993, Brunner had an answer for them. It was on the men's X-chromosome, one of the chromosomes that determine gender. He discovered that the men had inherited a version of a gene that encodes an enzyme called MAOA-L.[4] In the brain, MAOA breaks down important neurotransmitters, such as serotonin, dopamine, and adrenaline. MAO stands for monoamine oxidase; A designates a subtype of the enzyme (sort of like a car model), and L stands for low activity. Since 1993, the low-activity version of the gene—dubbed the "warrior gene" by the press—has been linked in several studies to increased aggressive behavior.[5] A tendency to get into fights or strike out at others is not the same as the goal-directed aggression often seen in criminal psychopaths, but the existence of the MAOA-L gene does strongly support the view that some psychopathic tendencies may be inherited.

Another genetic variation that may be linked to the development of psychopathy affects the metabolism of the neurotransmitter serotonin. Inheriting two long versions of the gene that produces a protein that transports serotonin back into brain cells after it has been released may be a risk factor for the development of psychopathic traits.[6]

Prior to checking the status of his own DNA and brain images, Fallon says he analyzed the brain scans of over seventy people, which according to the *Wall Street Journal* were sent to him by colleagues, psychiatrists, and criminal defense lawyers.[7] It started back in the 1990s when people began sending brain scan images to Jim for him to analyze. "I knew the human brain very well but I wasn't an expert on murderers or psychopaths or anything like that. . . . It was just a side thing," he recalled.[8] Then in 2005, he received a large group of scans to look at. "At this point, Jim knew his colleagues were sending him brain scans of murderers so he decided to make a story. He asked his associates not to identify the scans. He also asked them to include scans of non-violent patients along with those of murderers."

He easily identified ten normal brain scans. Then he saw a group of scans from patients with major depression and some with schizophrenia. "It was a mixed bag," he said. He didn't know there was a pattern in psychopaths, because it wasn't his main field of study, but he did notice a group of scans that showed inactivity in the prefrontal orbital cortex. Fallon later learned he had correctly identified the thirty murderers whose scans had been included in the collection of scans.[9]

"There was one subgroup of those that had a lot of amygdaloid and cingulate cortex type of activity, so they stood out." When the code was broken, this subgroup turned out to be psychopaths. "I think because I am not really an expert in this area, it made it easier for me not to be biased. I did not expect any pattern," he said. "I think that is where it helped." The first group with prefrontal cortex differences without amygdala and cingulate involvement turned out to be impulsive or reactive murderers. These people killed in a hot-blooded emotional manner as opposed to the cold-blooded manner characteristic of criminal psychopaths.

Fallon's observations are consistent with some small-scale experiments first published in late 1987[10] and early 1994.[11] The preliminary studies demonstrated the potential usefulness of PET-scanning the brains of people with personality disorders and violent tendencies. Adrian Raine and his co-workers used the technology to look at the brains of twenty-two men accused of murder in 1994.[12]

The darkness they saw indicating impaired metabolism in the prefrontal cortices of murderers and accused murderers was obvious, compared to an equal number of non-murderous controls. It suggested that the lack of neuronal activity in this part of the brain was a factor in murderous behavior. A follow-up study three years later found that 41 murderers who pled not guilty by reason of insanity also had reduced glucose metabolism in their frontal lobes compared to 41 controls. This mixed group also showed signs of reduced metabolism in half a dozen other brain regions.[13]

These pioneering early studies of violence-prone individuals led the way to current fMRI studies in which people undergoing brain scans are more likely to belong to similar groups: for example, those with psychopathy scores in the certifiable psychopathic range. The earlier studies, like Fallon's unpublished studies, captured mixed populations of violent individuals and murderers.

Despite a general impression to the contrary among many people, not all—in fact surprisingly few—murderers are high-scoring psychopaths. Some people kill as a result of stress or an isolated, uncontrolled emotional reaction such as anger or jealousy. More than half of the nearly 13,000 people murdered in 2010 in the U.S. were killed by someone they knew. Nearly one-quarter were killed by a family member. Nearly 43 percent were killed during arguments and just over 23 percent were crime victims. Circumstances surrounding the rest are unknown.[14]

Many criminals have antisocial personality disorder but do not reach the amoral or immoral depths of clinical psychopathy. Others kill because their criminal lifestyle forces them into situations where they must use violence. Most criminals—75 percent or so—have antisocial personality disorder, the personality disorder the American Psychiatric Society created to include sociopaths, which the Society still equates with psychopaths. Only a quarter or so of jailed criminals with antisocial personality disorder, however, are true psychopaths as indicated by the standard diagnostic test for that type of personality. This means about one in five prison inmates are estimated to be true psychopaths.

The search database of the U.S. National Library of Medicine and the National Institutes of Health, PubMed, lists 105 articles co-authored by J. H. Fallon. His published papers reflect his scientific interests which, according to his UCI faculty profile include "Alzheimer's disease, Human Brain Imaging, art, law, culture, and the brain." He has made significant contributions in several of these areas, including the use of imaging technology to locate genes associated with mental disorders, and research on growth factors and stem cells. He acknowledges that he has not published in the field of psychopathy. His finding is anecdotal.

He described his intriguing anecdotal studies in a TED talk titled *Exploring the Mind of a Killer* and in the BBC documentary *Are You Good or Evil?* He has also shared his scientific expertise in different areas of his research on the History Channel, Discovery, CNN, PBS, ABC, and the *Wall Street Journal*.[15]

Nevertheless, the images Fallon finds in the scans of the murderers he examines, and which he finds in his own distinguished, law-abiding brain, are often identical to those of certified psychopaths. (He has avoided releasing his scores on the Hare Psychopathy Checklist, Psychopathic Personality Inventory, and other formal psychological evaluations as well as some casual online tests, but he says they are just short of the cutoffs for psychopathy.)[16] The results like those he saw in his own brain scans are consistent with those reported in more controlled studies that have resulted in a better understanding of the abnormalities that appear to contribute to the cold-hearted nature of the most extreme psychopaths.

Front and Center

The same dark regions in Fallon's neuroimaging self-portrait that shocked him and instantly captured his attention, had captured the attention of other researchers interested in biological psychiatry years earlier. When Fallon points to the section of his brain scan that looks like the brain of a murderer, he points to a part of the frontal lobes called the prefrontal cortex (Figures 8 and 9).

The frontal lobes have been suspects in aggressive and criminal behavior since the 19th century. If you want to find your frontal lobes, imagine you have a bad headache. Place the palm of your hand on your forehead, fingers pointing up. Position the meaty part of your palm at eye level and lay your fingers over the top of your head. Fortunately, your skull prevents you from touching your frontal lobes directly, but if it were not in the way, you would have a pretty good grasp on this tissue that is so influential in determining the type of person you are.

Your frontal lobes are located immediately behind your forehead and extend halfway back across the top of your brain. They are part of the cerebral cortex, the outermost covering of the brain that processes higher brain functions. And the cerebral cortex of the frontal lobes controls some of the most sophisticated higher brain functions. Of course, other parts of your brain contribute to the mysterious task of generating consciousness, creating thoughts, and solving problems. But if you are the type of person who is even moderately successful at, for example, planning for your future retirement, weighing the risks of challenging your boss, worrying what might go wrong if you go sky-diving with an unlicensed instructor, "reading" people and getting along with them, and sublimating your sex drive when the time is not right, then you are doing a pretty good job of using your frontal lobes.

A lot of what distinguishes us from chimpanzees can be found in this relatively recently evolved addition to our central nervous system. We may share close to 99% of our DNA sequences with this ape,[17] but we seem to express more of certain genes in our brains than chimps do. (The code of an expressed gene is read and used to produce a protein encoded by the gene. An unexpressed gene is not decoded and produces no protein product.) We have genes specific to our species (some of which are associated with cognitive disorders) and a much more complex pattern of gene expression in our frontal lobes compared to apes.[18]

MRI scans show that prefrontal white matter increases during infancy dramatically in humans but not in chimps.[19] Apparently this contributes to our ability to plan, project, and out-problem-solve our fellow primates in such a way that we can dominate the globe for better or worse. Despite their outward similarities, human frontal lobes are more complex than chimpanzee frontal lobes. The signaling pathways and connections in human frontal lobes appear to be somewhat more elaborate than those of the great apes. Less white matter in the ape's temporal cortex might also reflect less connectivity between neurons. More connections between nerve cells is just what you want if you want to process information more efficiently and at a more sophisticated level. Such microscopic differences may be reflected in our good and bad behavior, and in our great and not-so-great accomplishments as a species.

One way to get an idea of the important function this part of the brain plays in thinking and planning, as well as in antisocial, criminal, and psychopathic behavior, is to consider medical reports describing injuries to this region. They are full of case histories of patients who suffered damage to the frontal lobe—beginning with a man named Phineas Gage. In 1848, Gage survived an accident in which an explosion sent an iron rod through his cheek and eye socket and out the top of his head, destroying portions of his frontal lobe. The *Smithsonian* magazine correctly referred to Gage, whose story is told in Chapter 9, as "neuroscience's most famous patient." He, and many unfortunate patients after him, could no longer balance their "intellectual faculties and animal propensities" after suffering damage to their frontal lobes, according to Gage's physician, John Martyn Harlow.[20]

Immediately above your eye sockets, behind your brow, is a subdivision of the frontal lobes called the orbitofrontal cortex (Figures 8 and 9) and adjacent ventromedial prefrontal cortex. The term orbitofrontal cortex comes up in the scientific literature devoted to the biological basis of psychopathy and antisocial behavior the way "weapon" comes up when you read about holdups. When it is damaged by a stroke or an injury—or even, as some neuroscientists believe, when it develops abnormally in the womb and during childhood—it appears also to fail in its job of influencing a sense of ethics, morality, and social cooperation. Its dysfunction can lead to impulsiveness and aggression, traits closely linked to psychopathy and antisocial behavior.

"The frontal lobes are the part of the brain that put a brake on impulses and drives," Georgetown University psychiatrist Dr. Jonathan Pincus told ABC News' Ned Potter. "It's the part of the brain that allows us to say, 'Don't do that! Don't say that! It's not appropriate! There are going to be consequences!'"[21]

If you know where to look, it's easy to see that something is missing when you look at a PET scan of Fallon's brain, and the brains of certified psychopaths. In most pictures of healthy brains, the orbitofrontal cortex glows with bright patches of red and yellow—colors added by the computer to indicate brain cells actively sucking up and burning glucose for energy as they keep nerve impulses flowing and neurons communicating with each other. That desirable glow is missing in the brains of unusual subjects like Fallon, who admits to having some non-violent psychopathic traits such as recklessness, and in the brains of people who tend to get into fights and victimize others. Their brain portraits show only a dull gray patch where the key part of the prefrontal lobe should be cheerily lit.

Even when this area is damaged, impaired, or inactive, intellectual ability is frequently unaffected. Fallon's distinguished non-criminal academic career is one example. High intellect among criminals does not appear to be the rule, but it is certainly not unheard of.

Smart Bad Guys

Literary intellectuals Norman Mailer and William F. Buckley, Jr. learned about the disconnection between psychopathic traits and intellectual impairment firsthand. Mailer was the celebrated, controversial author of eleven novels and twenty-eight books. He won Pulitzer Prizes for both fiction and nonfiction. Novelist Joan Didion described him as "a great and obsessed stylist, a writer to whom the shape of the sentence is the story."

Buckley, founder of *The National Review* magazine, was a leading figure in the American Conservative movement in the second half of the twentieth century and also a prolific author of conservative political commentaries and spy novels. He was known for his dictionary-like vocabulary and his inclination to use it.

Both the conservative Buckley and the liberal Mailer befriended convicts who wrote to them from prison. The jailed correspondents impressed the two famous writers with their writing skills. Eventually, the articulate prose of the convicts convinced Mailer and Buckley that the convicts deserved their freedom.

There are, of course, precedents for literary skill and even genius coexisting with ignorance in other areas. T. S. Eliot and Ezra Pound were, in addition to being leading literary figures and poets during the twentieth century, boorish anti-Semites. Leading American journalist H. L. Mencken and the industrialist Henry Ford were, too. Ernest Hemingway also made anti-Semitic comments. Holding such hateful, ignorant, and reprehensible views has never been inconsistent with accomplishment and fame, although it may highlight the limitations of ambition with intellect in the absence of wisdom. Buckley's and Mailer's assumption that intelligence and evil did not co-exist in criminal minds had lethal consequences.

Buckley's pen pal was a man named Edgar Smith. Smith was imprisoned for murdering Victoria Ann Zielinski, a fifteen-year-old cheerleader, in 1956. The murderer had crushed the girl's skull with a forty-four-pound rock after beating her with a baseball bat. While locked up for the crime—which he denied committing—Smith wrote to Buckley. He convinced Buckley he was a good writer. Smith told the conservative maven that he had been wrongfully convicted. Buckley appreciated good writing. How could anyone so intelligent, so capable of creating such cogent, well-crafted sentences and of marshaling such insights, be guilty? Buckley believed Smith was innocent and lobbied for his release. Fourteen years after his death sentence, Smith was set free. The legal justification for his release was the improper manner in which the police obtained his statement following his arrest. It is undeniable, however, that the efforts of Buckley and others who made him a cause célèbre played a big part in the decision to free Smith.

Smith made a short career of talking and writing about the injustice done to him. He authored *Brief Against Death* before his release from prison and *Getting Out* after his release. Once freed, he lectured and made radio and television appearances while he was enjoying his fifteen minutes of fame. In his fifth year of freedom, however, he backslid. He abducted a woman and stabbed her with a butcher knife. When he contacted Buckley after the stabbing, Buckley phoned the FBI to report Smith. Fortunately, Smith's victim survived and testified against him. Smith went back to prison; Buckley lost a pen pal.

On opposite ends of the political spectrum, Mailer, the author of *The Armies of the Night*, did not have a lot in common with Buckley, the author of *God and Man at Yale*, ideologically speaking, but he too was easily charmed by skillful prose. And so Norman Mailer, like Buckley, was seduced by the prose of a clever convict. He began corresponding with Jack Abbott, a lifelong criminal who had experienced neglect and abuse in the foster care system, which he had entered at birth.

After a youth spent in juvenile-detention centers and reform schools, Abbott went to prison for forgery. When he was twenty-one years old, he stabbed a fellow inmate to death. Facing more than twenty years for the murder, he escaped in 1971. He robbed a bank, was captured, and was sentenced to an additional nineteen years. Five years later, he began writing to Mailer and, as Smith had done with Buckley, succeeded in impressing the famous author. His letters to Mailer describing life in prison were published, with Mailer's help, in Abbott's book, *In the Belly of the Beast*.

Mailer helped Abbott again by supporting his efforts to gain parole, a goal which they realized in 1981, despite serious doubts by Abbott's jailers. Once freed, Abbott too made the rounds of New York literary society for a month or so. But then he got into an argument with restaurant employee Richard Adan over the use of a staff-only restroom. The two took the argument outside, where Abbott stabbed the 22-year-old victim—a fledgling actor and writer himself—to death. Abbott's plea of self-defense didn't convince anyone; he went back to prison. Mailer, like Buckley, lost a pen pal.

Hare wrote that the lack of depth in Abbott's conscious feeling about the murder is indicated by his statements that "There was no pain; it was a clean wound" and "He had no future as an actor—chances are he would have gone into another line of work."[22]

Abbott hanged himself in prison in 2002. His suicide note was never published.

The naiveté of Mailer and Buckley was perhaps, at the time, understandable. They could not conceive of high intellect and verbal intelligence being associated with psychopathic or criminal tendencies. Vicious murderers were, after all, ignorant, dumb thugs—not polished, skilled writers. Although we have an extraordinary amount to learn about the neurobiological basis of psychopathic behavior, we nevertheless know quite a bit more now than we knew then. We know that intelligence and writing skills are not incompatible with criminal or psychopathic behaviors. The brain is big enough and small enough, active enough and inactive enough, to accommodate both traits. We know that a man or woman may be able to write like a sage and still be a remorseless killer.

In the classic treatise on psychopathy, *The Mask of Sanity*, Hervey Cleckley placed "Superficial charm and good 'intelligence'" at the top of his list of psychopathic traits. This might be because the typical psychopaths Cleckley saw usually did "not commit murder or other offenses that promptly lead to major prison sentences."[23] Buckley's and Mailer's friends may have been exceptions, since the scientific literature doesn't dispute the argument that less-intelligent psychopaths get caught and sent to prison while more-intelligent psychopaths tend to move into corporate or political occupations, or else manage not to get caught.[24] Like the rest of the population, psychopaths range widely in intelligence.

While we don't know what their brain scans would have looked like, or what genes Smith or Abbott inherited, we know they displayed classic behavior of criminals with antisocial personality disorder and psychopathy. Neuroimaging studies of violent offenders with records similar to Smith and Abbott, along with neuropsychological test results, point convincingly to problems in the frontal lobes.

Adrian Raine and collaborators, for example, found using structural MRI that there was less gray-matter volume in the frontal cortex of people with antisocial personality disorder and high psychopathy scores around 28 out of 40.[25] His co-author psychologist Todd Lencz said that the 11 percent difference was "modest but noticeable when comparing groups."[26]

Back in the year 2000, the researchers couldn't be sure exactly which parts of the frontal lobes were short on gray matter, but later studies clearly pointed to the orbitofrontal cortex. That's the same region Fallon was surprised to see was dark in his brain, as well as in the brains of the murderers he studied. The association of reduced activity and gray-matter volume in this part of the brain is significant because it appears so often in studies of this type of psychopathology.

Sometimes it's easy to forget when discussing individual brain regions that the brain is a highly complex structure consisting of billions of interconnected units. What might look like a lesion causing a problem in one area all by itself might really be contributing to troubling behavior by interrupting communication pathways that run through it. So, the true source of the dysfunction might not lie in the prefrontal cortex alone, but instead in a circuit of brain regions and structures, all affected by an apparent lesion or flaw in one part of the brain.

The Emotional Brain

The overall trend of the research so far clearly indicates a strong connection between psychopathy and impaired function in parts of the brain that play a central role in regulating emotions and in how we react to emotions in ourselves and others. Neuroanatomists call this network the prefrontal-temporal-limbic system. This descriptive jargon describes a network of interconnected brain structures that, in addition to the prefrontal cortex, includes structures like the amygdala, hippocampus, superior temporal gyrus, and anterior cingulate cortex. In most cases studied so far, the problem linked to psychopathic behavior in this "emotional brain" is associated with decreased metabolic activity, lower volume of gray matter, and disruption in the communication pathways that link parts of the prefrontal-temporal-limbic system.

Yet these anatomical "usual suspects" are implicated by more than circumstantial evidence. The fact that identical or closely related brain structures produce antisocial behavior when they are impaired by disease, injured by accident, or perhaps in some cases even present at birth, strongly supports the argument that these regions are intimately involved in promoting psychopathic behavior in people born with a predisposition to psychopathy.

Based on his case studies, including his own, Fallon concluded that damage to the orbital prefrontal cortex and parts of the brain to which it is closely linked (including a neighboring part of the prefrontal cortex called the ventromedial prefrontal cortex and a fold of cortex found above and behind the orbital cortex called the ventral anterior cingulate) are clearly and unequivocally associated with psychopathic and even violent behavior. The list of neuroanatomical suspects also includes structures found beneath the brain's outer cover, the cerebral cortex. These evolutionarily older, more "primitive" structures lie deeper in the brain, toward its center. They include the amygdala and parts of the basal ganglia connected to these limbic cortices (Figures 10 and 11).

Poor Test Results

Why do these parts of the brain get so much attention from scientists looking for neuroanatomical links to really bad behavior? Aside from the fact that they keep calling attention to themselves in neuroimaging studies—which by itself would be enough to generate a reputation for involvement in pathological behavior—they also affect a person's ability to successfully interact in social settings. The orbitofrontal cortex, in collaboration with other structures such as the amygdala, helps regulate responses in psychological tests as well.

One test, for example, measures a person's ability to learn to respond to a stimulus voluntarily when it is linked to a reward and to not respond when it will result in a punishment. For example, every time you press a key on a keyboard when you see something you should respond to, you get some money. Every time you do *not* hit a key when you see something you should *not* respond to, you also get some money. But every time you press a key when you should not, you *lose* some money. Both groups do equally well learning to press the key when they should. But psychopaths make significantly more errors by pressing the key when they should not.[27] These and other results suggest that psychopaths don't do well when it comes to learning to control their reward-seeking behavior, even if it costs them money.

Psychopaths also perform differently from non-psychopaths on tests that measure fear conditioning, startle reflexes, word and language processing, and responses to distressing cues. Multiple studies show that psychopaths, compared to non-psychopaths, have trouble picking up emotional clues in facial expressions, voices, and words. When something grabs all of their attention, they don't respond as much to threats with subtle increases in perspiration and heart rate as non-psychopaths do.

Other studies point to the involvement of brain regions that influence, control, or tone down impulsive behavior. They implicate parts of the brain responsible for influencing both actions and thoughts that reflect a sense of morality, ethics, guilt, regret, and reflection. They suggest with problems balancing the risks of punishment versus reward, and problems predicting likely future consequences of current actions. In short, they point to the involvement of neural pathways that include the orbital prefrontal cortex and associated brain regions capable of producing recklessness and manipulative behavior with shallow emotions and extreme callousness toward others.

Brian Dugan, whose story is told in detail in Chapter 11, is one individual whose test results strongly suggest that biology has influenced his fate—and, tragically, the fate of two young girls and one woman who were unlucky enough to have encountered him. He has the unenviable distinction of being in the Psychopath Top 1 Percent; he has more psychopathic traits than 99.5 percent of the population. He has scored between 37 and 38.5 out of a possible maximum of 40 on the Hare Psychopathy Checklist. His IQ is also exceptional; it is greater than 140, according to a profile that aired on National Public Radio in 2010.[28] It is, to be sure, intelligence devoid of empathy or deep emotions, a deficiency he himself admits. But it is still intelligence intact enough to recognize and identify what psychologists call a "moral violation" in a psychological test.

In the test, subjects rate a picture on a scale of one to five, based on how much they think it represents a moral violation.[29] The NPR profile used a picture of a racist group, the KKK, burning a cross as an example. To the surprise of some, psychopaths like Brian, who is serving three life terms for rape and murder, rate these images the same way non-psychopaths do. In other words, they can indicate that the photos are morally objectionable.

But whether or not they actually *feel* that moral objection, as most people do, is unlikely. This is where men like Brian diverge from the rest of humankind. fMRI results show that the brain of a psychopath does not *respond* to the morally objectionable image the way the brain of a non-psychopath does. In psychopaths, parts of the brain involved in processing moral judgments, regions like the amygdala and posterior temporal cortex, show a different pattern of activation compared to non-psychopaths. You would not see, for example, increased activation in the amygdala and decreased activation in the temporal cortex in non-psychopaths, but that is exactly what you see in psychopaths.[30] This may be an anatomical correlate of the psychopath's inability to feel and process emotions like people without psychopathic traits.

It doesn't matter how these brain abnormalities occur. There are many ways people can suffer damage to their brain's emotional circuitry: stroke, head trauma, or genetics combined with a damaging environment. In the case of born or developmental psychopaths, bad luck with regard to genetics and upbringing can impair function in the key brain regions.

In the case of acquired sociopathy or "pseudopsychopathy," we know stroke and impact injuries, infections such as herpes simplex and rabies encephalitis, and organic brain diseases such as temporal lobe epilepsy and fronto-temporal dementia can transform a pleasant personality into a seriously unpleasant personality in a very short period of time.

Although there are significant differences between developmental psychopathy and the pseudopsychopathy induced by injury or disease, the similarities are impressive enough to support a link between parts of the brain implicated in psychopathy and regions damaged in patients who develop antisocial traits.

In 1995, Dominique LaPierre and his co-authors from the University of Québec in Montréal described a seemingly inconsequential trait psychopaths share with patients who suffered orbitofrontal brain damage: people who have damaged frontal cortices have trouble naming odors. A comparison of thirty psychopathic and thirty non-psychopathic criminals revealed that the psychopaths had the same problem.[31]

This finding regarding odor-labeling skills is especially important, they explained, "in the sense that it cannot readily be explained socioculturally, thus presenting a new and convincing argument for brain-based etiology of this disorder." In other words, here is a subtle deficiency that psychopaths share with brain-damaged individuals. And the brain damage is in two different regions of the prefrontal cortex, the orbitofrontal and the ventromedial subdivisions. The findings provide an example of the similarities between some psychopathic behaviors and some features of prefrontal cortex damage.

Since it is possible to induce antisocial behavior in previously nice people by directly altering their brain tissue, it is less likely that a disorder like psychopathy can be traced solely to society's influence. Skeptics critical of this view may point to good people turned bad as a result of abuse. They cannot, however, dismiss the evidence that brain abnormalities caused by either brain injuries or developmental abnormalities can strongly influence and even determine antisocial behavior. Impaired function of the orbitofrontal or ventromedial regions due to injury or psychopathy may result in poor planning, poor judgment regarding social and ethical matters, impulsivity, preoccupation with sex, and promiscuity. One interesting case involved a previously sexually normal and law-abiding forty-year-old man who developed an uncharacteristic interest in pedophilia. Although he knew his interest was morally wrong, he felt helpless trying to control it. Eventually his behavior was traced to an egg-sized tumor in the right orbitofrontal cortex of his brain.[32] His sexual attraction to children vanished when the tumor was removed and reappeared when it grew back. A second operation succeeded in removing the entire tumor, together with his sexual interest in children once and for all. It is possible that the removal of the tumor allowed his frontal cortex to reassert its role inhibiting darker urges springing up from deeper brain regions.

Could similar "dark urges" be lurking in all of us? The answer, which depends on your interpretation of "dark urges," is probably yes. The patient with the tumor-induced pedophilia also exhibited an overall greater, uncontrollable interest in sex in general. It is possible his extraordinary and certainly abnormal interest in children was part of an aberrant, out-of-control preoccupation with sex itself. Limbic system activity, signals from the deeper brain regions, looks out for our basic individual survival needs—fear, food, aggression—as well as our species survival needs: sex. Perhaps, without the overseeing controls exerted by the frontal lobes, the checks are removed, like a car with a stuck gas pedal and no brakes. Symptoms may vary in individuals, however. Brain wiring varies somewhat. They follow a general plan, but brains are not constructed like identical integrated circuit boards. A tumor in the same location in a different person might not result in the exact same symptoms seen in the patient who developed a sexual interest in children.

It is not yet possible to prove a direct, one-to-one association of brain abnormalities to psychopathy in the same way that a blocked artery is recognized as the direct cause of a heart attack or stroke. It *is* possible to say, however, that brain abnormalities, and not just sociocultural influences, can play a major role in psychopathy.

It's important to keep in mind, however, that it is easy to over-emphasize the role of the particular brain region one is reading about or studying. The frontal lobes' executive function applies to executive *brain functions*, not just to executive *psychopathy functions*. It plays crucial roles in healthy brains capable of empathy as well as in unhealthy brains incapable of empathy. The orbitofrontal cortex, for example, also figures prominently in a condition that plagued writer, lecturer, and radio personality David Sedaris, who suffered from obsessive compulsive disorder (OCD). Consider the difference between the manifestation of orbitofrontal cortex involvement in OCD and in psychopathy. Sedaris's obsessive compulsive behavior during his childhood compelled him to repeatedly touch, count, and even lick objects. There was nothing psychopathic about his behavior, even though OCD involves a part of the brain also implicated in psychopathy.

"It started off with touching things and then I would have to touch things with my nose," he told an interviewer in 1998 on the Palm Springs show *More Than a Mouthful.*[33] "It would take me forever to get anywhere. Then I would go home and go to bed. Then I would have to get out of bed to go lick the light bulb in the refrigerator. So I'd lick the light bulb in the refrigerator and I [would] go back to bed and I would think I probably didn't lick that in the right place. So I have to get out of bed again and do it again, and go back to bed. And then I would think: how many peppercorns are in that spice jar? So I would have to get out of bed—this is like at 3 o'clock in the morning—count all the peppercorns and go back to bed. Then I was sure I had miscounted. So I had to get up again. It was exhausting." Compulsive head movements, tics, and beeping vocalizations followed.

Then Sedaris went through a phase during which, he says, "I had to take my shoe off and hit myself over the head with a shoe." Doing all of these things, things he "had" to do, left him a complete wreck. "If I was sitting in class, I had to lick the light switch that was beside the door." And he would do just that as he returned to his seat when called to the blackboard.[34]

"It lasted until I was twenty. Then I started smoking and it went away," he told an interviewer. (Jim Fallon's OCD also waned dramatically when he started smoking at age eighteen. Many people with schizophrenia take to smoking too; they are two to three times more likely to pick up the habit than the rest of the population. This might be an instance of self-medication, since nicotine causes an increase in an inhibitory neurotransmitter known as GABA.[35] GABA tones down neural activity and so could dampen brain circuits that are overactive in some mental disorders.)

If Sedaris indeed suffered from OCD as a child and young adult, there is a good chance that his symptoms could be traced to greater-than-normal activity in the orbitofrontal cortex of his brain. This is not just because the orbitofrontal cortex is a crucial piece of neural real estate involved in making decisions and linking rewards and learning. When an unmedicated Sedaris was in the thrall of his compulsions, there is a good chance that his orbitofrontal cortex, in a sense, had too strong a connection to a part of the brain that is intimately involved in movement, including movements involved in touching and licking things.

This is what Jan Beucke and his colleagues found when they scanned the brains of 92 subjects when researching OCD.[36] People who had not taken antidepressants to help them suppress their compulsions appeared to have brains that were hyper-connected between the orbitofrontal cortex and the basal ganglia, located deep in the center of the brain (Figure 11). This is the same region that is implicated in Parkinson's disease, which produces major symptoms of movement disorder. The researchers found that medication might even reduce the degree of connectedness between the brain region most associated with executive function, the orbitofrontal cortex, and one closely linked to movement, the basal ganglia. It is possible that it is the degree and specificity of the interactions between the prefrontal region and other parts of the brain that may account for symptoms of multiple neurological or mental disorders, including Alzheimer's disease, schizophrenia,

OCD, and psychopathy. However, Sedaris's prefrontal cortex issues clearly have nothing to do with psychopathy. It's not clear if Jim Fallon's childhood OCD, along with his childhood hyper-religiosity, were related to his psychopathic traits. Now, he says, they are just tendencies.[37]

The association of both OCD and psychopathy with the prefrontal cortex merely illustrates that brain regions implicated in one disorder can be just as involved with, or make contributions to, other disorders. For instance, based on MRI scans, some adults with bipolar disorder appear to have smaller and less metabolically active prefrontal cortices than adults who don't live with bipolar disorder.[38] There may be no single brain region solely devoted to OCD, bipolar disorder, or psychopathy. But they share brain structures that are intricately connected. When the circuits are disturbed or damaged to different degrees and in different ways, differing symptoms result depending on the nature of the interruption or flaw in the connections.

Sorting out the pattern of interconnections or brain circuits that underlie the brain's higher cognitive functions and—when they are compromised or impaired—dysfunctions or mental disorders has proven to be very difficult. It is, after all, brain science and, as the cliché goes, if it were easy, everyone would be doing it. But it is progressing, although slowly, thanks in part to brain-imaging studies.

An Exception that Proves the Rule?

One indication of the advances being made in the area of neurocriminology is the appearance of studies that are beginning to reveal differences in the brains of subgroups of psychopaths. In 2004, for instance, Raine and his colleagues used structural magnetic resonance imaging (MRI) to scan the brains of sixteen unsuccessful psychopaths who had not been able to avoid the law, thirteen successful psychopaths who had managed to avoid the law, and twenty-three control subjects or non-psychopaths who, of course, also managed to avoid the law.[39]

They found that psychopaths whose activities landed them in prison had 22 percent less prefrontal gray matter than non-psychopaths. Successful psychopaths, by contrast—those who managed to stay out of prison while still scoring high on the Psychopathy Checklist—did not share this abnormality.

Criminal or unsuccessful psychopaths additionally showed signs of abnormalities in the hippocampus (Figure 11), with the right side being larger than the left.[40] The hippocampus is closely associated with the transformation of short-term memory into long-term memory. It also plays an important role in social learning and, particularly relevant in these studies, in learning to fear the consequences of one's actions. This is a skill that keeps a person from doing something, out of the fear that they might get caught and be punished or suffer otherwise unpleasant consequences. That is exactly what jailed psychopaths are not very good at. The observation that unsuccessful psychopaths have abnormal hippocampi should not be too surprising; psychopaths who avoided prison time did not have abnormal hippocampi in this small study.

Raine's research raises the possibility that the different career tracks of successful and unsuccessful psychopaths may have their roots in these anatomical differences. It is possible that successful psychopaths have other abnormalities that leave them with no conscience but with intact brain function in other key brain regions. These neurobiological "gifts" or attributes might allow them to behave like psychopaths but not get caught, either because they are more clever than their jailed peers or because they limit their misdeeds to those less likely to land them in prison.

Their unsuccessful cousins, on the other hand, are more seriously handicapped. Their impairments, both in brain structure and function, may predispose them to commit more thoughtless crimes, to impulsively engage in more overt criminal behavior. They may also be less skillful at masking their inability to empathize with others and hide their emotional deficits.

A potential problem with this study is that the unsuccessful psychopaths scored a bit higher on the Hare Psychopathy Checklist than the successful psychopaths. But other researchers have observed differences between successful and unsuccessful psychopaths as well, so that may not weaken the implications of this research.

We know, for example, that psychopaths who land in prison have reduced stress reactions and reduced ability to think like an executive in psychological tests when compared to non-psychopaths. Jim Fallon, perhaps not so coincidentally, reports very little response to pain, anxiety-provoking situations, and violent, horrifying images that other people find disturbing.

A lot of the frontal cortex is devoted to "big issue" questions like: What happens now? Where will this get me? What are we going to do next? And what will happen if I do this?

This part of the brain weighs options, compares potential outcomes, and examines multiple choices whenever a person makes a decision. Similar to a CEO, it functions like an executive. People with injured prefrontal lobes have significant problems acting as an effective CEO. But successful psychopaths, including some real CEOs,[41] have increased stress reactions and in some cases possibly *better* executive function.

If successful psychopaths have fewer abnormalities in the prefrontal cortex and other parts of the brain that evaluate and handle executive decisions than incarcerated psychopaths do, it is easy to imagine how they can avoid getting caught or taking risks likely to lead to capture.

Apparent differences between successful and unsuccessful psychopaths suggest that psychopathy may include two distinct personality disorders with great similarities but significant distinctions. Another possibility is that psychopathy describes a spectrum of behaviors. Psychopathy may not be a single disorder, just as schizophrenia or autism are not single disorders. The standard test used to define psychopathy, Hare's Psychopathy Checklist, itself includes multiple categories of traits. For example, one measures emotional detachment and another measures antisocial behavior. It would be possible, for instance, for a successful psychopath to have high scores in emotional detachment and low scores in antisocial behavior, while an unsuccessful psychopath could have a different profile. Both could still score high enough to be classed as psychopaths but with emphasis on different psychopathic traits.

This, along with studies on brain-injured people, implies that having an impaired prefrontal cortex is one way to end up an unsuccessful psychopath. Other, more subtle changes could lead to a more "successful" life in those with psychopathic features.

As with most complex medical conditions, and particularly mental and personality disorders, multiple factors appear to contribute to the development of psychopathy. Genetics evidently can predispose some people to psychopathy. And the environment in which the brain develops could play a role. This might be related to inheritance, or it might be related to other factors affecting the fetus, as is suspected in schizophrenia. Finally, early life experiences may promote the development of psychopathy in some susceptible individuals.

Why Isn't Dr. Fallon a Practicing Psychopath?

Why doesn't Jim Fallon charm, threaten, manipulate, exploit, and use people for his own ends and amusement? Why isn't Jim, with his quiet orbital prefrontal cortex and amygdala, multiple "warrior-like genes," and low empathy genes, a practicing psychopath, a murderer, or both, like more than half a dozen of his ancestors? He has, as he has said, "the exact brain pattern of a psychopathic killer," but he is not a psychopath by any testable standards. He has some personality traits in common with psychopaths and his brain scans raise interesting questions about the origins of psychopathy.

A person who was abused as a child and who inherited genes that predisposed him to psychopathy may have a greater chance of becoming a psychopath than someone who did not inherit the same genes but suffered the same abuse; he would also have a greater chance of becoming a psychopath than someone who inherited the same genes but was raised in a loving and supportive home. Fallon says that he was lucky enough to be raised in a loving, supportive home.

"It's an unlucky day when all of these three things [genes, abnormal brain function, and abuse] come together in a bad way," Fallon said on NPR, "and I think one has to empathize with what happened to them [psychopaths]."

Often, of course, it would require the compassion of the Dalai Lama to empathize with criminal psychopaths while thinking about their victims. And this is the source of the growing controversy about the liability of psychopaths in light of recent findings indicating that the problem lies, to a significant degree, in their brains which seem to be incapable of processing emotions and relating to others.

Chapter Five

Troubling Developments and Genes

"My mother was cancer," murderer Richard "The Ice Man" Kuklinski said in Trenton State Prison. "She slowly destroyed everything around her. She produced two killers—me and my brother Joe."[1]

Richard lied routinely to his family and his associates during his forty-year-long criminal career, and he lied to journalists after it ended. But he was deadly accurate when he summarized himself and his twenty-five-year-old brother, Joe, who was indeed a killer too.

Joe lured twelve-year-old Pamela Dial, with her black-and-white mixed breed dog "Lady" in tow, into a building on Central Avenue in Jersey City, New Jersey on September 15, 1970. The weather had been clear and comfortable that day, nearly 74°F. As midnight approached and the three of them ascended the stairs to the roof of the four-story building, the temperature was cooling down to the high 50s. Pamela had found Lady wandering in the neighborhood around 11:30 P.M. and was returning home when she encountered Joe and accompanied him into the building.

When they reached the top of the building and stood on the roof, Joe attacked. He sodomized the girl, strangled her, and threw her body off the roof. Then he threw Lady after her.

Joe had been seen with the girl. The next morning, as the day heated up and the temperature began to climb to 92°F, police found him in the house he shared with his mother at 434 Central Avenue. It was just around the corner from the murder scene, two doors from where Pamela was found after the injured dog crawled to her body and howled to wake the neighborhood.[2] At the police station, Joe confessed under interrogation. It led to his rapid conviction, and he was soon sent to Trenton State Prison to serve out a life sentence.[3] He finished serving it thirty-three years and one week after raping and murdering the child; he died in prison on September 22, 2003.

Joe's older brother Richard was thirty-five years old when Joe killed Pamela. Richard managed to stay out of Trenton State Prison for sixteen more years before he joined Joe inside. During those years, he raised his son Dwayne and daughters Chris and Merrick while supporting his wife Barbara, whom he married in 1961. They thought he was a businessman with a terrifying temper. They knew he was an abusive husband. They did not know that he killed people when he went to work.

"He would set up business deals and when the people arrived with their side of the bargain, he would kill them," New Jersey State Attorney General W. Cary Edwards said when Richard was arrested on December 17, 1986.[4]

After his conviction, Richard actively sought attention and publicity. He had the time to pursue it since he wouldn't be eligible for parole until he was 110 years old. He agreed to take part in three HBO documentaries and spent days speaking to two biographers. During one of the interviews, he admitted to killing New York City police detective Peter Calabro. That got thirty more years added to his sentence. He promoted his image as "The Ice Man," a cold-blooded, emotionless, ruthless, highly efficient killer. The nickname came from his attempt to hide the time of death of at least one of his victims by storing the body in a freezer before disposing of it.[5]

"I was a person who was able to hurt somebody at any given time with no remorse and who could do it over and over again without it bothering them," Richard told forensic psychiatrist Park Dietz, M.D., M.P.H., Ph.D., who had been hired by HBO to interview the murderer in 2002. They talked over a four-day period for a total of thirteen hours. Part of the interview was included in HBO's documentary "The Iceman and the Psychiatrist."[6]

Dietz, a consultant to the FBI and now president of the forensic consulting firm Park Dietz & Associates, asked Richard if he thought of himself as an assassin. The question amused Richard. "Assassin; it sounds so exotic. I was just a murderer."

He hinted that he had killed at least 200 people during an unlikely career as a contract killer working for organized crime families in New York. He said he committed his first murder when he was 13 or 14 years of age. Solid evidence, however, points to half a dozen or so victims, mostly low-level criminal associates. Two were his accomplices, three were drug or pornography dealers, and one was a police detective. It would surprise no one if he killed more, perhaps many more, but without strong evidence who is going to believe Richard Kuklinski's unsubstantiated claims? He also claimed he used everything from a crossbow to hand grenades, from garrotes to pistols, from cyanide to strangulation to kill in the triple digits.

It's hard to tell while watching the documentary when Richard was lying and when he was telling the truth. This is not surprising, since he had, in the professional opinion of Dietz, two personality disorders that accounted for his behavior. Dietz saw evidence of paranoid personality disorder in Richard. The more dominant feature of his personality, however, was antisocial personality disorder, which Dietz later made clear he considered the same as psychopathy. The psychiatrist explained that he was referring to "someone who does not have a conscience, does not have remorse, does not feel a sense of guilt about most of the bad things they do, is impulsive and violent."[7] This diagnosis might also explain Richard's embrace of the media a few years after he went to prison for the rest of his life. The attention and widespread reputation it earned him is consistent with a trait common in psychopaths: grandiosity. Richard also displayed another trait that is a characteristic feature of psychopathy: fearlessness. Richard said he rarely felt anything that approached nervousness or fear. There was, the psychiatrist explained, a genetic basis for that.

Fearlessness may be one reason some psychopaths do extreme things and take dangerous risks. Those whose emotional life is very empty, who feel little except anger, may seek extraordinary experiences just to feel something more than the emptiness that comes with an innate inability to feel many emotions the rest of us take for granted. For psychopaths, Hare wrote, "Fear—like most other emotions—is incomplete, shallow, largely cognitive in nature, and without the physiological turmoil or 'coloring' that most of us find distinctly unpleasant and wish to avoid or reduce."[8] Richard said he had gotten a bit of a thrill from sex, but not much else.

Resorting to murder at least six times might suggest that he may have also experienced some stimulation from planning, executing, and getting away with the act. In some cases, it is conceivable that the act of murder was a response to someone who angered and/or disrespected him. He was subject to violent outbursts of anger, according to his wife and children. Dietz himself saw the anger start to build when he questioned Richard about the appropriateness of killing three men he claimed to have killed in South Carolina after a car they were riding in cut his car off. After some tense moments followed by some gentle questioning, Richard attributed his anger to Dietz's appearing to speak down to him, as his abusive father Stanley Kuklinski had half a century ago.[9]

Although his claims of being a hit man extraordinaire are suspect, few question Richard's claims that he had a horrible childhood. His wife and children attested to it. His father Stanley was known as an abusive alcoholic who beat his children and wife. Richard said he always regretted not adding him to his list of victims. But "Richard sometimes thought his mother was even meaner than his father—no small thing," his biographer wrote, "Anna tried to stop Richard from stealing, hit him with most everything she found in the house: shoes and broom handles, hairbrushes, wooden spoons, pots and pans. She often hit him on the head—this even after [Richard's other brother] Florian was killed that way [by his father]—and knocked Richard out cold. She'd come up behind Richard and strike him when he didn't expect it."[10]

Besides being inhumane and illegal, abusing children this way may have blowback that the abusers never imagine, if they even care. Psychologists have been gathering data for years that suggests that mistreatment of children can have severe consequences. It has been linked to drug abuse, depression, and suicide, as well as antisocial behavior. Several studies suggest that psychopathy can be added to that list. It is possible that the stress accompanying abuse in susceptible people alters the development of their brains as they grow and mature.

The Widening Circle of Abuse

Back in 2002, a trio of Swedish psychologists led by Britt af Klinteberg of the Karolinska Institute ventured into the files of a group of 199 males from a bad neighborhood in Stockholm.[11] They all had criminal records. Researchers had kept track of these boys from the ages of 11 to 14 years until they were adults, 32 to 40 years old. The authors found that children exposed to a high level of victimization were more violent and had higher psychopathy scores on the PCL test than a control group of 95 children from similar backgrounds who were not victimized as children.

Children who were exposed to lower levels of abuse had no, or only minor, histories of violence and lower PCL test scores. The Swedish study replicated the results of a similar study completed six years earlier involving 652 neglected and abused children living in a metropolitan area of the United States Midwest.[12] These results indicated "a clear connection between early childhood victimization and psychopathy," according to the authors of the U.S. study, Barbara Weiler and Cathy Widom, Ph.D. They also suggested that the connection between childhood abuse and later violence in some individuals might be traced to the presence of psychopathy.

A decade before this study, criminologists and psychologists recognized that having a father like Richard Kuklinski's father, a father who was an alcoholic, a psychopath, or who displayed antisocial behaviors, was one of the best predictors of future psychopathy in a child.[13]

Although it is clear that childhood abuse or victimization is a risk factor for the development of psychopathy, it is not necessary for the development of psychopathy. Eric Harris, for example, was raised by decent parents who never abused him. He was raised in the same household as his psychologically healthy brother.[14] It appears that it is possible to be born, as forensic psychiatrist Michael Stone, M.D., of Columbia University says, a "bad seed."[15] The expression of an unfortunate combination of still unidentified genes may be enough to produce a criminal psychopath without the unwanted and unwarranted addition of beatings or other mistreatment.

While it is true that abuse is not necessary to bring out psychopathic traits in some individuals, it is also true that abusing children does not guarantee that they will grow into adults who can fake but not experience the feelings and emotions that allow humans to care about others. Without a predisposition to psychopathy, it is not at all certain that psychopathy will follow abuse. Other emotional and psychological damage from childhood abuse, though horrific, would not be the same thing as clinical psychopathy.

DNA's Contribution

Despite the rare exceptions, there are strong indications that genes influence the development of personality traits that set criminal psychopaths apart from non-psychopaths in many cases. In fact, the heritability of psychopathy is estimated to be around 50%, a respectable contribution.[16] This does not mean that half of a person's psychopathy can be attributed to his or her genes. In fact, it tells us nothing about any particular person, whether it's Richard Kuklinski or Richard III. Heritability applies only to populations. It means that around 50% of the individual differences in psychopathy observed in a population can be traced to genetic variations. (Choosing the word "heritability" to describe this concept has unfortunately led to confusion with the word "inherited," which does apply to individuals. The two words are not the same, despite their seeming linguistic similarities. Sadly, this is one of many instances where the public's difficulty understanding scientific concepts can be traced to poorly chosen and unnecessarily obscure jargon.)

Scientists redeem themselves from poor word choices, however, when they devise elegant experiments. A good example is when they compare traits in identical and fraternal twins. Identical or monozygotic twins inherit the same DNA. Fraternal, or dizygotic twins, are like any pair of non-identical siblings; they have about half of their genes in common. By comparing the frequency with which traits show up in identical-twin pairs to the frequency with which they show up in fraternal-twin pairs, researchers can estimate the influence of genetics on a trait in a population.

There are some assumptions associated with twin studies that need to be considered. For example, do identical and fraternal twins really share the same environment? Or do people treat identical and fraternal twins differently? And, do some parents choose each other as mates because they have similar traits? If so, their fraternal twins might have more than half of their genes in common.[17] But twin studies still provide some of the most valuable and revealing insights into the relative contributions of genes and environment to behavior.

For example, a study of 838 identical and 1,360 fraternal twins points to the existence of a psychopathic personality factor that is highly heritable.[18] The results derived from a self-report questionnaire indicated a strong genetic influence in the development of psychopathic traits in 16- to 17-year-old Swedish twins.

The genes that might influence psychopathic behavior have not been identified. In fact, even mental disorders that have received years more research time and billions of dollars more in funding—disorders like schizophrenia, major depression, bipolar disorder, autism, and attention deficit hyperactivity disorder—have not been linked to "disease-causing" genes. Instead, clusters of genes appear to influence the development of these illnesses.

Multiple genetic variations in these genes are now known to increase the risk of developing these disorders. In fact, some of the same genetic variations show up in all five of these serious psychiatric conditions.[19] Interestingly, some of these variations involve genes that affect how brain cells communicate by regulating the movement of calcium into and out of cells. Calcium's importance in biology extends to a lot more than bone health; it is a very influential factor in nerve-cell function and, seemingly, in achieving mental health.

If psychopathy is indeed a mental disorder, as many experts believe, then psychopathy research too might benefit from being included in genetic studies like those that have already linked five major mental disorders (schizophrenia, bipolar disorder, autism, major depression, and attention deficit hyperactivity disorder) to each other through the genetic variations they have in common. Psychopathy may share some biology with them, just as they appear to share some biology with each other.

Above Genes

For many criminal psychopaths, part of the answer to the question "How could someone be so evil?" may lie somewhere in the genetic material the perpetrator came into the world with, his genome. Another part of the answer apparently lies above his genome, in his epigenome. (Epi in Greek = "above.") There is, it turns out, much more to genetics than DNA.

The key is what turns genes on and off. Environmental factors can influence how genes are regulated. It is now commonly believed that environmental influences can play a part in the development of mental disorders such as schizophrenia, bipolar disorder, and major depression. Stress, which victimized children experience in abundance, is one such environmental factor.

Canadian researcher Patrick McGowan and his colleagues reported in 2009 that childhood abuse leaves an epigenetic mark on the brains of those who endure it and then take their own lives.[20] They detected evidence of epigenetic changes affecting the function of a stress hormone receptor (a glucocorticoid receptor) that is found specifically in neurons. People who took their lives but who were not abused did not show these changes. This study linked findings in rats with those in people, since rat pups who fail to receive normal attention from their mothers have similar epigenetic changes in their brains.

There are different ways environmental factors like the stress produced by physical abuse may tell genes what to do. They may lead to the modification of DNA itself by adding a methyl group (a carbon atom bonded to three hydrogen atoms) to a specific site on the giant molecule. The addition of this chemical tag to just the right spot in DNA on or near a particular gene can change the way that gene is expressed. There is a virtually unlimited supply of tags like these in the body, ready to respond to events that originate far from the cell's nucleus where DNA is stored.

Events and things you encounter in your environment can also cause chemical tags to attach to proteins called histones. DNA doesn't routinely hang around in the nucleus fully extended like a string floating in water; it is wrapped around histones and so condensed to save space and regulate access to the genes it contains. Adding a methyl group to a histone can make it harder or easier for DNA to be read or accessed by the cellular machinery that turns its encoded instructions into amino acids, the building blocks of proteins. Adding an acetyl group (that's a methyl group with two additional atoms, another carbon and an oxygen) often makes it easier for a gene's encoded information to be converted into a protein. Removing an acetyl group often has the opposite effect.

RNA, a molecule similar in structure to DNA and involved in many crucial cellular processes, including turning DNA's coded instructions into functioning proteins, can also affect gene expression. It can also turn genes off by interfering with several of the processes that read the message encoded in DNA. It might also promote the addition of methyl groups to DNA and the modification of histones.[21]

The pattern of use of these chemical tags creates an epigenome. Diet, smoking, exercise, infection, toxic chemicals, and many other things you encounter in your day-to-day life can affect your epigenome. It is highly likely that the stress of being terrorized as young child does the same. The epigenomes of middle-aged identical twins don't look much alike despite their identical genes, because experience has changed the factors that control the expression of those identical genes.

"We've got to get people thinking more about what they do," epigenetics authority Randy Jirtle, Ph.D., of Duke University asserted in 2010. "They have a responsibility for their epigenome. Their genome they inherit. But their epigenome, they potentially can alter, and particularly that of their children. And that brings in responsibility, but it also brings in hope. You're not necessarily stuck with this. You can alter this."[22]

Epigenetics is a potentially game-changing avenue of research for behavioral geneticists. It may help explain why it is so difficult to find genes involved in complex disorders and to identify the factors that explain complex behaviors like those associated with mental diseases and psychopathy.

A Remnant of Abnormal Development

Take a look at Figure 10. This half of a human brain was "fixed" or hardened and preserved in formaldehyde before being cut lengthwise down the middle. The front faces left so you are looking at the right hemisphere. You are also looking at a structure that may provide a marker for the development of psychopathy, the jelly-like material marked with an asterisk, the "septum." The fluid-filled chambers or ventricles in the brain are separated by a transparent wall or enclosure. In Latin, that is septum pellicidum, the full anatomical name for this see-through membrane of nervous tissue.

Around three months after conception, a space or gap called a cavum (Latin for hollow) forms between the two sheets of the septum (see Figure 11). A couple of months later it normally begins to close and finishes closing three to six months after birth. The closing of the gap is related to the proper development of parts of the limbic system and other nearby structures. If the limbic system structures don't develop normally, the gap doesn't close. When this happens, the resulting condition is called cavum septum pellucidum (CSP).

Adrian Raine and his colleagues[23] reasoned that looking for CSP in antisocial types would be a good way to find evidence that psychopathy and antisocial personality might be related to improper or flawed development of the brain, since complete development normally includes closing the gap. The presence of the gap is a marker for abnormal fetal brain development. But where can you readily find a supply of people with considerable psychopathic traits outside of a prison? Some people will swear they have psychopaths in their workplace, and they very well might, but the authors of this study turned to a temp agency instead.

Raine maintains that temporary employment agencies are good places to find psychopaths, as psychopaths often have a difficult time maintaining full-time employment. Based on one of his studies, he claims that 13.5% of those he tested were psychopathic based on the North American criterion of a score of 30 on the PCL–R diagnostic test. This estimate jumped to about one third of the temps if the European PCL–R cutoff of 25 was used. But why would psychopaths be hanging around temporary job agencies?

Raine suggests it is because they "provide wonderfully safe havens—almost a breeding ground."[24] The benefits for psychopaths may include the less-rigorous background checks typically given to temporary compared to permanent employees, and freedom of movement. The former lessens the risk for psychopaths that their past behavior will catch up with them, and the latter lessens the risk that their present behavior will. Temporary jobs allow them to pack up and leave after, or perhaps even before, they get caught exploiting, victimizing, or otherwise taking advantage of a temporary employer. Impulsivity is a frequent trait seen in people with high psychopathy scores, and changing jobs is easier at a temp agency.

The researchers used MRI to look for CSP in 87 persons recruited from temporary employment agencies. They found it in 19 of them. The presence of the brain abnormality, according to Raine and his co-authors, is associated with more antisocial personality, psychopathy, and run-ins with the law compared to those people without the marker. This, they concluded, is evidence for neurodevelopmental involvement in later antisocial behavior.

Developing the Right Connections

If psychopathy is, as Raine and many other scientists believe, a neurodevelopmental disorder, then we might expect to see other signs of it in the structure of the brain. Since the function of the brain depends on its internal connections, the connections between two brain regions that both figure prominently in biological theories about the cause of psychopathy is a good place to look.

Many psychopathy researchers think they have a pretty good idea of what might be happening in the brains of psychopaths. The orbitofrontal cortex, especially the middle part (called the medial orbitofrontal cortex) in a normal brain suppresses the aggressive tendencies of the amygdala and prevents the entire interconnected network from recognizing and processing emotions and acting, or not acting, on them accordingly. If the orbital cortex or its communication pathways are hindered, the amygdala is free to promote its rather primitive agenda of animal-like passions, including different forms of aggression, violence, rage, and sexual promiscuity. At least it appears to do so in the most dangerous psychopaths.

The amygdala and the orbitofrontal cortex are connected by a bundle of nerve fibers called the uncinate fasciculus or UF. Uncinate fasciculus translated from Latin is "hooked small bundle", which aptly describes the way it looks when you trace its path from the frontal cortex to the amygdala.

The prefrontal cortex, which includes the orbitofrontal cortex, and its connections to other brain regions are not completely developed until late adolescence. This has been offered as one reason some teenagers act "without thinking," as some parents have noted. This part of the brain is involved in decision-making, solving problems, foreseeing the outcome of actions, and other "executive" tasks. It's easy to imagine problems related to the development of this part of the brain and its connections contributing to psychopathic traits, including impulsivity.

Interfering with gene expression, environmental inputs or both can disrupt the normal development of the brain and its connections. Brain imaging studies suggest that inheriting genes linked to psychopathy might contribute to psychopathic behavior by affecting brain development before and after birth, according to Yu Gao, Ph.D., of the University of Pennsylvania and her colleagues.[25] And there is plenty of time to alter this development. The brains of preschoolers quadruple in size. By six years of age, they are ninety percent on the way to reaching their final volume. Both gray and white matter in the brain continue to develop all the way into late adolescence.[26] With this development come changes in behavior. Interfering with this development with something as drastic as abuse can indeed affect behavior.

All neurons communicate, sometimes making thousands of connections to other brain cells. It is not only the cell clusters and brain subdivisions that show signs of dysfunction in the brains of psychopaths; there appear to be problems with the wiring that connects brain regions closely involved in generating the characteristics that make humans humane.

Wiring in the nervous system consists of long extensions called axons. These neuronal extensions make contact and communicate with other neurons. The axons are covered by glial cells. Glia cover and insulate axons with a fatty covering called myelin. The fatty sheath is white. That is why neuroscientists call the communication pathways in the brain "white matter." Clusters of neurons are referred to as "gray matter" to distinguish them from white matter.

Researchers at the Institute of Psychiatry at King's College London used DT-MRI, or diffusion tensor magnetic resonance imaging tractography—the technique of choice for imaging fiber bundles in living subjects—to examine the connection between the amygdala and the orbitofrontal cortex in nine criminal psychopaths whose psychopathy (PCL–R) scores ranged from 25 to 34. These volunteers, ranging in age from 22 to 46 years, had been convicted of false imprisonment, multiple rape with strangulation, manslaughter, and murder. Their IQ scores ranged from 87 to 101. Nine healthy, non-criminal men of similar ages and IQ scores served as controls. The screening version of the Hare Psychopathy Checklist (PCL–SV) indicated they were not psychopaths.

The British scientists looked at the communication pathway between the frontal cortex and the amygdala, the uncinate fasciculus (UF). In the high-psychopathy group, the UF was broken down or structurally impaired. Furthermore, the degree of the structural problems in the UF was correlated with the degree of psychopathy in these psychopathic criminals.

The results indicate that the worse the quality of the connection between brain regions like the frontal cortex and others that process the ability to relate to others, the greater the psychopathic behavior.[27]

Although this British study was small, it is part of a growing and increasingly convincing body of research that links psychopathy to the interconnected regions that comprise the "emotional brain," including the prefrontal-temporal-limbic system. For example, Michael Koenigs, of the University of Wisconsin-Madison, and co-workers used DT-MRI to compare the connections in the brains of 14 criminal psychopaths to those in 13 non-psychopathic criminals. They too found evidence of reduced structural integrity in the UF connecting part of the frontal cortex (the vmPFC or ventromedial prefrontal cortex, to be exact) to the region of the temporal lobe that contains the amygdala. fMRI results provided further evidence that impaired connections between the vmPFC and the amygdala are a biological feature of psychopathy.[28] These and other studies have found abnormalities in the communication pathways linking the frontal lobe with other brain regions and between the two sides of the brain.[29] Scientists have also found differences in the thickness of the massive white matter bundle, the corpus callosum (Figure 11) that connects the right and left halves of the brain.[30] It is through this massive bundle of connections that the two sides or hemispheres of the brain communicate with each other.

It looks as if, in the small-scale studies that have been conducted so far (nine to fifteen subjects), greater impairment of the connections between brain regions implicated in psychopathic behavior leads to greater psychopathy scores.

If the differences are related to mis-wiring of neuronal connections during development, no one knows for certain what causes them. In many, but not all, individuals with psychopathy, inheritance of unknown genes combined with stresses such as physical abuse during childhood are thought to be the major factors. It is possible that one or more of the hypothesized genes that can influence a person's susceptibility to psychopathy may have a role in guiding nerve-cell projections to their final targets before and after birth. Scientists suspect that this is a factor in the development of brain disorders like schizophrenia and autism. If psychopathy is actually a brain disorder and not a disturbing, disconcerting variety of personality that lies on the extreme end of the empathy spectrum, it is possible that the problem originates with faulty circuitry laid down in the fetal brain.

We are all born with far more neurons—billions more—than we end up with in our prime adult years. A few weeks after conception—brain cells are produced at an astounding rate, thousands per second, in a process called neurogenesis—you have plenty of brain cells, but neurogenesis doesn't connect them. And it is the interconnections in the brain that give it its remarkable abilities.

The connections in much of the brain really start to form after an infant is born, during a dynamic process called synaptogenesis, which isn't completed until young adulthood. This is when immature neurons "sprout." The long, thin projections, axons, which will carry electrical signals between brain cells, seek out their targets to form synapses. These are the contact points between neurons where the electrical signal carried along the axon is converted into a chemical signal when neurotransmitters are released. These chemical messengers carry the signal across the gap in the synapse that separates one neuron from another. Synaptogenesis is influenced by both experience and genetics. This is one obvious place where something can go wrong in the brain's development, resulting in serious consequences later in life.

At the end of an axon finding its way toward its synaptic target is a growth cone. This is an expanded, splayed-out extension of the axon, and it contains chemical sensors. These sensors respond to chemicals in the environment and use them to direct its progress. Watching its progress would be like watching the developing axon move through a three-dimensional map making turns right, left, up, and down based on the chemicals it senses in its immediate environment. The signals are received by proteins that stick out of the growth cones. These proteins act like antennas to pick up signals in the environment. Different proteins are produced at specific times during the migration process, based on instructions provided by RNA molecules.

If everything goes right, the RNA is degraded at the right time, after it has served its purpose by producing a specific protein needed at a specific time during the journey. Other RNAs, with precise timing, then produce other proteins which pick up different signals and continue to guide the axon to its proper target. Now, what if an RNA molecule hangs around too long, when it isn't wanted or needed?

Scientists at the Weill Cornell Medical College in New York[31] found evidence that this is where synaptogenesis can go wrong. Axons responding to signals they should no longer be responding to can take wrong turns. This can result in faulty brain wiring. The researchers investigated neurons traveling from the spinal cord into the brain, but the same mechanism could result in mis-wiring in other regions of the central nervous system.

This finding is consistent with reports that have been appearing since 2007 or so, which suggest that mutations that affect the control of RNA degradation can interfere with normal brain development. So far, these mutations have been associated with movement disorders linked to abnormal brain development.

It remains to be seen if problems with RNA degradation contribute to mental disorders that are believed to be related to faulty brain development. Even if they don't, there are other key players in the formation of synapses that can be affected by mutations. For example, special cells that guide developing neurons in the neocortex produce a signaling molecule, another protein, called reelin.[32] Some researchers believe problems with reelin signaling in humans might play a part in the development of schizophrenia, autism, depression, and Alzheimer's disease. If psychopathy is indeed a developmental brain disorder influenced by genetics, as recent findings suggest, then it too might be added to the list of disorders like autism, major depression, bipolar disorder, attention deficit hyperactivity disorder, and schizophrenia that could be linked to faulty wiring in the brain.

Chapter Six

Back Again? Predicting Bad Behavior

2011 was the first year since the terrorist attack on the World Trade Center in 2001 when more police officers died at the hands of criminals than died in automobile accidents. The toll: 72.[1] By some estimates, half of these officers may have been killed by criminal psychopaths.

Jump ahead to the fictionalized year 2054. John Anderton is the head of the "Pre-Crime" police unit that has pretty much wiped out crime in Washington, D.C. Unlike police officers 40 years before, Officer Anderton and his colleagues clean up the capital by arresting individuals *before* they commit crimes.

This scenario is from the film *The Minority Report*, in which Pre-Crime cops get their tips from two male twins, Arthur and Dashiell, and one female, Agatha, who have been genetically modified to possess the gift of pre-cognition; they are full-time psychic "Pre-cogs." With no labor union, these pasty, and no doubt water-logged, people lie passively in a shallow tank of what must be carefully maintained Pre-cog-sustaining fluid while awaiting visions of future crimes which they pass along to the officers of the special police unit. The minority report of the title refers to a dissenting prediction by one of the Pre-cogs: Agatha. This crucial report is generated when Anderton, played by actor Tom Cruise in the film version of the story, is himself fingered as a future murderer.

The movie predicted the ubiquity of personalized advertising, electronic newspapers, and the potential widespread use of self-driving cars and retinal or iris scans years before many filmgoers had much if any experience with them. But there is a theme that is more important than these technological developments for a rapidly changing society. Anderton's efforts to evade his fellow Pre-crime cops, find out why he has been accused of a future crime, and prove his innocence, are the stuff of entertainment, but it is the ethical issue raised by the story that makes the film interesting, especially with regard to psychopathy research. What are the rights and obligations of society, and of a pre-accused offender, if a "future" crime is predicted?

The basis of the film is a science fiction short story with the same title. It appeared in the January 1956 issue of *Fantastic Universe Science Fiction*. The author, Philip K. Dick, was called a pulp fiction hack in *Wired* magazine[2] and "one of the most influential science fiction writers of the 20th century" in the *New York Times*.[3] He had been writing for four years when *The Minority Report* appeared in the 35-cent pulp magazine. Dick's name and the title of his story appear on the front cover, but *The Minority Report* is not the subject of the magazine's cover illustration. To grab the attention of readers, the editor chose an image of giant flea-like creatures threatening a blond female, dressed in a yellow jumpsuit, encased in a protective bubble with all parties floating in the vacuum of space.

Despite the cover art of the magazines that published much of Dick's work, he didn't write about giant insects or depend much on aliens or spaceships in his stories. His approach to science fiction stressed alienation more than aliens. He tended toward stories with issues concerning the nature of reality, the reliability and unreliability of the senses, and the controlling influences of powerful entities like corporations and governments. He had to write fast and often because he struggled most of his life trying to live on pulp fiction fees, which he once compared to eating dirt.

Despite, or because of, his poverty, Dick succeeded in creating a large body of work—45 novels and 121 shorter pieces—before he died in 1982 at age 53 of a massive stroke. The plots of many of the stories, like their author, contain significant elements of paranoia, which may have been related to his fondness for amphetamines and to their side effects.

Dick once intended to say in a speech he never delivered: "We live in a society in which spurious realities are manufactured by the media, by governments, by big corporations, by religious groups, political groups—and the electronic hardware exists by which to deliver these pseudo-worlds right into the heads of the reader, the viewer, the listener."[4]

A few paragraphs later, he planned to tell his audience: "So I ask, in my writing, What is real? Because unceasingly we are bombarded with pseudo-realities manufactured by very sophisticated people using very sophisticated electronic mechanisms. I do not distrust their motives; I distrust their power. They have a lot of it. And it is an astonishing power: that of creating whole universes, universes of the mind. I ought to know. I do the same thing." He wrote this before the Internet, before Facebook, before news and entertainment became confused in increasingly Corporate-owned media outlets and before brain-scanning technology became so common that it became a tool for marketing and public relations firms.

Although he never benefited from it, his oeuvre has and will continue to provide material for Hollywood films and some wealth at least for his estate. The films *Blade Runner*, *Total Recall*, *Screamers*, *A Scanner Darkly*, *Next*, *Paycheck*, and *The Adjustment Bureau* as well as *The Minority Report* are all inspired by or based on his stories.

Despite Dick's imaginative scenario, many people doubt that science will provide a basis for arresting people before they commit a crime in the near future, or ever. Nevertheless, although some psychologists and statisticians are skeptical of the progress so far, research funded by the MacArthur Foundation Law and Neuroscience Project, the National Institute of Mental Health, the National Institute on Drug Abuse, and the National Institute of Biomedical Imaging and Bioengineering is now under way to identify brain activity patterns that could, in the opinion of the scientists doing the research, be used to at least help predict if someone is likely to end up back in prison.

There is more than one goal attached to the expensive and time-consuming effort required to scan and explore the brains of criminal psychopaths in the hope of one day understanding the influence biology has on their behavior. One is purely intellectual: to satisfy our curiosity by answering one version or another of the question "How could anyone be so evil?"

A goal more likely to attract research funding is to learn enough about the brains of human predators so we can perhaps change their behavior and protect innocent people from becoming their victims. Using emerging insights into how the brains of criminal psychopaths function or malfunction to predict and prevent future crimes inevitably raises references to *The Minority Report.*

To Free or Not to Free

How can we know who will reoffend and who won't? Who do we release on parole and who do we lock away forever, certain they will always be dangerous? Parole boards and judges rely on a convict's age, past history, prison record, and on the opinions of prison psychologists, the availability of social supports such as family and friends, and the word of convicts themselves when they decide who will be retained and who will be released. When they make the right decision, a rehabilitated convict is released back into society. When they make the wrong decision, something as, or almost as, serious as a crime is committed: a rehabilitated convict is detained when he is no longer a threat. Or, if a deceptively unrepentant prisoner fools the parole board, he is released into a population of potential victims. One only need to remember Edgar Smith and Jack Abbott, the murderers who fooled William Buckley and Norman Mailer respectively, with disastrous—and in one case fatal—consequences.

Fool Me Twice

Ironically, some traits of criminal psychopaths, such as the ability to con and manipulate, may get them released sooner than criminals without these traits. That is what Stephen Porter and his colleagues at Dalhousie University in Nova Scotia concluded after reviewing the files of 310 Canadian men who spent two or more years in prison after being convicted of federal crimes.[5] They categorized the men according to their PCL–R test results, and found that 90 of them scored 30 or higher out of 40 points. Thirty, you'll recall, is the cut-off for a diagnosis of psychopathy in Canada and the U.S.

The prisoners in the Canadian study were also categorized according to their crimes: non-sex offender, child molester, mixed rapist/molester, or rapist. Then the researchers coded the results. No one (except the offenders) knew who was who until all the results were in. Not surprisingly, the men with high psychopathy scores were more likely to commit violent as well as non-violent offenses like burglary than were the men with low psychopathy scores. They were not, however, more likely to commit sexual offenses, except in one subcategory: sex offenders who were also psychopaths were linked to more cases of child molestation in this particular group of criminals.

One of the study's findings suggests that the ability of criminal psychopaths to manipulate others by faking feelings, and by putting on convincing shows of remorse for parole boards, works for them. Or at least it helps with the "out" part for those who have an "in-and-out-of-prison" lifestyle.

"They use non-verbal behavior, a 'gift of gab,' and persuasive emotional displays to put on an Oscar award-winning performance and move through the correctional system, and ultimately parole boards, relatively quickly despite their known diagnosis," Porter told the BBC.[6]

A sexual or nonsexual psychopath offender sitting in front of a Canadian parole board was nearly 2½ times more likely to convince the board members to let him out on conditional release than a non-psychopath. It appears that his ability to con and lie, to charm and deceive, can work well even for a criminal psychopath who can't figure out how to keep from getting caught and thrown into prison in the first place. His typically antisocial behavior on the outside, of course, brings him back to prison more often—and brings him back sooner—compared to those with fewer psychopathic traits, yet he still had the ability to charm or convincingly lie his way out to begin with.

The psychopaths on average took a year to return to prison while the non-psychopaths took two. According to Hare, psychopaths have a recidivism rate twice as high as non-psychopaths and triple the rate if you measure the times that their violent behavior, versus something like drug dealing or theft, lands them back in prison.[7] A review conducted in 1998 found that psychopaths were three times more likely to return to prison after a year than non-psychopaths.[8] And they were four times more likely to be sent back for committing violent crimes. But, of course, no one knows how many were not caught after committing crimes. The researchers concluded that "specialized education and training in dealing with psychopathic offenders is urgently needed," something with which many victims would agree.

Disagreements among academics about the diagnostic validity of the PCL–R extend to its ability to predict antisocial behavior. Nevertheless, "there is clear evidence that the PCL–R is predictive of violent behavior and both general and violent recidivism," Michael Vitacco, Ph.D., and his co-authors declared in one review.[9] This, however, doesn't mean it can predict future behavior for a particular individual with certainty. It is one factor among others, including a criminal's age, which can be a useful indicator of risk of reoffending after release. Antisocial behavior in persons with high psychopathy scores may decline with advancing years. Or not.

As they approach age 50, "psychopathic offenders seem to 'fall off the radar,' in terms of showing a dramatic drop in convictions," Julia Shaw of the University of British Columbia and Stephen Porter observed.[10] But it's not clear why. They could, the authors suggest, have actually stopped offending. Or they might be spending more time in prison and so lack the opportunity to continue committing crimes. It is possible that they die sooner because risk-taking is common among many psychopaths. It is also possible that some gain a bit more experience controlling their impulses as they age. And, of course, fatigue and illness that often accompany aging may make violent acts less likely.

"Ultimately," forensic psychologist Luisa Williams of the Northumberland, Tyne and Wear NHS Trust said in 2009, "the acid test of whether an offender will reoffend lies only in their future behavior."[11] That is still the case and helps explain why the hunt continues for better ways to predict the future behavior of offenders being considered for release from prison.

Impulsive Insights

Many features of psychopathy can contribute to antisocial behavior, but it would be hard to imagine traits better designed for landing someone in prison repeatedly than a predilection for impulsive behavior combined with a lack of remorse and a lack of guilt.

The consequences of psychopathic impulsivity are what you might expect. Hare's experience revealed that "jobs are quit, relationships broken off, plans changed, houses ransacked, people hurt, often for what appears as little more than a whim." A revealing and common response is: "I did it because I felt like it."[12]

Unsuccessful psychopaths, those who can't avoid prison, either don't devote much mental energy to predicting likely outcomes of their behavior, or else are somehow impaired and so unable to foresee or appreciate the consequences of their actions.

Hare illustrates psychopathic impulsivity with a story one of his high PCL–R scoring subjects told him.[13] While walking to a party, this man decided to buy some beer. When he discovered he had left his money at home, he felt it was too much trouble to walk the six or seven blocks back to retrieve it. Instead, he found a heavy piece of wood and used it to rob a gas station that was conveniently nearby. It's not difficult to trace the gas station attendant's serious injuries in part to the attacker's impulsivity issues.

Many neuroscientists believe a part of the brain called the anterior cingulate cortex (ACC) plays a role in such impulsive behavior. More specifically, this part of the cortex seems to be active when the brain is making a choice, detecting errors, monitoring conflicts, and learning what to avoid.

Figure 10 shows the location of the ACC in the frontal lobe, tucked beneath other folded layers of the cortex located closer to the inner surface of the skull. The ACC is also highlighted in the MRI image in Figure 12, which makes the cortex look a bit like a maze. (This might be an apt analogy for anyone entering the brain with the intention of coming out with answers about philosophical questions related to some of its most intriguing and mysterious functions such as consciousness, free will, self-awareness, and the nature of good and evil.)

The folds that make up the cortical maze allow much more brain tissue to fit into the limited space inside the skull. Since the skull could not expand as brains evolved and still safely pass through mammalian birth canals, the evolutionary solution was to crumple up the expanding cortex like a sheet of paper scrunched into a ball. If you could spread out the cortex, it would cover an area about 2½ square feet, about the size of a sheet of newspaper, and between only 1⁄16 and 1⁄6 of an inch thick.

In 2013, a team of researchers including Eyal Aharoni, Ph.D., Michael S. Gazzaniga, Ph.D., and Kent Kiehl, Ph.D., announced that they had detected something promising in the folded cortex of the ACC. They published the results of a preliminary study called "Neuroprediction of Future Rearrest" in the *Proceedings of the National Academy of Sciences*. The inspiration for the report's title was not a story by Philip K. Dick: the inspiration was the result of a brain-imaging study involving 96 prisoners between the ages of 20 and 52. The images suggested to the authors "a potential neurocognitive biomarker for persistent antisocial behavior."[14]

A press release prepared by the Mind Research Network in Albuquerque, N.M. and released by Duke University began with the claim: "A new study conducted by The Mind Research Network in Albuquerque, N.M., shows that neuroimaging data *can* predict the likelihood of whether a criminal will reoffend following release from prison." Its headline was more qualified: "Brain scans *might* predict future criminal behavior [emphases added]."[15]

The findings had "incredibly significant ramifications for the future of how our society deals with criminal justice and offenders," Kiehl said in the statement. "Not only does this study give us a tool to predict which criminals may reoffend and which ones will not reoffend, it also provides a path forward for steering offenders into more effective targeted therapies to reduce the risk of future criminal activity."

PsychCentral's headline was as optimistically circumspect: "Brain Scans *Could Predict* Future Criminal Behavior" but the opening was a bit more conservative: "Neuroimaging data *could help* researchers *predict* whether a criminal will break the law again once released from prison [emphases added]."[16]

Kiehl, a hardworking and ambitious researcher, has gone far since getting his Ph.D. in psychology and neuroscience at the University of British Columbia in 2000. One of his goals is to discover an effective treatment for psychopathy, which no one has yet managed to do. "If you could target the brain region involved, then maybe you could find a drug that treats that region," he told John Seabrook in a 2008 *New Yorker* profile. "If you could treat just five per cent of them [psychopaths], that would be a Nobel Prize right there."[17]

In graduate school, Kiehl's mentor was Robert Hare, the pioneer psychopathy researcher and developer of the Psychopathy Checklist (PCL–R). By 2013 at age 43, Kiehl was a tenured professor of psychology with secondary appointments as professor of law and professor of neuroscience at the University of New Mexico. He is also the Executive Science

Officer and Director of the Mobile Imaging Core and Clinical Cognitive Neuroscience at the Mind Research Network in Albuquerque. The latter appointment provides him with a mobile fMRI brain-scanning machine, which he helped design.

fMRI Delivered to Your Prison

The mobile brain scanner is a crucial tool in Kiehl's work. It gives him an advantage over researchers without an fMRI machine-on-wheels. Most of the multi-ton, multi-million-dollar machines that take snapshots of living brains are confined to hospitals or research facilities. For most studies, criminal volunteers like Willem Boerema, shackled and under guard, are transported to the machines to have their brains scanned. This is done with significant inconvenience to administrators, researchers, and guards.

Kiehl's brain scanner goes to the criminals. Kiehl and his collaborators use a semi-trailer to transport the mobile fMRI machine to the prisons and adolescent correctional facilities of the New Mexico Corrections Department. So far, they have taken more than two thousand brain scans of volunteer prisoners, many of whom are psychopaths or minors whose behavior suggests they could someday develop into psychopaths. Nobody has more scans of criminal brains than Kiehl and his team of forty investigators and staff at the Mind Research Network.

The scans that Kiehl and his co-authors claim hold the promise of predicting re-arrests indicate to the scientists that something is not quite right in the ACC, the anterior cingulate cortex. This is just what you might expect, since the ACC is one of the regions reported to show increased activity whenever someone makes a decision involving an impulsive behavior.

For example, let's say you agree to look at a screen and press a button every time the letter "X" appears but not when the letter "K" appears. It sounds simple, but it takes concentration because a "K" is just a modified "X" with its left limbs pointing straight up and down as if it were performing a half jumping jack. Since the letter "X" appears more than 80 percent of the time in this test, it takes some effort to not press the button when "K" pops up on the screen. An impulsive person would be expected to make more errors and hit the button more often when "Ks" appear than a less impulsive person. If someone has trouble controlling the impulse to respond when a letter pops onto the screen, scientists figure this trait might be reflected in a brain structure like the ACC which has previously been implicated in this type of task.

This is the test Kiehl and his colleagues asked their convicted volunteers in two New Mexico prisons to take while the prisoners underwent brain scans in the Mind Research Network's mobile scanner. After following these volunteers for four years, the scientists report that those with relatively low activity in their ACCs during the test were roughly two times more likely to get re-arrested after being released from prison than were convicts with relatively active ACCs. Kiehl said "This means we can see on an MRI a part of the brain that might not be working correctly—giving us a look into who is more likely to demonstrate impulsive and anti-social behavior that leads to re-arrest."[18]

A co-author of the report, Walter Sinnott-Armstrong, Ph.D., a Professor of Philosophy at Duke University, believes that "These results point the way toward a promising method of neuroprediction with great practical potential in the legal system. Much more work needs to be done, but this line of research could help to make our criminal justice system more effective."[19]

Not surprisingly, this paper received more press coverage than most journal articles, which receive none. Many accounts in the mainstream media repeated the information in the press release. Bloggers tended to be more skeptical. Many wondered if spotting decreased blood flow to a particular region of the brain could really predict who will commit future crimes, or, more accurately, who will get caught and re-arrested for committing crimes in the future. Some neuroscientists doubted if low activity in the ACC could be a useful marker for antisocial behavior.

Kiehl has found that the ACC shows the greatest change in activity when someone is trying to control their impulses. That is why he zeroed in on this region when he and collaborators designed the experiment. Other parts of the brain suspected of being involved in controlling impulses include the dorsolateral prefrontal cortex (Figure 8) and the basal ganglia (Figure 11). The ACC may not be the main player in this type of mental activity. It is more likely part of a network and it could be responding with increased activity to subtle inputs from other brain regions.

One model presented in 2002, for instance, includes the ACC as a control filter in a network or circuit that processes information about errors.[20] If this model is accurate, the ACC may receive information from the amygdala, basal ganglia, and parts of the frontal cortex and pass it along to the motor cortex (Figure 8) and other regions involved in movement. These motor areas could feed updated information back to the frontal cortex and basal ganglia. This scheme outlines a wiring diagram that might underlie one way we learn by making mistakes.

Such interconnectedness does not contradict Kiehl's assertion that "we can see on an MRI a part of the brain that might not be working correctly—giving us a look into who is more likely to demonstrate impulsive and anti-social behavior that leads to re-arrest."[21] But, just because it might not be working correctly doesn't mean it is structurally impaired either. One comparison of a couple of dozen psychopathic subjects and an equal number of non-psychopathic subjects found no group differences in the size or volume of the ACC.[22] It is possible that the ACC itself is not impaired in psychopaths. The ACC reduced activity in Kiehl's and others research might reflect reduced input from other parts of the brain, a possibility that still leaves the ACC as a potentially useful marker for defective impulse control in affected individuals.

Kiehl someday hopes to capitalize on the apparent involvement of the ACC in impulsive decision-making by developing a way to train prisoners to improve its function and so improve their ability to control their impulses. This, most of us would agree, would be preferable to seeing a criminal psychopath who left his wallet at home look around for a heavy piece of wood, as the psychopath who robbed the gas station did on the spur of the moment when he suddenly found himself out of cash.

Of course, in such a controversial field of research, not everyone agrees with the statements in the press release.

"The problem with this work is that it fails to consider core principles of psychological measurement," Christopher Patrick said.[23] One of the most basic of these is that the brain response during the test (psychologists would call it the predictor or independent variable) must be reliable if the prediction is to be valid or useful. This requires proof that the test yields consistent scores for individuals across time. The result of one scan is not meaningful in scientific terms until it has been demonstrated to be reliable. Considering these and other basic principles of psychological testing, "the likelihood that recidivism can be predicted from ACC activation within a single-session lab task in any way that would be practically useful is extremely low," Patrick concluded.

Any brain scan or test used to predict the future behavior of an individual has to meet rigorous criteria to satisfy skeptical psychologists like Patrick. To ensure that the test results are meaningful and accurate, it is also necessary to take into account the limitations of the technology. Craig Bennett has learned a lot about these issues based on his investigation of how emotional information is processed and integrated with higher cognitive processes in the brain. His research combines his interests in developmental cognitive neuroscience and magnetic resonance imaging methods.

"While statistical classifiers can sometimes pick up on activity levels or patterns of activity that might be predictive, there is still a lot about how individuals vary that we can't explain," he said. "For example, if we gather data from a group of 200 prisoners and generate a classifier that can predict psychopathy, how do we know that prisoner #201 is really a psychopath if our classifier says he is? Could there be other, mitigating activity in other parts of the brain that our classifier is not trained on? Is 200 people really a big enough sample size to extrapolate to all people who are and are not psychopaths? Have we captured all possible variations in regional brain activity with 200 people? These are sticky questions without good answers."[24]

Bennett's comments were not specifically made in response to the claims made in the neuroprediction paper but rather directed at anyone who views or evaluates fMRI results and claims. As mentioned previously, most colorful fMRI images are combined group results placed on a single representative image of a brain. Making the leap from that group-accurate image to a single person's fMRI scanning result may not be as easy as people outside the field assume.

"If you compare the group fMRI results to those of the individuals that comprise the group, you will typically find that they look almost nothing alike," Bennett explained. "While the group map detects similarities that are generally consistent across the group, there is a wide range of variation in terms of the individual differences in regional brain activity."

Jim Fallon agrees but adds that part of the problem is not carefully defining the person you are studying. He used schizophrenia as an example. Once you diagnose someone correctly and know something about their genome, he has found, "you can get a pretty consistent look to those scans."[25] The same would apply to a population of carefully defined and diagnosed psychopaths.

The human brain is not static. It is always consuming glucose and oxygen at fairly high rates compared to other organs. Depending on the nature and design of their experiments, neuroscientists are sometimes trying to pin down a dynamic system.

As Bennett puts it: "Our brains are constantly changing, and are never the same from hour to hour, day to day, month to month, or year to year. If I give you a cognitive test at 2 P.M., you will perform differently than you would at 2 A.M. Your brain activity will be somewhat different too. You could hypothesize a situation where a psychopathy classifier is very accurate when the subject's data was acquired at the same time of day as the training data, but would misclassify if the subject's data were acquired in the wee hours of the morning, or if some other bit of context were different."

Bennett uses as an example the effect on men's testosterone levels associated with the success or failure of their favorite sports teams. "As a male, if your team loses then your testosterone level tends to fall lower. Conversely, if your team wins then your testosterone level goes up. If testosterone level was part of a measure of future tendency toward violence, then what you watched on TV a few hours before could make a difference in your sentencing."

Kiehl and his fellow authors, of course, know that they have much more work to do before they have validated their approach to predicting the chances a freed criminal will break the law again and return to prison. They acknowledge in their paper that future attempts to replicate their findings "should examine the robustness to variations in task, sample characteristics, sample size, anatomical region of interest (ROI), and analytic procedures."

After the paper was published, Kiehl told *Time* magazine that "There are more papers coming out that show how MRIs predict who reoffends. We are examining treatments that increase activity in the anterior cingulate. The goal is to see if we can help identify the best therapies to reduce recidivism."[26]

Flanking Maneuvers

The neuroprediction report from Kiehl's lab makes another interesting and potentially useful observation about how researchers may be able to progress in their search for clues about criminal behavior, psychopathy, and potential treatments.

It refers to a promising way to attack the challenge of reducing criminal behavior to pages of graphs and illustrations in scientific journals. Finding the biological and genetic bases of mental and personality disorders has been a frustrating experience for researchers. For instance, after years of research and millions of dollars in costs, no clear-cut examples of individual genes solely responsible for complex diseases have been identified. This includes schizophrenia, depression, and bipolar disorder, even though these disorders clearly have strong genetic influences. Even less is known about the nature of psychopathy.

This is one reason in recent years scientists have begun to look for biological markers or traits associated with complex disorders versus searching for particular genes. They call these traits endophenotypes to distinguish them from genotypes, the genes a person is born with. Endophenotypes may be more easily identified, observed, and measured than the complete, complex genetic bases of psychiatric conditions with their complex behaviors.[27] This makes endophenotypes potentially attractive targets for getting at some of the root causes of complex psychiatric disorders.

The same outflanking, divide-and-conquer approach may be a way to dissect complex behavior patterns like criminal behavior and psychopathy. If the ACC can be shown to be underactive in impulsive criminals, it might be looked upon as a neurocognitive endophenotype, a defect or abnormality linked to criminal impulsivity but more readily accessible to study than the criminal behavior as a whole.

Turning Up the Power

The 96 subjects in the neuroprediction study conducted by Eyal Aharoni, Kent Kiehl, and their co-workers in 2013 was large by past standards of psychopathy research, but more subjects will be needed to convince the scientific community that this preliminary study is valid. Many neurobiological studies of the psychopathic brain, however, have involved far fewer subjects. This might have drawbacks some researchers hadn't considered, or else hadn't spent much time thinking about, before Katherine Button and her colleagues pointed them out in a paper they published in *Nature Reviews Neuroscience* called "Power failure: why small sample size undermines the reliability of neuroscience."[28] Small sample sizes, the authors remind readers, make it more likely that results that appear to be statistically significant actually are not, and they also increase the chances that true effects are missed.

It is impossible to slide every criminal with a Hare psychopathy score near 30 into an fMRI machine even if you have one ready to go on a semi-trailer within a reasonable driving distance. The best researchers can do is sample the population of criminal psychopaths. Then they must use mathematical manipulations and statistics to determine whether or not the effect they see—for example, decreased activity in a part of the brain involved in impulsivity—reflects what they would observe if they could test every criminal psychopath. To do this accurately requires something called statistical power. If a study has enough statistical power, then it is capable of finding a result in a sample that accurately reflects what exists in the entire population (which, as noted, is too large to test and still get home at a decent hour).

The statistical power of a study depends on the sample size and on the magnitude of the real effect. Not surprisingly, studies involving many subjects can pick out smaller effects. Studies involving fewer subjects can't reliably pick out smaller effects, but they may be able to spot larger effects. Large studies are more powerful than small studies, but are more difficult to organize and cost more.

Button, a psychologist at the University of Bristol in the UK, together with her statistician, geneticist, and neuroscientist co-authors, analyzed 49 research papers in the field of neuroscience. Each of these papers had analyzed and combined results from multiple other studies to determine if a particular finding was real. (Such studies are called meta-analyses.)

They found that "the median statistical power in neuroscience is 21 per cent." That means half of the studies have a power below 21 per cent and half above. Low-powered studies miss too much. If the power estimate of 21 per cent is correct, many neuroscience studies could be missing around 80 percent of the real effects. These are called false negatives. Low power also increases the chances of obtaining false positive results; that is, a "statistically significant" effect reported in a small study has a good chance of mistakenly looking real.

This finding doesn't mean that you can point to any particular paper and say it is poorly designed and provides false results. It means instead that as a whole, the scientific literature in the field of neuroscience is underpowered, and alarmingly so.

Underpowered research studies also make it more likely that any detected real effects will look greater than they actually are. These and other conclusions concerning the drawbacks of small, underpowered research lead Button to conclude:

"The current reliance on small, low-powered studies is wasteful and inefficient, and it undermines the ability of neuroscience to gain genuine insight into brain function and behavior. It takes longer for studies to converge on the true effect, and litters the research literature with bogus or misleading results."[29]

These problems, of course, would apply to any field of scientific research that publishes results of studies involving small numbers of subjects. They are not specific to neuroscience or to psychopathy research, although the authors conclude that "small, low-powered studies are endemic in neuroscience."[30]

Between September 2012 and April 2013, nineteen Editorial, News and Analysis, Comment, or Perspectives and Review articles in research journals published by the Nature Publishing Group highlighted "failures in the reliability and reproducibility of published research" in different areas of biological research.[31]

In the future, the Nature Publishing Group, the publisher of the prestigious journal *Nature* and other influential publications, will allow authors much more space to describe how they carried out their studies. At the same time, authors who want to publish in *Nature* journals will have to document and justify more fully how they designed their studies and how they analyzed their results. Statistics will be looked over with more critical

Figure 1. LEFT: American psychiatrist Hervey Cleckley, M.D., established the basis for modern studies of psychopathy in the U.S. with his 1941 book *The Mask of Sanity.* RIGHT: Canadian psychologist Robert Hare, Ph.D., extended Cleckley's work and created the Psychopathy Checklist (PCL), which for the first time allowed clinicians and researchers to measure psychopathic traits in individuals.

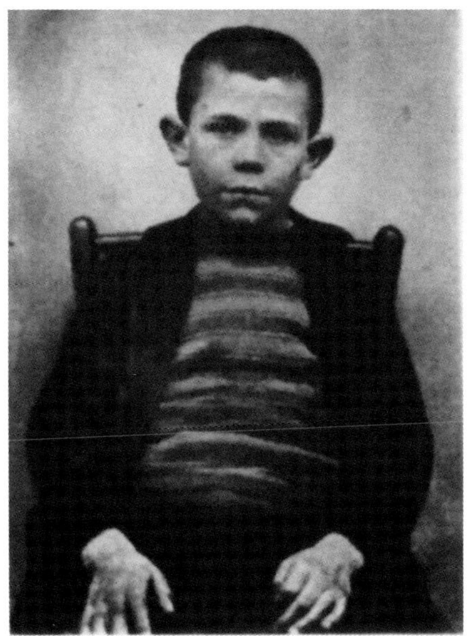
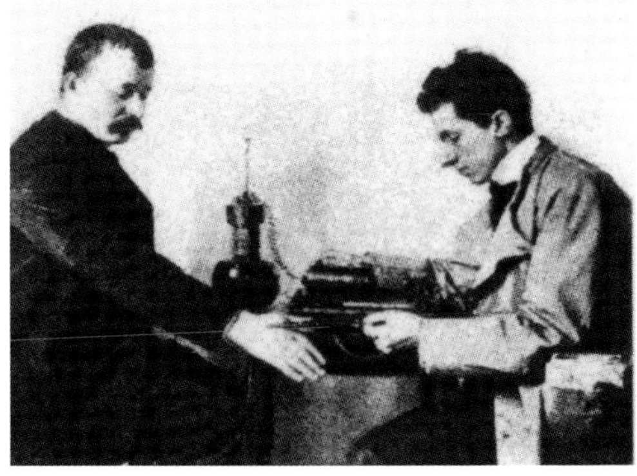

Figure 2. LEFT: Rav, described by Cesare Lombroso as "Boy Morally Insane." RIGHT: Testing a criminal's pain sensitivity using an electrical device adapted by Lombroso in the second half of the 19th century. More recently, scientists have found that psychopaths' nervous systems have a decreased response to the threat of pain compared to non-psychopaths.

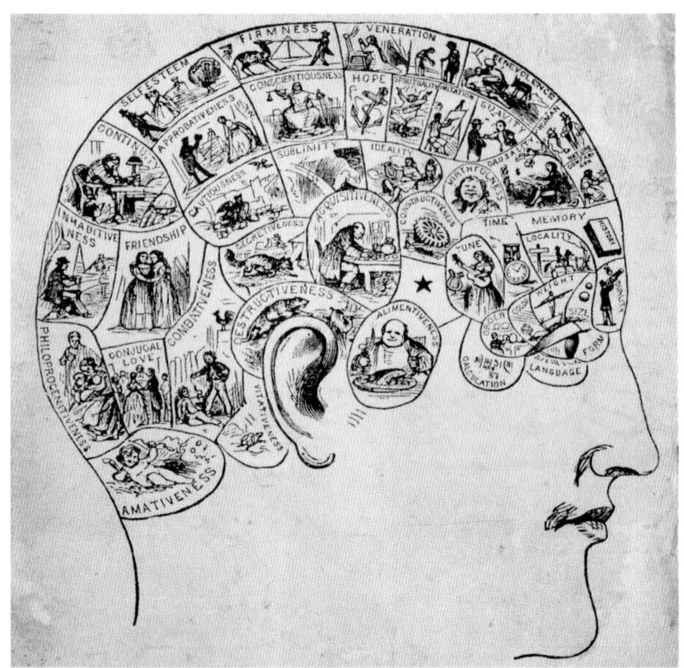

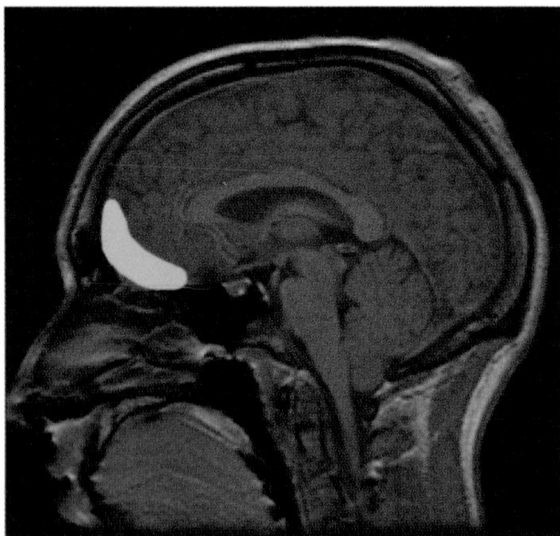

Figure 3. TOP: An illustration from *The Phrenological Journal* showing the locations of mental functions as understood in 1876. Traits were reflected in the shape of, and bumps on, the skull. Today, neuroscientists have the advantage of looking inside, rather than outside, the skull in their quest to understand brain function. BOTTOM: The orbitofrontal cortex, reportedly underactive in psychopathy, is highlighted in green in this MRI scan. The upper two thirds of the highlighted region, Brodmann area 10, is reportedly less dense.

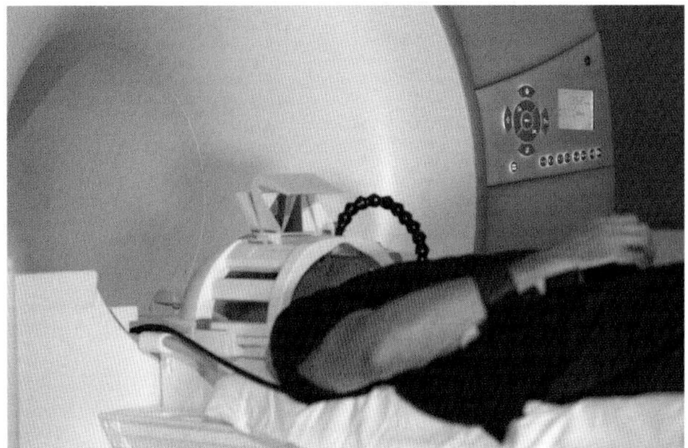

Figure 4. A model demonstrating a functional magnetic resonance imaging (fMRI) brain scan procedure at the Mind Research Network in Albuquerque, New Mexico. He can see a written or visual stimulus using a system of mirrors positioned above his face. The mirrors are positioned on a head coil which is part of the mechanism that detects changes in blood flow in the brain. Head movement is limited by padding and restraints to assure a sharp image. The subject can indicate his responses to the stimuli he sees in the mirror by pressing different buttons or keys on a device positioned under his hand. As he makes decisions based on what he sees, the fMRI machine detects differences in blood flow to different parts of his brain. Increased brain-cell activity is reflected in increased blood flow. The signals containing this information are detected by the machine, processed by computer, and used to produce images like those in Figures 5 and 13.

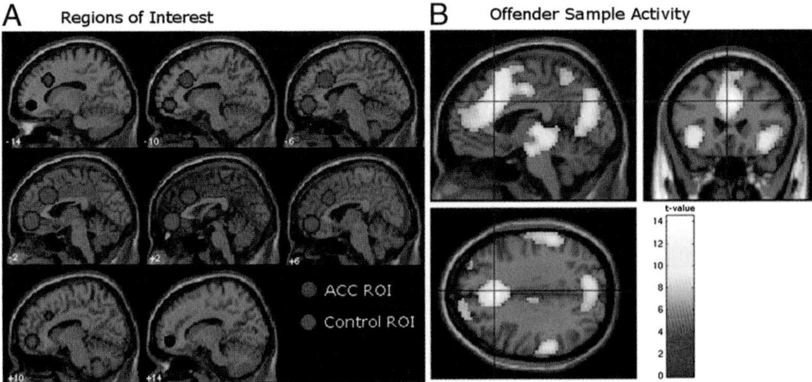

Figure 5. The results of fMRI brain scans of criminal offenders performing a cognitive task that requires decision-making and impulse control (B). Offenders with low brain activity in the anterior cingulate cortex have approximately double the risk of future arrest compared to offenders with high activity in this part of the brain, according to Eyal Aharoni of the Mind Research Network in Albuquerque, New Mexico and his co-authors. The images represent the average response obtained from the scans of 96 offenders overlaid onto a single brain scan image. The crosshairs are centered on the anterior cingulate cortex as seen from the side (B upper left), front (B upper right), and top (B lower left). One hundred and two non-offenders took the same test. Their pooled results (A) were used to select the precise target areas or regions of interest during the study. ACC = anterior cingulate cortex. ROI = region of interest.

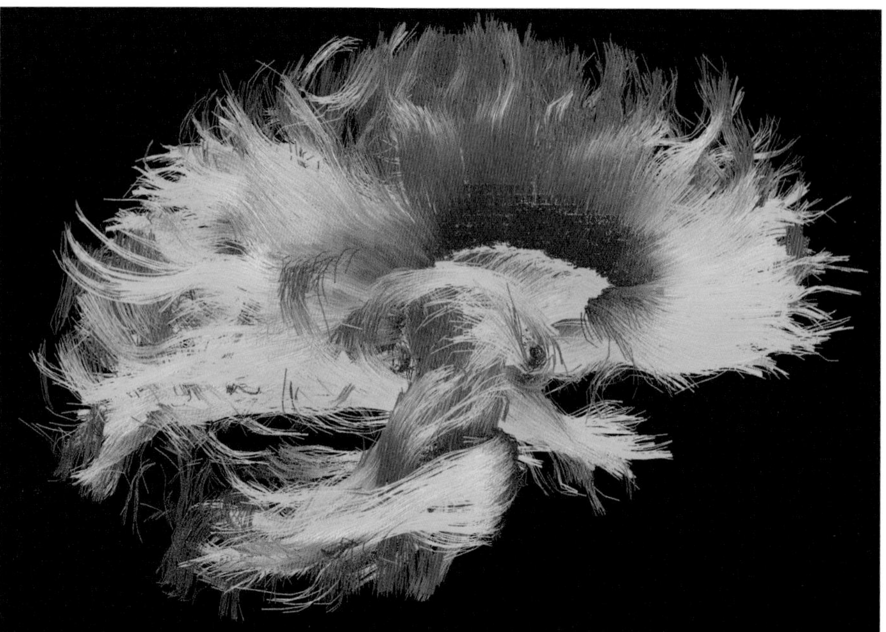

Figure 6. A DT-MRI scan showing white-matter nerve fibers in the brain. Reports suggest that a key bundle of fibers connecting the amygdala with the frontal cortex may be impaired in the brains of persons with high psychopathy scores. In this image from the Human Connectome Project, red fibers make right-left connections, green make front-back connections and blue make up-down connections.

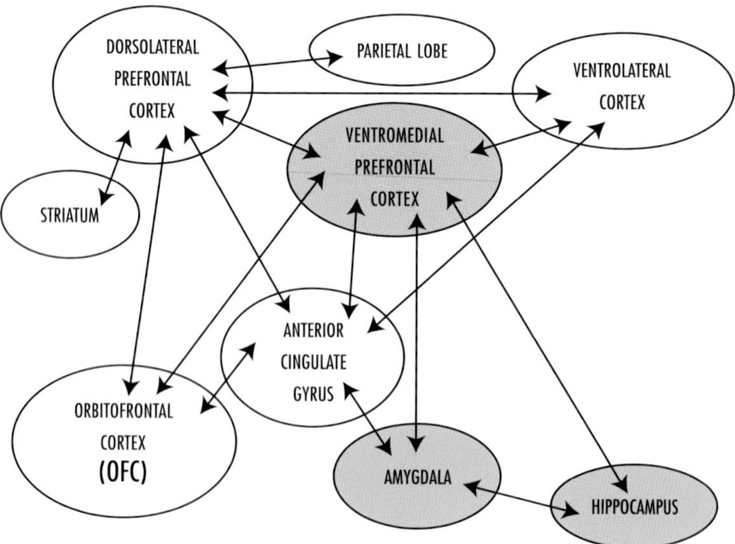

Figure 7. Circuits of the "moral" brain? In this model showing the interconnections of possible brain neural circuits that might underlie behavior associated with moral judgments, the ventromedial prefrontal cortex acts as an important integrating hub or center. Stroke damage affecting this area can change the moral choices a person makes.

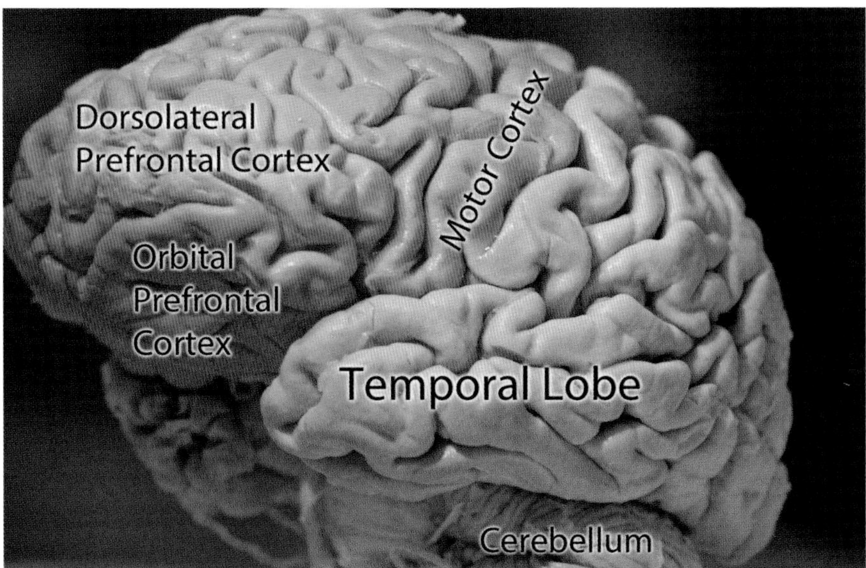

Figure 8. The whole brain, with the front facing left. The entire frontal lobe has been shaded orange. The amygdala is hidden deep the temporal lobe. The motor cortex is involved in planning, controlling, and performing voluntary movements. Much of the rest of this region is involved in high-level executive functions.

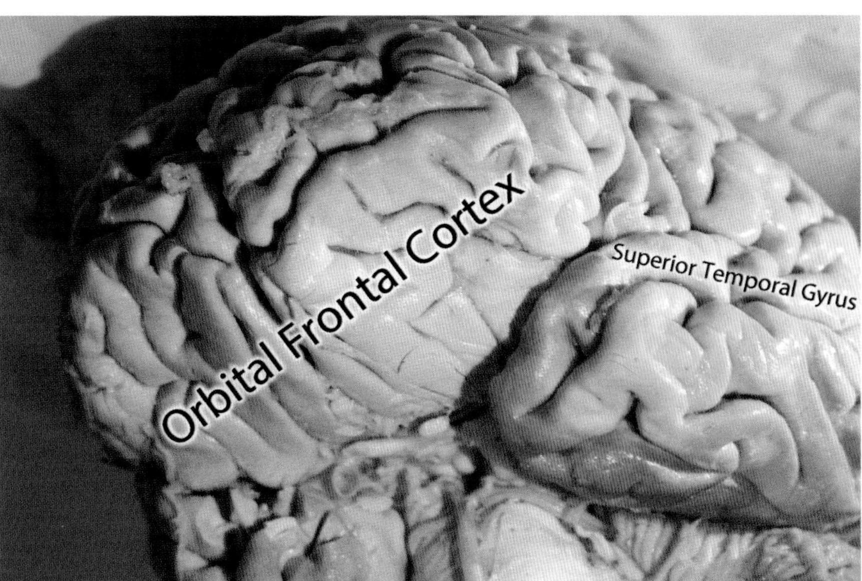

Figure 9. The orbital prefrontal cortex dominates this view from underneath the brain. Some research indicates that "cold-hearted" criminals with antisocial personality disorder AND psychopathy have reduced gray matter in the prefrontal cortex and parts of the temporal lobe (indicated by orange shading). "Hot-blooded" criminals with antisocial personality disorder WITHOUT psychopathy do not show this abnormality.

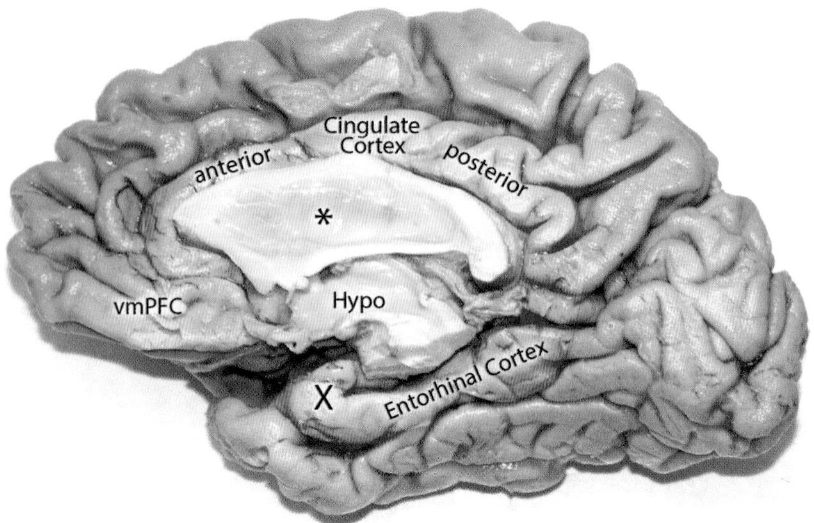

Figure 10. The inside right half of a brain split down the middle. Evidence suggests that the ventromedial prefrontal cortex (vmPFC) may be a major processing center for the neural circuitry underlying moral decision-making. The amygdala lies below the X. The colored regions are all part of the limbic lobe. The * = septum pellucidum. Hypo = hypothalamus.

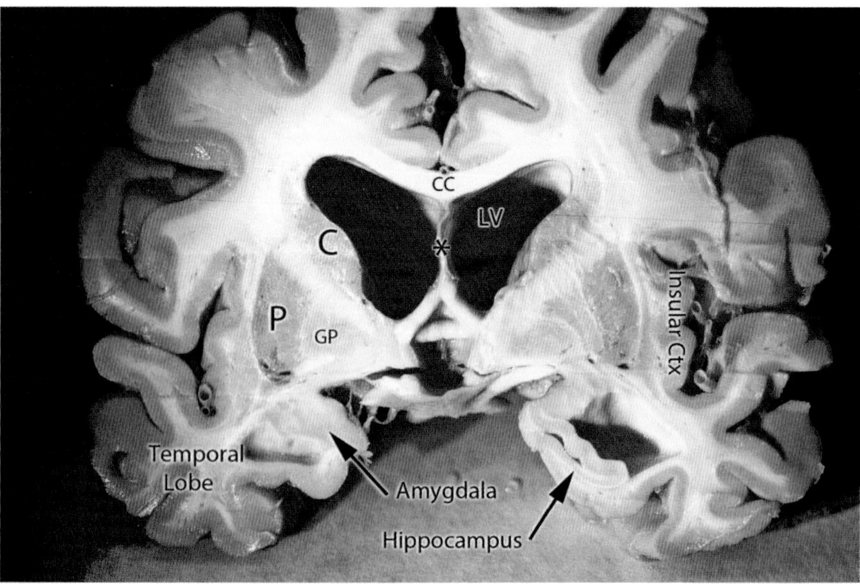

Figure 11. A human brain sliced crosswise as seen from the front. The amygdala is in the temporal lobe on the left. * = septum pellucidum. CC = corpus callosum. LV = lateral ventricle. Insular Ctx = insular cortex. P, GP, and C (putamen, globus pallidus, and caudate) make up the striatum, another region in which abnormalities have been linked to psychopathy.

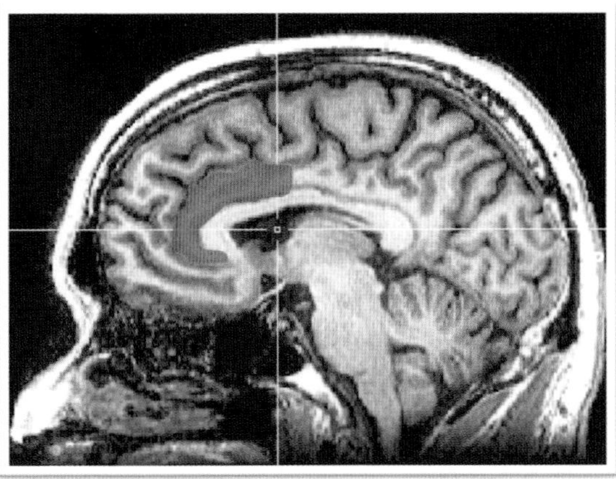

Figure 12. Magnetic resonance image (MRI) of the brain as seen as if sliced down the center from front to back. The anterior cingulate cortex (ACC) is highlighted. Under and behind it is the massive bundle of nerve fibers (the corpus callosum) that carries nerve signals between the right and left sides of the brain. The crosshairs are centered on a chamber (the lateral ventricle) that is filled with cerebrospinal fluid.

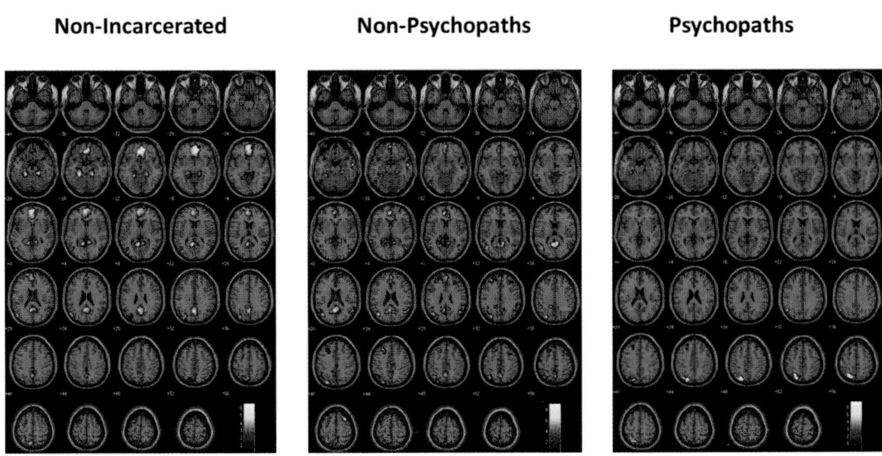

Figure 13. An fMRI compilation of activity patterns evoked by viewing images with moral versus non-moral connotations. The results of multiple individuals have been overlaid on a single brain image showing 29 levels of the brain as seen from above, looking down. The left set compiles the activity of 28 non-antisocial, non-incarcerated persons. The middle shows the responses of 16 non-psychopathic incarcerated criminals; the right, 16 psychopathic incarcerated criminals. Note how both the free and the jailed non-psychopaths differ from the criminal psychopaths.

98-5504

Harris2

http://members.aol.com/rebdomine/pissed.htm

Philosophy:

My belief is that if I say something, it goes. I am the law, if yo
u don't like it, you die.
If I don't like you or I don't like what you want me to do, you di
e. If I do something
incorrect, oh fucking well, you die. Dead people cant do many thin
gs, like argue, whine,
bitch, complain, narc, rat out, criticize, or even fucking talk. S
o thats the only way to
solve arguments with all you fuckheads out there, I just kill! God
I cant wait till I can
kill you people. Ill just go to some downtown area in some big ass
city and blow up and
shoot everything I can. Feel no remorse, no sense of shame. Ich sa
ge FICKT DU! I will rig up
explosives all over a town and detonate each one of them at will a
fter I mow down a whole
fucking area full of you snotty ass rich mother fucking high strun
g godlike attitude having
worthless pieces of shit whores. i don't care if I live or die in
the shootout, all I want
to do is kill and injure as many of you pricks as I can, especiall
y a few people. Like
brooks brown.

America:

Love it or leave it mother fuckers. All you racist (and if you thi
nk im a hypocrite, come
here so I can kill you) mother fucking assholes in America who bur
n our flags and disgrace
my land, GET OUT! And to you assholes in iraq and iran and all tho
se other little piece of
shit desert lands who hate us, shut up and die! We will kick your
ass if you try to fuck
with us or atleast I will! I may not like or government or the peo
ple running it or things
like that, but the physical land and location I DO fucking love!. S
o love it or leave it!

Society:

I live in denver, and god damnit I would love to kill almost all o

Figure 14. "Feel no remorse, no sense of shame." Entries from Eric Harris's webpages, together with his personal history, helped convince experts that he was at least a budding psychopath well on his way to becoming a full-blown psychopath.

eyes and authors will be encouraged to publish their unprocessed or raw data. This will allow reviewers and other researchers to analyze the results for themselves.

Why did the publisher of *Nature* scientific journals need to change its publishing guidelines? Their many reasons reflect specific weaknesses in graduate-level education and scientific research in the U.S. One of the most obvious is that hiring, tenure, and grant-review committees have long valued a long resume or curriculum vitae (CV) over a short one. Long CVs mean more publications. It is easier to get a long list of publications by publishing small amounts of data. The researcher who carefully completes a long and powerful project that results in one publication likely will lose out to a researcher who breaks the work up into several papers. Quality often suffers for the sake of quantity in a research environment where grant money is scarce and competition is intense. The fault, of course, lies with the hiring, tenure, and grant-review committee members; that is, with the most influential scientists themselves.

Button's University of Bristol colleague and co-author Marcus Munafò told an interviewer from the blog *Neurobonkers* that his "big concern is with the incentive structures that scientists have to work within. We are incentivized to crank the handle and run smaller studies that we can get published, rather than take longer to run fewer studies that might be more authoritative but aren't going to make for as weighty a CV in the long run because, however much emphasis there is on quality, there is still an extent to which promotions and grant success are driven just by how heavy your CV is."[32]

The length of a scientist's list of publications may even be more important than the prestige of his or her alma mater. A close look at the careers of 182 academic biologists suggests that those who published early, before being awarded a Ph.D., and often, are more likely to be successful a decade after graduation than those who delay publishing.

"It doesn't matter if you go to Harvard or a low-ranked university. If you begin publishing scientific articles when you're still a graduate student, you are far more likely to succeed in the long run," first author William Laurance, Ph.D., said in a press release issued by the James Cook University in Cairns, Australia.[33] And thus the cycle of publishing more but shorter studies versus fewer but longer and more substantial ones is renewed.

A second reason is that researchers receive little encouragement or reward for publishing results that report successful or unsuccessful attempts to reproduce findings from other labs.[34] Researchers also are not encouraged by editors and peer reviewers to tone down the significance of their results, to describe them as exploratory or speculative. Reading nearly any press release issued by a university or research institution describing recently published results shows the emphasis placed on stressing the excitement of the finding rather than the exploratory and less-than-definitive nature of the research. The combination of pressure to publish lots of papers and to hype them has resulted in what the editors at the Nature Publishing Group consider worrisome "failures in the reliability and reproducibility of published research."[35]

The field of psychopathy research is just as reliable and suffers from the same concerns as other fields of neuroscience. Often in the past, and in many cases to this day, researchers out of necessity have had to make do with small numbers of subjects. They, like scientists in other fields, need to look more critically at how they design their experiments and investigations to suit that availability. One reason some reports of brain-imaging studies involving psychopaths have not been accepted by the highly competitive top-tier journals like *Nature* is because they could not include enough subjects to satisfy the reviewers and/or editors. Kent Kiehl and his colleagues at the University of New Mexico and the Mind Research Network are tackling the problem by using grants from the John D. and Catherine T. MacArthur Foundation, the National Institute of Mental Health, and the National Institute of Drug Abuse to create a database containing thousands of personal and medical histories with matching brain scans of individuals with psychopathy.

Despite the challenges of getting enough brains scanned during an expensive scanning session, psychopathy researchers over the past two decades have nevertheless managed to lay the groundwork for someday explaining the biological reasons one percent of our species differs so much from the other 99 percent in terms of morality. When working toward this goal, identifying specific brain regions that might be targeted for therapy someday is obviously important. So, too, is identifying the brain circuits that might underlie the processes that will explain how the psychopathic mind works.

Chapter Seven

Missing Fear and Empathy

The Haukeland University Hospital in Bergen, Norway covers a lot of land. The trees lining the streets of Bergen can't hide its buildings, which cover over two million square feet of space. The single main building alone covers more than 1⅓ million square feet. The Hospital employs around 11,000 people who treat or assist in the treatment of nearly 600,000 patients per year. If you find yourself in Norway and incur severe burns, develop a brain tumor, or experience decompression sickness or the bends while scuba diving in a fjord, this is where you should ask to be taken for the best specialist care. The Hospital also has a Center for Research and Education in Forensic Psychiatry and a Regional Security Unit. If you are a criminal psychopath and volunteer for a brain scan, you might have it done at Haukeland.

This is where LTK, a 25-year-old Norwegian man who impressed researchers as "somewhat grandiose" as well as manipulative, conning, and superficially charming in his social interactions, had his brain scanned. Like most individuals described in medical case reports, LTK is known to readers only by his initials.

It would be nice for his fellow Norwegians if LTK's psychopathic profile were limited to the classic traits of manipulative conning behavior, superficial charm, and the grandiose sense of self-worth his doctors saw in him. Sadly, his score of 36.8 out of 40 on the Hare Psychopathy Checklist (PCL–R) reflects some far more troubling traits—and convictions. The worst was for rape. Helge Hoff, who works at Haukeland University Hospital's Center for Research and Education in Forensic Psychiatry, and his colleagues described LTK, who agreed to have his brain scanned while processing emotional information as part of an experiment, as a "prototypical criminal psychopath."[1]

We know that a key way in which LTK and other criminal psychopaths differ from non-psychopaths is the way their brains deal with emotions. They don't respond to emotional images or situations in the same way people who lack psychopathic features do. For the most part, they have impaired ability to process or personally relate to the emotional content of words or emotional experiences.

For example, consider the following scenarios or situations. You are waiting to be called into a dentist's office for a procedure you fear. You discover that a creepy insect is under the bedcovers with you. You see a companion run down by an automobile. You hear sounds of a break-in when you are in the shower.

If your brain processes emotions like most people, seriously considering all of these scenarios is liable to produce some subtle but predictable and measurable effects. This ability to re-create or feel someone else's discomfort is not "just in your head." Your body responds as well. Your heart beats a little bit faster and you sweat more as you become more emotional. Even a small increase in moisture can be detected, because it makes it easier for an electric current to pass between sensors placed on your skin. Scientists measuring this skin conductance see it increase when a person with a conscience and a sense of empathy reads about, or views a disturbing picture of, a person experiencing fear, pain, or grief.

Attach the electrodes to men like Richard Kuklinski, Ted Bundy, or LTK and you will see that they are literally unmoved. And so is the recording device that's measuring their skin conductance. They hardly respond emotionally to stimuli that make the rest of us uncomfortable and a little bit sweaty. These stress- and fear-inducing situations also affect brain and body so the heart beats two or three beats per minute faster than normal. But in the one percent of the population with significant psychopathic features, these physiological responses are significantly toned down.

That is what Christopher Patrick and his fellow researchers found in 1994 when they presented 54 criminals, including some with psychopathic features like LTK's, with imagined fearful and neutral scenarios.[2] Regardless of their Psychopathy Checklist scores, all of the criminals rated themselves about equally capable of fear and equally capable of imagining themselves in described situations. But the physical responses of the criminal psychopaths in the group showed significantly decreased changes in heart rate and electrical skin conductance compared to the criminals who had lower psychopathy scores.

In fact, you can predict which criminals will have the least response to fearful images by looking for those who have the highest antisocial behavior factor scores on Hare's psychopathy scale. These differences suggest that something is deficient or at least different—depending on how you regard psychopathy—in the brains of psychopaths.

These and other studies in the past twenty years suggest that there seems to be a disconnection between words and emotions in the brains of criminal psychopaths. Their brains do not process them the way non-psychopathic brains do. High psychopathic traits come with emotional disability. The oft-quoted, pithy characterization of this deficit made by psychologists John H. Johns and Herbert Quay more than a half century ago bears repeating: "Psychopaths know the words but not the music."[3]

Hare expanded on this insight for Dick Carozza of *Fraud* magazine: "It means that psychopaths understand the denotative, dictionary meanings of words but do not fully appreciate their connotative, emotional meaning. Their language is only 'word deep,' lacking in emotional coloring. Saying 'I love you' or 'I'm truly sorry' has about as much emotional meaning as saying 'have a nice day.' This lack of emotional depth in language is part of their more general poverty of affect as described by clinicians and observed in neuroimaging studies."[4]

People like LTK, however, often act as if they have emotional *ability*. They can often convincingly fake recognizing and experiencing emotions, for example, when they think the act will help them con others. But, in reality, it is fake. The quality of the acting differs among individuals, but in some it can be very convincing. The practiced deceitfulness can routinely fool naïve victims. For a short period of time, skillful psychopaths can even fool experienced researchers upon first meeting, according to Robert Hare. But repeated studies over the past fifteen years indicate that psychopathy is harder to hide in the laboratory.

Before LTK entered the lab to have his brain scanned to see how he responded to emotion-related stimuli, Hoff and his colleagues needed to find out more about their volunteer. The history they gathered about his family background uncovered little that would have predicted his future career as a psychopathic rapist. While there is evidence that psychopathy has a genetic component, it wasn't an obvious factor in LTK's case.

According to his parents, his mother had an unremarkable pregnancy and an unremarkable birth. LTK seemed like a normal baby: he seemed to respond to people as any baby does. He was born too soon to take part in an experiment that tested skin conductance activity in 1-year-old infants exposed to a fear challenge. Skin conductance, as described earlier, reflects the body's automatic response to fear or stress by increasing perspiration. The study found that infants who showed low levels of skin conductance activity at age one year were more likely to act aggressively at age three years.[5]

LTK wasn't a particularly fussy infant either, a trait that has been linked to later conduct problems in boys.[6] When conduct problems lead to a formal diagnosis of conduct disorder during childhood or adolescence, it may precede a diagnosis of psychopathy in adulthood. Reportedly, LTK's family was not much different from other families that did *not* produce a psychopathic son. There were no signs that LTK had been abused or subjected to extreme stress as a child. In this regard, LTK differed from many criminal psychopaths who claim, or are known, to have been abused early in life.

The Homicidal Triad

He also had no history of setting fires or abusing animals. Arson and animal abuse, together with bed-wetting, are known as the "Homicidal Triad," "Hellman and Blackman Triad," or the "Macdonald Triad"[7] among forensic psychologists and psychiatrists, criminal profilers, and many readers of true-crime books. Because they are frequently associated with psychopathic behavior in the public's mind, it makes sense to ask: why didn't they appear in LTK's medical history? They are, after all, frequently said to predict a child's future as a psychopath. According to forensic psychologist Karen Franklin, Ph.D., a careful examination of the evidence indicates a weaker connection between the Homicidal Triad and future violence than the original FBI profilers who made the link assumed.[8] More likely, with the exception of bed-wetting, they are indications of severe stress or abuse. In other words, future violent individuals, psychopaths, or serial killers who have suffered childhood abuse may indeed include the Homicidal Triad in their list of youthful experiences, yet other abused children who show the same set of behaviors do not grow up to be violent or to become serial killers.

It is every caring parent's nightmare if her child displays the Homicidal Triad by any of its names. But the presence of the Triad by itself doesn't guarantee that the child will follow in the footsteps of Ted Bundy or John Wayne Gacy, who have become the twin faces of psychopathic serial killing in popular culture. Nor does its absence, as illustrated by LTK, guarantee the absence of psychopathy.

Who Are You Calling a Psychopath?

The Homicidal Triad is often linked to serial killers in popular culture. There is an interesting, uncertain, and somewhat controversial relationship between serial killers and psychopaths. We know that not all psychopaths are serial killers and that not all serial killers are psychopaths. Of the estimated one to two million criminal and non-criminal psychopaths in the U.S., a minuscule number are serial killers: estimates range from 35 to 100.

U.S. federal law makes no mention of psychopathy in its definition of serial killers: "The term 'serial killings' means a series of three or more killings, not less than one of which was committed within the United States, having common characteristics such as to suggest the reasonable possibility that the crimes were committed by the same actor or actors."[9] The FBI recognized the complexity of serial killer motivations and their relationship to psychopathy when it declared that "psychopathy alone does not explain the motivations of a serial killer."[10]

Christopher Patrick questions what many people assume is obvious: that all serial killers are psychopaths. He used Jeffrey Dahmer as an example.

Dahmer sexually abused and killed seventeen young men and adults over a thirteen-year period ending in 1991. He also ate some of their body parts.

"On some level," Patrick said, "Dahmer's compulsive behavior may have been driven by probably dopaminergic reward tendencies in a way that addicts are driven. The impulse is so strong that it almost engulfs them. Jeffrey Dahmer's case is way over the top; you've got a typical case [of addiction] dressed in alcohol, and you've got Jeffrey Dahmer's dressed in blood."[11]

Park Dietz, who examined Dahmer, agrees that he was not a psychopath, although, he pointed out, many serial killers are indeed psychopaths. He doesn't, however, agree with the suggestion that Dahmer's problem could be traced to compulsive behavior.

"Dahmer had several mental disorders, diagnosed by nearly all forensic evaluators who saw him," Dietz wrote. "His inability to find a sexual partner who shared his interest in prolonged cuddling was a function of his personality disorder, which I believe I diagnosed as Schizotypal Personality Disorder."[12]

Features of this disorder include social isolation and superstitious, odd beliefs. Dahmer's sexual tastes reflected paraphilias, which, Dietz explained, "included necrophilia, what was once called 'Pygmalionism' (a taste for dolls and mannequins), and what I named 'splanchnophlia' (an attraction to the shiny membranes covering the viscera); for him, cannibalism was never erotic." [Paraphilic behaviors entail extreme, dangerous, and abnormal sexual desires.]

Dahmer was an alcoholic, a problem that impaired his judgment and made it more difficult for him to avoid getting caught. Of Dahmer's disorders, Dietz regards only alcoholism as an addiction. "There are those who want to view paraphilias as an addiction, but I do not share their view. Paraphilias are more or less stable configurations of erotically arousing imagery and activities, probably learned in late childhood by the time of puberty," the psychiatrist explained.

In fact, apart from drinking, there is little in Dahmer's behavior that qualifies as compulsive behavior, in Dietz's view. "He did not regard his sexual desires, preferences, or behavior as senseless activities that he sought to stop or that relieved anxiety (which is the psychiatric concept of compulsion). Nor was I impressed with anything about his behavior—apart from drinking—that could be called impulsive or reflective of impulses any stronger than the sex drive of normal men his age."

"Did he seek rewards? Of course! Don't we all?" Dietz summed up. "He found it rewarding to lie next to a man with nice biceps all night long, and he wanted one who wouldn't leave him and wouldn't rob him. If that's dopamine at work, okay, but this doesn't mean there was anything pathological about his dopaminergic system."[13]

Psychiatrist Michael Stone is also skeptical of a link between serial killing and addiction. He points out that addiction is associated with physical withdrawal. He believes it is more likely that most serial killers have sexual urges combined with psychopathic traits, both of which are responsible for their behavior.[14]

What's Left Behind

At the Society for the Scientific Study of Psychopathy meeting in Washington, D.C. in 2013, a young graduate student approached former FBI special agent and criminal profiler Mary Ellen O'Toole and told her very adamantly that many serial killers are not psychopaths. "Really?" O'Toole replied. "Interesting, because I worked on hundreds of these cases."[15] The young student had not visited the scene of a single case, but she was nevertheless very certain that she was correct.

O'Toole explained what it looks like in the trenches: "When we analyze a crime scene, we look at the pre-offense behavior, the crime scene behavior, and the post offense behavior. In my research, I was looking at manifestations of behavior that could be indicative of the 20 traits [which are part of the Hare Psychopathy Checklist]. We are looking for predatory behavior. We are looking for the hunting behavior, which is associated with psychopathy. We are looking for instrumental violence, which has a very strong presence in these kinds of cases. [Instrumental violence is goal-oriented, premeditated, and "cold-blooded." Reactive violence is impulsive and "hot-blooded"]. We are looking for a lack of empathy for the victim. We are looking for callousness."

That is what she often found when she visited the scenes of serial killer-related murders. "You have the presence of this cold-blooded, instrumental violence. It is well planned out. The victims are treated as objects, and there is a level of callousness that is incredible. There is a high risk component to it. There is impulsivity to it. So we don't just focus on [something like] an addiction and whatever the addiction is associated with." It is not simply an urge that they need to have satisfied, or a "fix." "We know there are a lot of other things going on with these people."

She frequently sees a level of organization in the work of many serial killers that is quite remarkable and unlike what an addict would display, which might betray desperation. "That behavior shows some level of cognitive functioning that allows these individuals to think under pressure, under stress, under anxiety. But again, when you start seeing traits like predatory behavior—they are hunting humans—and instrumental violence, you can see behaviors that manifest traits of psychopathy. We look at the whole gestalt. We don't just look and try to explain one behavior."

O'Toole understands that some people who don't investigate crime scenes as a day job may look at some of the weird, strange, sickening behaviors perpetrated by some serial killers and be tempted to explain it as something other than psychopathic sexual sadism. "But if you ask somebody like me who has seen this behavior over and over again, you are less likely to get a reaction because I've seen cannibalism, I've seen necrophilia, I've seen all of those things. And then I've ended up meeting the people that have done these things. So when you start talking about compulsions, I certainly respect the opinions of people who have different explanations for this behavior, but I start looking for paraphilic behaviors." O'Toole acknowledges that paraphilic behaviors can sometimes be compulsive. "But that is part of what sexual offenders are: they are motivated by their paraphilic behaviors so it is that sexual pathology in the embodiment of somebody who basically does not care about other people; they have no conscience." Their actions are done to serve themselves and to satisfy their own desires. In these cases, the desires are sexual, but other criminal psychopaths are driven by desires for personal gain. We don't know enough about the brain to explain why a very small number of criminal psychopaths become serial killers with paraphilia and others follow other criminal pursuits.

O'Toole cannot say a particular serial killer is a psychopath unless he (or—rarely—she) has been evaluated. But when she applies her analysis to many of the cases she has worked, it allows her to say "in my opinion, this person manifests traits of psychopathy."

Conduct (Disorder) Unbecoming

Although LTK apparently avoided the Homicidal Triad and a career as a killer or serial killer, according to his clinical history, he nevertheless began to display plenty of other disturbing behaviors from a very young age. In kindergarten, he did not play cooperatively with other children. Perhaps it was his hyperactivity; he was often uncontrollable and unruly. He troubled his teachers and parents in school by skipping classes, by lying, and by stealing. He behaved the same way at home. Although there is no record of him acting violently toward any classmates, he reportedly "committed minor vandalism at home, in kindergarten, and in school," Hoff and his co-authors learned.

LTK's bad-boy lifestyle accelerated at the age of twelve. While many of his classmates were playing video games and thinking about girls, LTK was already having sex with older girls. Perhaps his smoking and drinking impressed them. About two years later, he ran away from home for the first time and managed to stay away for several days. Later, the local police started to get to know him when they picked him up for stealing, drunkenness, and disturbing the peace.

Around age sixteen, they arrested him for stealing a car. They added drunk driving to the charge. Shortly after his arrest, he apparently attempted suicide and was taken to a hospital. He escaped. Following his recapture, he entered a special social services program offered by the Norwegian Child Protection Service. Leaving the program at age eighteen, LTK got back together with a former girlfriend, whom he soon made pregnant.

According to the girlfriend, impending fatherhood did nothing to tame LTK's behavior. He cheated on her, lied to her, continued to drink, and failed to provide financial support. Violent thoughts may have been simmering in LTK because two years later, he attacked a young teenager. He raped her as he held a knife to her throat. He was caught after a second teenaged victim identified him after he raped her.

In prison, LTK again made a suicidal gesture and was again taken to a hospital. He escaped. Again. This happened several more times. Ultimately, he was released and lived freely as a vagrant while he waited for the results of his legal appeal. Details are unavailable, but the researchers did learn that while LTK was waiting for his appeal to be resolved, he returned to his old habit; he was caught in the act of trying to rape yet another victim.

Back in custody, he resumed his suicidal gestures and claimed he both saw and heard things that were not there. Despite these claims of hallucinations, a psychological exam failed to find an indication of psychosis. There is a good chance LTK was faking it, trying to manipulate the system to his benefit.

He spent some time in a prison and some in a medium-security forensic psychiatric ward. He continued to escape and be recaptured, and was eventually sent off to a psychiatric ward with greater security. Under the constraints of the maximum-security ward, where it was harder to get away with misbehavior or to escape, he appeared to settle down. His behavior in the ward gave no indication that he was intellectually impaired. His history indicates that "Here, he showed good behavioral control, no dramatic mood fluctuations, no self-harming, and no violent or threatening behavior toward others." In short, his "psychosis" had disappeared.

Such shifts in behavior are not uncommon in confined psychopaths who can appear to control their behavior if they have no opportunity to take advantage of others in a highly structured setting. It can provide an opportunity to scheme in a different way. In LTK's case, his good behavior—combined with the belief on the part of authorities that he did not pose a threat of violence in the short term—earned him some privileges and a bit more freedom. He exploited his more privileged status in the psychiatric unit by arranging to have contraband, including drugs, brought into the ward and by arranging to have sex with more than one woman from outside his ward.

He impressed Hoff and his colleagues as someone who "does not seem to experience normal depth of emotions." They added that "he lacks genuine guilt and remorse. Behaviorally he is an impulsive and irresponsible sensation seeker who lives on others and lacks realistic long-term goals." Like many psychopaths, his behavior suggested that he sought sensations instead of emotional connections to others, and used parasitic behavior to get what he wanted. He gave no indication he could feel love or sorrow or happiness, but, like Richard Kuklinski, he could experience the physical pleasure of sex and enjoy gaining power over others. One thing no one yet knows is why LTK was a serial rapist but not a serial killer. Perhaps he would have devolved into one given time, or perhaps he would have continued to rape. What would he have become if the knife he used in his attacks had slipped?

Volunteer

All we know is that if he had used his knife to slice instead of coerce, he would still be a psychopath. His personal and criminal history more than qualified LTK to be a subject for an fMRI demonstration of emotional disability in the brain of a criminal psychopath. Specifically, the study he volunteered for investigated how his brain responded when asked to process information involving the recognition of emotions. Lying on his back, his head rested in the fMRI machine as he looked at images of line drawings depicting variations of happy, sad, angry, or neutral faces. The test also included faces in which the line-drawn features were scrambled like bad Picasso imitations drawn by a not particularly talented child. The scrambled versions obliterated any resemblance to a face or facial expression. A response button rested on LTK's chest. Before the testing began, the researchers explained the rules of the testing procedure to him and he previewed the images so they would be familiar.

In the first phase of the experiment, he pressed the button like a game-show contestant when he saw a "target image," one particular facial expression or scrambled facial image he had been asked to spot in a sequence. In the second phase, he was asked to press the button only when he recognized a target image that had appeared twice in a row. In the third phase, he was asked to press the button only when the target image appeared after it had shown up two images prior in the sequence. He did this for six conditions: three with images of facial expressions and three with scrambled faces. Only a third of the sequences required him to press the button to perform the task correctly. He looked at 18 presentations in each block of testing. Between testing sessions, he rested in the fMRI machine.

LTK's brain scan results, like those of other psychopaths, were very different from those of the dozen non-psychopaths who served as controls for the study. For example, when LTK looked at the facial expressions,

24 different regions of his brain were activated compared to only eight in the brains of the six men and six women of comparable age who served as non-psychopathic control subjects. Perhaps even more interesting is the fact that he seemed to process the information in evolutionarily older parts of his brain than did the controls. The non-psychopaths showed signs of activation not only in fewer brain regions but in more recently evolved regions of the neocortex.

LTK's brain, by contrast, responded to the image-processing tasks by increasing blood flow to parts of the thalamus, insula, putamen, cingulate, and medial frontal gyrus on the left side of his brain, parts of the substantia nigra and caudate body on the right side, and the cerebellum.

The cerebellum—or "little brain" if you translate it from Latin—is located in the back of the skull and sits below the overhanging neocortex of the occipital lobe like a mollusk seeking shelter from the rain. For many decades it was associated with the control of fine movements, like those required for walking, learning dance moves, and fine motor tasks like rapidly and sequentially touching the tips of four fingers to the tip of the thumb on the same hand. Today it's not surprising to page through neuroscience journals and come across reports linking this part of the brain with cognitive function and disorders that affect it. For example, some genes associated with autism influence the development of the cerebellum and others appear to be overexpressed in this part of the brain.[16] Simon Baron-Cohen points out in his book *The Science of Evil: On Empathy and the Origins of Cruelty* that lack of empathy is a feature of autism, borderline personality disorder, narcissism, and psychopathy.

Why does LTK's brain respond to the task of processing images of faces by activating older brain regions? Hoff and his fellow researchers speculate that LTK and other psychopaths do not use higher cognitive functions when analyzing facial expression. LTK's brain, like that of other psychopaths who have taken part in similar experiments, seems to make use of more primitive mechanisms for processing information about facial expressions and emotions.

The authors of the LTK study remind us that LTK's brain-imaging results are presented as a case study. Case studies are instructive and frequently interesting in a medical sense but may not apply to large populations. An essential criterion of useful scientific research is reproducibility. If no other researchers working in independent labs can reproduce your results, then your results don't amount to much until the discrepancy is resolved. This observation is often not stressed in popular accounts of research studies. But this does not mean that case studies like LTK's are not important.

One valuable feature of LTK's story is the extensive background information provided about him in combination with his brain-scanning results. More importantly, the results are consistent with those of other studies that correlate emotional disability with unusual neural responses. Repeated studies indicate that the ability of psychopaths to recognize and respond to emotional stimuli is impaired. Psychopaths, as we have seen, are also generally unmoved by anxiety-provoking situations that cause most people to squirm. It is one of the most important and noticeable features of the criminal psychopath. LTK, so different from 99 percent of the human race in terms of having a conscience, is much like his fellow criminal psychopaths in terms of having trouble processing emotions.

Another clue is provided by the way many psychopaths process language. Instead of processing it predominantly on one side of the brain—the left side in the case of right-handed people—many of them process or control language on *both* sides of their brains.[17] This unusual lack of distribution of labor in the brain suggests that everything does not go according to schedule during brain development in these individuals, just as developmental problems are suspected in people who go on to develop schizophrenia.

Psychopaths also don't do well on tests that rely on familiarity with abstract feelings. This may explain why complex emotions like remorse, compassion, love, guilt, and empathy are foreign to them and why they have to fake these feelings, mimicking the corresponding outward behavioral signs of these emotions when interacting with people, while all the while not actually feeling any of the emotions themselves. They don't have problems relating to non-abstract feelings like hunger or sexual desire.

I Don't Feel Your Pain

Another salient feature of psychopathy is lack of empathy; it is central to any description of this type of personality. You probably are not completely comfortable when thinking about closing a door on your finger. Just considering the prospect may make you uneasy, because past experience has taught you that it hurts so much, it should never be repeated. Thanks to your sense of empathy, you feel the same way when you see someone else on the verge of having their finger crushed in a door. Empathy allows you to imagine the pain that person would feel when a finger is mangled.

You may wince when you think about seeing such an accident because a specific neural network involved in processing the feeling of empathy is activated in your brain. These pathways include parts of the brain's cerebral cortex, as well as parts of the brain located beneath the cortex. The cortical regions that have been implicated in the process of sharing the feelings of another person include the orbitofrontal cortex and the ventromedial prefrontal cortex (vmPFC). These are connected in a network with each other and with the subcortical regions of the amygdala, the hypothalamus, and the brain stem. Working together, these and perhaps other parts of the brain allow you, from childhood, to "feel" someone else's pain and share their emotional state.

Consider now the psychopathic version of empathy that Richard Kuklinski showed his daughter Merrick, who related the exchange to Richard's biographer, Philip Carlo. The exchange followed one of the killer's violent outbursts in the home he kept with his abused wife and three children: "There were times at home when Richard would have one of his outbursts and break things and then lock himself in his office. Merrick would ask him to please calm down, to 'please relax, Daddy.' During these episodes, Richard would then explain in a matter-of-fact way, 'You know if . . . if I kill Mommy, if something happens and she dies, I'll have to kill you all . . . I can't leave any witnesses. . . . But you, Merrick . . . you'll be the hardest to kill. You understand that?'"[18]

Perhaps this approach to parenting was Richard's way of expressing his warped concept of affection and reassurance. But even here, Richard puts what would be an unthinkable concept for most parents into terms describing how it affects him and him alone, not his potential victim. It would be hardest for him to kill her compared to other members of his family. With this mind-boggling exchange, he revealed the value system of a man who lacked empathy.

Richard's behavior is certainly more typical of a real criminal psychopath's behavior and outlook than that of the fictional psychopath Tony

Soprano. Soprano had a sincere affection for his children, whom he would never harm in the television show *The Sopranos*. For Richard Kuklinski and other real criminal psychopaths, family members are possessions. It would be inconvenient to have to destroy them, but, in their minds, there is no question they would do it to protect themselves. That is what distinguishes real criminal psychopaths from fictional psychopaths. Counting on sincere sentimentality from a criminal psychopath would be like expecting a hungry shark to pass up a meal. Such grotesque demonstrations of morally deficient reasoning convince many researchers that psychopathy is indeed a mental disorder that renders psychopaths not liable for their actions. Others say that since they know right from wrong, they are responsible for their actions, no matter how they think, no matter how different their brains are.

The results of the brain-imaging studies discussed so far strongly suggest that the biological material that generates and regulates emotions and feelings is closely associated with a set of structures in the brain collectively known as the limbic system. It is located "inside" the brain, deep under the wrinkly surface of the brain's outer cortex, and includes the thalamus, amygdala, hippocampus, hypothalamus, cingulate gyrus, and basal ganglia (Figures 10 and 11).

The limbic system is occasionally referred to as the "emotional brain" because so many of its diverse functions are related to emotionality and to the "fight-or-flight" response. The motivations for fighting or fleeing, after all, include anger or fear and frequently the desire to survive a threat.

Behaviors related to survival also can be linked to the motivation to have a good time. Neurobiologists call it "reward seeking." It translates into behaviors that increase the chances of an individual getting some food or having sex. Even the memory storage functions that have been linked to this part of the brain frequently involve a strong emotional component.

Three Brains in One

The psychiatrist who named the limbic system, Paul MacLean, was intrigued by human beings' ability to be rational, caring, and thoughtful as well as primitive, violent, and selfish. This led him to begin studying how the brain controls emotional behavior when he began his research career after the Second World War.

His work provided a helpful way to think about how our brains are organized. His Triune (three-in-one) Brain Theory, which he introduced in 1970, is based on the evolution of its different parts. MacLean referred to the oldest part of our brain as the reptilian brain. Its history goes back 500 million years, to when fish used it to survive. Reptiles thrived 250 million years later with a more sophisticated version. It still controls essential tasks that we mostly perform without conscious effort, such as breathing, balancing, maintaining body temperature, and keeping our hearts beating. It consists of the brain stem, which sits atop our spines, and the cerebellum, the large structure that looks like a mini-brain tucked under the back of the larger brain. If you have ever tried to relate to or bond with a turtle or lizard, you know that this part of the nervous system is not liable to impress or surprise you with warmth or spontaneity. It is rigid and predictable.

The development of the second component of the Triune Brain, the limbic brain, coincided with the evolution of mammals. That means it was at least 150 million years in the making. It includes many of the brain structures that show abnormal functioning in fMRI scans of criminal psychopaths.

The third component, the majority of the cerebral cortex called the neocortex, evolved with primates just 2.5 million or so years ago. Many people assume that the neocortex is more important than other brain regions in its contributions to what makes humans unique in the animal kingdom. It is credited with making language, culture, imagination, abstract thought, and consciousness possible. But this might not be the most accurate way to describe its relationship to the limbic system.

Psychiatrist Thomas Insel, the director of the National Institute of Mental Health, said MacLean's Triune theory was "outside the mainstream of scientific effort," according to the *New York Times*.[19] He did, however, give it credit for opening "the door for neuroscience to 'ask big questions about consciousness and philosophy, instead of the more tractable questions about vision and movement.'" Since its introduction, the Triune Theory has propped open the door for neuroscience, which is now exploring these big questions with brain-imaging technology.

Limbic system theory divided the brain into old and new subdivisions. The more primitive parts (in terms of cognition) consisted of the evolutionarily older regions of the brain. The more sophisticated parts (again, in terms of cognition) consisted of evolutionarily more recent developments, like the neocortex, the gray matter that is responsible for our higher intellectual abilities. Early on, the limbic system was thought to be the seat of emotion. It was thought that the separation was definite: the older limbic system took care of emotions, and the newer cortex took care of high-level thinking. But the limbic system is highly connected, if you follow enough connections, to the entire brain. So where do emotions originate? Does one part of the brain run the show?

> "I used to think that the brain was the most wonderful organ in my body. Then I realized who was telling me this."
>
> —Emo Philips

Its outer, wrinkly surface is the brain's public face. That is what most people picture when they think of the brain. It consists of gray matter, a synonym for the stuff that makes us smart, allows us to paint pictures, compose symphonies, write novels, and solve equations. It enables us to plan and organize and learn. It allows most of us to master our baser emotions, desires, and drives. Most of us.

Many people assume that the brain represents a culmination of primate evolution since it includes the recently evolved frontal lobes, the portion of the brain most closely associated with higher, executive functioning. It is a common assumption that the cerebral cortex is the dominant and most significant part of the central nervous system. It is seen as overseeing and controlling the evolutionarily more primitive brain structures lying beneath it, the structures whose counterparts we share with reptiles, the part of the brain devoted in large part to survival, fighting, eating, and sex.

This view is consistent with that of many people who consciously or subconsciously regard humans as the ultimate in evolution, as if evolution was leading to us. In fact, squirrels, deer, beetles, and millions of walking, flying, creeping, crawling creatures are the ultimate in evolution as long as they are well-adapted to their environments. They may not have produced novels, symphonies, scientific theories, or reality television shows, but their accomplishments are still impressive enough to have ensured their survival—the number one end goal of the evolutionary process.

In a similar sense, the human brain, which has evolved by adding new layers of complexity over old, may not have *culminated* in the neocortex, the most recently evolved component. There is another way to look at the brain's hierarchy, according to neuroanatomist Charles Ouimet, Ph.D., of the Florida State University College of Medicine. Perhaps the limbic system, the emotional brain, is not lower down in the brain's hierarchy. Instead, the neocortex might be seen as something that evolved to assist or improve the function of the "more primitive" limbic brain.

"I think the limbic system, including thalamic components, is primary," Ouimet said.[20] "The function of the forerunner of the neocortex in reptiles, for instance, is to provide finer sensory discrimination and finer motor control so the limbic system can make better informed choices and responses. With evolution, I think it is likely that that system did not change; the neocortex is still there to give finer discrimination and motor control so the limbic system can be better informed."

The job of the limbic system, after all, is to keep the animal alive and breeding. "The job of the neocortex," Ouimet suggests, "is to help the limbic system do just that." He doesn't think the limbic system was ever superseded by the neocortex. "It's just that the neocortex likes to think so: 'I think, therefore I am in charge.'"

This leads Ouimet to wonder about the issue of consciousness, which is often thought of as a cortical phenomenon. "But," he asks, "aren't feelings one aspect of consciousness? You never read about that." He considers the prefrontal cortex, with its close connections to the limbic system, an extension of the limbic system. He sees its function to be making "good" choices. "Good" means conducive to survival and breeding. It is a subjective term used to meet very concrete ends.

"One mistake we make," Ouimet observes, "is in thinking that the limbic system is one thing and the neocortex is another, whereas in fact one is a functionally differentiated outgrowth of the other. The limbic system did not get 'overrun' by the neocortex during evolution; it just got a better computer."

Based on wide-ranging evidence from neurology, neuroanatomy, paleontology, and neuropsychology, Antonio Damasio and his colleagues at the University of Iowa suggested back in 1982 that changes in the limbic system may have played a key role in our evolution.[21] They noted that our limbic system differs from that of other primates with less-developed mental capabilities. Our limbic system appears to influence "higher" brain functions associated with the cerebral cortex. Furthermore, they suggested that changes in the limbic system during the evolution of our human ancestors may have come before changes in the neocortex and were central to the development of our current behaviors, including social and sexual behaviors.

Joseph LeDoux, Ph.D., a Professor of Science at New York University, is an authority on the biological mechanisms of emotional memory as well as being the lead singer for the rock band "The Amygdaloids," for which he also writes songs. After studying the neurobiological underpinning of emotion for much of his forty-year-long career, he concludes that: "There is no emotion system. There are systems that are responsible for the various functions we label as 'emotional' but there is not an emotion system."[22] The inspiration for LeDoux's rock band is an important component of many of these systems. But it is also one of the most misrepresented in popular media.

The Limbic System Celebrity

The amygdala has become a celebrity among the limbic structures of the brain. If it were a person, it would have an entourage. The hypothalamus and the frontal cortex sometimes join it on the pop-neuroscience A-List, but other regions of the brain, like the cerebellum, never walk the red carpet of popular neuroscience with the amygdala, which makes frequent appearances in the popular media. A search for "amygdala" on the Huffington Post website, for example, delivered more than 5,100 hits in the fall of 2013, making it far more popular than the prefrontal cortex and the hypothalamus, which scored 722 and 221, respectively.

You may not yet have heard of the criminal Aaron "Amygdala" Helzinger. Batman has. Aaron once overpowered the comic book hero after Aaron's amygdalae were removed (his incompetent neurosurgeon was aiming for his hypothalamus) in an attempt to reduce his violent rages.[23] Incomprehensibly, this psychosurgery left Aaron with extraordinary strength.

A character on the other side of the law, a district attorney, accused a police officer of being a racist on "Attack of the Xenophobes,"[24] an episode of the television series *Boston Legal.* The officer faced prosecution after he shot and killed an unarmed black youth whose can of soda he mistook for a pistol. The evidence against the officer came straight from a hospital/neuroscience lab. He was shown pictures of people of different ethnic backgrounds while having an fMRI brain scan. The fictional scientist/expert witness testified that he "measured the response in the part of his brain that controls fear. It's called the amygdala." The defendant's response to pictures of African-Americans, according to the fictional witness and fictional prosecutor, proved the officer was guilty.

Asked if fMRI allowed him to tell what someone is thinking, the expert explained, accurately, that it did not. Instead, it allowed him to tell how someone is feeling "and specifically, we can identify responses associated with sociopathic tendencies. Here we determined the defendant was racist" because his amygdala lit up during the test. Furthermore, the expert swore he could measure it "with extreme accuracy."

Like Batman's opponent, "Amygdala" Helzinger, the case brought by the *Boston Legal* prosecutor is a good example of bad neuroscience. Many popular cultural and infotainment accounts of neuroscience are oversimplified. The fictional jury in the television show and their creators, the show's writers David Kelly and Craig Kurt, clearly knew this. Perhaps they were up on the scientific literature, because they seemed to know that there is no credible evidence showing that fMRI can be used in this way to "tell how someone is feeling." It shows blood flow patterns in the brain, which reflect brain-cell activity. Neuronal activity in an isolated part of the brain is not the same thing as a feeling or an emotion. It is an indication of activity in one component of an emotion system, as LeDoux points out. It is an indication that a specific part of the brain appears to be involved in the perception, recognition, analysis, or other cognitive function related to viewing an image.

It's true that this cluster of nerve cells in the temporal lobe is activated when someone is afraid. But few amygdala stories also mention that this brain region is also activated when you look at pleasant pictures that interest you. It is possible that the police officer on *Boston Legal* accused of racism was attracted to African-Americans. His amygdalae might have responded the same way if he looked at a happy face.

Find Your Amygdala

Joseph LeDoux provides easy directions for locating your amygdala.[25] Point a finger at your ear. Point another finger at your eye, on the same side of your head. If both fingers projected a beam of light that could pass through flesh, bone and brain, then the two beams would intersect at one of your amygdalae. You have another one in the same relative position on the other side of your brain.

If you could illuminate all of the cells in the amygdala with the beam of light, part of the structure might remind you of an almond, amygdala in Latin. That is what early anatomists thought it looked like. Neuroanatomists have since decided that there is more to the amygdala than first recognized. More subsections, a dozen or so subnuclei, are included in the structure so, on the whole, it has lost its almond shape but, thanks to its Latin name, it has retained its almond identity. "Its actual shape resembles more a strap carrying an old style dumbbell," according to neuroanatomist Jim Fallon, whose own brain we've already discussed as an interesting example of a brain that looks like it belongs to a psychopathic murderer but has never produced criminal behavior.

Like Batman and the *Boston Legal* district attorney, many people connect the amygdala exclusively with fear, and it definitely plays a key role in this important emotion. This small group of brain cells has a role in the processes that allow people to recognize fear and initiate aggression, among other emotional responses. But, like its size and shape, its role in other functions has expanded as neurobiologists have learned more about it. It appears to help integrate emotional processing, behavior, and motivation. All of the senses communicate with the amygdala. This is something to at least keep in the back of your mind when you consider that the amygdala has been reported to be less active and smaller in the brains of criminal psychopaths.

If the amygdalae are damaged in a person, that person may have trouble recognizing fear in facial expressions,[26] a trait seen in psychopaths.

Multiple studies indicate that high psychopathy scores are associated with an impaired ability to recognize emotional expressions in faces and to link clues to fearful situations. Psychopaths just don't process fear the way most people do. Harvard Medical School associate professor of psychiatry Jordan Smoller points out in his book, *The Other Side of Normal*,[27] that a few unfortunate individuals born without psychopathic traits show the same response after their amygdalae are damaged.

Yaling Yang, Adrian Raine, and their collaborators tapped five temporary employment agencies to find subjects for their study which measured the volume of the amygdalae in 27 people with PCL–R psychopathy scores ranging between 23 and 40. They compared them to 32 controls with psychopathy scores ranging from 5 to 14.[28] Their finding that the amygdalae of higher-scoring psychopaths are around 18 percent smaller in volume than they are in low-scoring or non-psychopaths, suggests that the amygdala has a role in the brain processes that work differently or are defective in psychopaths.

The amygdala, as discussed in Chapter 6, is connected to another brain region that has been linked to an impaired ability to identify emotional states and lack of empathy, the ventromedial prefrontal cortex (vmPFC) in the frontal lobe. James Blair, Ph.D., of the U. S. National Institute of Mental Health proposed that a deficit or deficits in the function and interaction of the vmPFC and the amygdala provides an explanation for the development of psychopathy.[29] His suggestion is based on brain scanning and psychological testing results of psychopathic individuals that researchers have been gathering for at least two decades. It is supported by observations that the vmPFC plays a highly influential role in decision-making processes. It is also supported by the knowledge that the amygdala's role goes beyond processing fear and driving aggression. In addition to processing emotional expressions, the amygdala plays an important role in forming associations between a stimulus and a reward, and between a stimulus and a punishment.

Rounding Up the Usual Suspects

But brain-imaging studies have suggested that associations appear to exist between multiple brain regions and psychopathy. In addition to the amygdala and the vmPFC, other regions of the frontal lobes as well as the hippocampus, thalamus, basal ganglia, cingulate cortex, insula, and parts of the temporal lobe all appear to function differently in psychopaths. This has led Kent Kiehl to propose a paralimbic dysfunction model to explain the development of psychopathy.[30] It proposes that decreased activity in, and underdevelopment of, a group of closely interconnected brain structures that form a ring around the inside, center of the brain (see Figure 10) can account for the characteristic features of psychopathy. He calls it the paralimbic model because it includes structures that formally belong to the limbic system and some that are closely associated with it.

The paralimbic model is similar to the model Jim Fallon proposed based on his unpublished research. He believes the deficits seen in psychopaths: imperfect communication between the amygdala, orbital/ventromedial prefrontal cortex, and mostly anterior cingulate cortex are intimately involved in psychopathic behavior. Fallon's work, he said, "was based on case studies. Some [of the subjects] were impulsive murderers. Some were psychopaths. It was kind of a mixed bag. I was just putting together what I thought might be true. Kent really did the scientific study. I took a guess that turned out to be pretty good."[31] If it was a guess, it certainly was not a wild guess. His model is consistent with others that imply psychopathy is a developmental disorder.

It is possible, of course, that there is more than one way to develop a psychopath. Problems during development may result in different flaws or physical deficits in different individuals but still produce behaviors we call psychopathic. While it is still not possible to establish a cause-and-effect relationship between brain abnormalities and psychopathic behavior,[32] the correlations that have been established so far—combined with what we know about the psychological effects of brain injuries in patients—strongly suggest that the answers do indeed hide in the dark regions of the brain that appear on fMRI scans.

Chapter Eight

Successful, Unsuccessful, and Other Types of Psychopaths

The new job and the new life start today. It's the beginning of a career that will present new experiences and new challenges. And it will involve face-to-face encounters with people like you have never faced before. Last month you left San Francisco and drove 225 miles south to Atascadero, California, where you signed a lease for your new apartment. The next day, you unpacked. The day after that, you drove over to the Atascadero State Hospital to have a look. This is where you'll work in exchange for a $40,700 annual stipend and necessary experience in preparation for your budding career in forensic psychology.

Although it was established sixty years ago, this maximum-security forensic hospital looks nothing like the snake pits people associated with psychiatric hospitals in the first half of the 20th century. In daylight, the pinkish façade seems to lighten the image of the 1,275-bed hospital, which has around sixty doctoral psychologists on staff. At night, however, when the exterior spotlights cut through the darkness and illuminate the security perimeter fencing, it is unmistakably a maximum-security facility. Inside the main building you find, as NPR reporter Ina Jaffe did, that "the hospital appears more blandly institutional than dangerous," and "the halls seem endlessly long."[1]

You are one of four interns selected from 48 applicants. Today, having completed a three-week orientation, you will begin your rotations. You'll start in the admissions unit, where you'll pick up experience in the psychological assessment of mentally ill criminals. After 3½ months, you'll begin spending time in the treatment units. Before you are done, you will have completed sixteen psychological evaluations of your patients, including forensic evaluations, psychological testing batteries, behavioral analysis, and the PCL–R, the Hare psychopathy checklist, evaluation.

All of your patients are male, all are dressed in khaki pants and khaki shirts, and none of them is here voluntarily. Some are clearly mentally ill. Some are here because they have been found not guilty by reason of insanity or being incompetent to stand trial. And others are classified as mentally disordered offenders. They are being confined after their scheduled parole date because they are believed to still pose a threat. And many do pose a threat. In March of 2013, a dozen employees of the hospital were injured by aggressive patients, according to a local newspaper account.[2]

All varieties of mental illness are present in the inmate population. Those with high psychopathy scores are always noted. In 2011, hospital director Jon De Morales told Ina Jaffe that the inmate population of his institution seemed to consist of two groups. "There are criminals who happen to exhibit symptoms of a mental disorder," he said, and then "there are mentally ill people who happen to have committed crimes. They all end up in the same place."[3]

Those with high psychopathy scores tend to cluster in the first group. And the longer you observe and interact with them, the more you notice distinct differences that suggest they are not all the same. This is despite the fact that popular references to criminal psychopaths often suggest that the only difference between them is their address: in or out of prison.

So how can you explain the big differences in behaviors among psychopaths you observe in the hospital? It seems to you that at Atascadero, the patient/inmates with PCL–R scores in the psychopathy range fall into one of four distinct subtypes. When describing your new job to your friends and family, and to preserve confidentiality, you create four composite hypothetical patients whose behaviors capture what you see on the job five days a week. Call them Lawrence, Barry, Zach, and Andy.

Lawrence impresses you as insufferably stuck-up. His attitude, body language, and behavior announce that he considers himself to be privileged by the nature of his existence. He has no problem insulting anyone on the staff or any of his fellow inmates, as long as they pose no physical threat to him. You have even seen him insulting another patient with a high psychopathy score, Barry.

Barry tends to whine and alternate easily between agitation and depression. He frequently complains to the staff about slights and petty injustices he feels he has suffered. Barry, as well as many non-psychopathic inmates, has been the target of another inmate who, like the others, easily meets the cutoff score for a diagnosis of psychopathy: Zach.

Zach will lean against a wall, savoring the conflicts or discomfort he observes in a common room. His amusement at the agitation and the trouble he sometimes instigates is clear. It reveals the pleasure he gets from observing and causing the discomfort of others. His file includes testimony that Zach once pulled a sleeping handicapped man from his wheelchair and set him gently on the floor in an empty classroom. He offered to help the man back into his wheelchair if he would pull himself halfway across the room to reach the spot where Zach had moved the empty chair. When the man reached his chair, Zach chuckled and walked away. He watched from the hallway as a teacher eventually arrived to help after hearing the man call for assistance.

Yet even Zach is leery and tries to steer clear of Andy. Charged with assault, robbery, rape, and attempted murder, Andy showed intermittent signs of mental illness in the past including hallucinations, but claims to be "in remission" now. The last time he claimed he heard voices, he blamed them for urging him to severely beat up a weaker fellow inmate. Andy claimed his victim owed him his dessert after losing a bet which his victim denied making. Andy's gaze reminds you of an animal watching prey. Far too often, it is.

Lawrence, Barry, Zach, and Andy, as different as they appear to be, all share key features of psychopathy, including childhood behavior problems, lack of guilt or remorse, failure to accept blame or responsibility, shallow affect, lying, and irresponsibility. That is how they all scored high on the PCL–R test. They all "are criminals who happen to exhibit symptoms of a mental disorder."

Psychopathic Subtypes

Psychologists Carolyn Murphy, Ph.D., and James Vess, Ph.D., noticed significant differences in behavior among the psychopaths confined to Atascadero State Hospital back in 2003.[4] Even though they shared core traits of psychopathy, patient/inmates with strong psychopathic traits included some individuals who were more sneaky than confrontational and others who were more aggressive and hostile. The psychologists divided them into four subgroups:

1. The Narcissistic Psychopath, with superior airs, self-absorption, a sense of entitlement, and who is likely to put down or belittle others.
2. The Borderline Psychopath, who is impulsive, needy, and liable to change moods frequently and easily.
3. The Sadistic Psychopath, who seems to take cruel pleasure in observing or making people suffer.
4. The Antisocial Psychopath or remorseless criminal, who is not attuned to the suffering of others and acts aggressively toward others.

Of course, any group, psychopathic or non-psychopathic, will contain individuals with different personality traits, but the forensic psychologists thought that subdividing the inmates with psychopathy confined inside a forensic hospital might have benefits for the staff who have to deal with them. Perhaps the knowledge could provide clues about what to expect from them and aid in communicating with them. Staff will know what to watch out for as they work with the different types of psychopaths, and better protect both themselves and other inmates. It is also conceivable—if a longed-for and long-sought treatment for psychopathy is ever developed—that identifying the behavioral subtype of a psychopathic inmate might improve his or her chances of responding effectively to a therapeutic approach that might take this information into account.

The presence of mental disorders in addition to the personality disorder of psychopathy would be expected to affect their behavior. It is also possible that they reflect variations in personalities of men who score high on the psychopathy checklist. Anxiety, for example, could be one factor that distinguishes these individuals. It's also possible that they represent examples of a more widely recognized system for classifying psychopaths first suggested over seventy years ago.[5]

I Come First, You Come Second

In 1941, psychiatrist Ben Karpman suggested that psychopathy consisted of two distinct groups, each with its own cause. The first group consists of idiopathic or primary psychopaths who have no identifiable conditions that can explain their "psychopathic indulgence." They might have psychopathic traits because they were born with them. Eric Harris and LTK may belong in this group. Despite supportive upbringing, good socioeconomic status, and average or above-average intelligence, rare individuals may develop psychopathic traits that leave the rest of us perplexed and astounded. Andy from the hypothetical study above would fit into this group.

The other group consists of symptomatic or secondary psychopaths. In Karpman's scheme, these individuals behave like psychopaths because they have other conditions, something that psychologists can identify such as anxiety disorder, bipolar disorder, borderline personality disorder, or brain damage. Someone like Barry would be a good candidate for this group.

"For decades, there's been some concern about there being different types of psychopaths," Robert Hare recalled.[6] "The common way of looking at it is to call one group primary psychopaths that have all the psychopathic features, and the other group secondary psychopaths who have the features but also who experience or exhibit signs of some sort of neurosis, anxiety, or underlying conflicts."

According to Hare, the secondary psychopath is not really a psychopath in Karpman's conceptualization. "These are people who exhibit some of the behaviors [of psychopathy], but for some underlying reason—maybe they are psychotic, have another psychiatric problem, brain damage, all sorts of thing—but they're clearly not psychopathic. They put on a façade somehow." Such a façade gives them "the mask of sanity" seen in primary psychopaths, but it hides different underlying pathologies.

In fact, Karpman was so concerned about the façade element that he tried to introduce a new term for primary psychopaths to distinguish them from secondary psychopaths: he called them anethopaths. The term never caught on. "But among the so-called anethopaths or primary psychopaths," Hare remembered, "Karpman identified one variation that he referred to as 'the passive parasitic.'" These individuals are very manipulative; they con and suck you in. The other variation is antisocial and aggressive. In Hare's words: "They don't talk, they do." In the hypothetical group discussed above, this describes Zach.

In 1941, the same year Karpman announced the need to separate psychopaths into two subtypes, a 27-year-old doctor from Italy named Silvano Arieti began his residency at Pilgrim State Hospital in West Brentwood, Long Island.[7] He had come to the U.S. in 1938 to escape from Benito Mussolini's fascist regime. Arieti would go on to earn a national reputation based on his writings about schizophrenia and about creativity. He also talked about psychopaths in much the same vein as Karpman.[8]

"He started talking about psychopaths and then pseudo-psychopaths," Hare said. "And pseudo means just what it means: pseudo." Pseudo-psychopaths seem psychopathic in terms of their aggressive, antisocial behavior, but they differ from psychopaths in other ways: they don't con, manipulate, or lack feelings or emotions, as true psychopaths do.

Furthermore, Arieti divided true psychopaths, those Karpman wanted to rename anethopaths, into two main variations: the simple and the complex. "The simple psychopath had all of the characteristics of psychopathy and was highly aggressive. His motto was: 'How do I do this?'" Hare said. "The motto for the complex psychopath was: 'How do I do this *and* get away with it?'" Unsuccessful or criminal psychopaths would seem to fall into the simple category. Successful psychopaths—the businessmen, politicians, and con artists who get away with conning—would fall into the complex category.

"So, the division had been set perfectly [over seventy years ago]. People forgot all of this. Now in the literature, people are talking about primary and secondary psychopathy as if they are both forms of psychopathy, and it's driving me crazy," Hare said.

It is easy to understand why Hare is distraught at the confusion and lack of consensus regarding subtypes of psychopaths that characterize the field today. There is order in Karpman's distinctions between Primary (true) psychopaths and Secondary (pseudo) psychopaths and more order in the breakdown of Primary psychopaths into Complex (successful) and Simple (unsuccessful) psychopaths.

More than half a century later, Jennifer Skeem and her colleagues looked for subtypes of psychopaths among 123 criminals with PCL–R scores of 29 or higher. They assumed that psychopathy is hereditary in primary psychopaths and due to environmental influences in secondary psychopaths.[9] The assumption was that they are all true psychopaths. Those called secondary psychopaths—those with identifiable past experiences that seemed to be risk factors—turned out to be more anxious than primary psychopaths. Although these criminals had fewer psychopathic traits, their antisocial behavior was on the same level as that of primary psychopaths. Furthermore, the secondary psychopaths were more likely to have symptoms of major mental disorders, to have features of borderline personality disorder, and to have more trouble successfully interacting with other people. Although the authors assumed that primary and secondary psychopaths were indeed subtypes of one population of psychopaths, their results support the view of Karpman, Arieti, and Hare that secondary psychopaths may actually be pseudo-psychopaths.

Other researchers claim primary psychopaths are those with strong traits of callousness, arrogance, and manipulative behavior, while secondary psychopaths are more likely to be antisocial and impulsive. In this take on psychopathic subtypes, corporate psychopaths would belong in the primary category and criminals in the secondary category.

Thus, it depends on who you talk to and which research papers you read to make sense of psychopathic subtypes, as long as you are willing to dismiss competing classifications. Other assumptions may influence which classification system you prefer. Some people claim psychopathy exists on a spectrum or is dimensional. In other words, it is a variable trait like height or skin tone; some people can have a little psychopathy and some can have a lot. Others think psychopathy is an all-or-none trait, like being a shark; you are either a cold-blooded predator or you are not. You cannot be 50 percent shark and 50 percent Labrador retriever.

Different research results point to different profiles of psychopathy. No one knows enough yet to determine if one of these models is correct or not, because the nature of psychopathy has not been agreed upon. Should the term psychopath be reserved for those with the extreme psychopathic behaviors? Or does it apply to anyone with more than an average psychopathic profile? Perhaps small research groups working independently and arguing with one another will not be able to resolve these issues. A large cooperative project, as proposed at the end of this book, might speed understanding along.

One and the Same but Different? Successful and Unsuccessful Psychopaths

A few neurobiological studies of non-criminal psychopaths have been published in recent years. The result has been more references to another way of subdividing and classifying psychopaths: successful versus unsuccessful.

It's not clear how many successful psychopaths end up successful in life in the traditional sense. Full-blown psychopathy is characterized by antisocial traits that often create disadvantages for an individual. Just because a person doesn't have a criminal record doesn't mean they haven't screwed up their lives and the lives of those around them. Is that success? Also, it's important not to confuse full-blown psychopathy, which is often self-destructive, with the presence of some psychopathic traits, like James Fallon has, which, as Oxford University research psychologist Kevin Dutton points out, can contribute to success in many careers as diverse as surgery and military Special Forces.[10]

Despite the confusion and debate surrounding psychopathic and anethopathic, primary and secondary, pseudo and not-pseudo, simple and complex, if you have strong psychopathic traits and end up in prison, you are, in nearly everyone's opinion, unsuccessful. You got caught. You can't take more than four or five relaxed, straight-line steps in your six-by-eight-foot cell. And when you are allowed to leave your cell, you are confined to a cell block in the company of many similarly confined people of the same sex with resentful attitudes, all kept there by thick, strong walls, bars, and guards.

Outside those walls, other people with strong psychopathic traits have managed to avoid 48-square-foot cells to live instead in 3,000-square-foot or larger Manhattan condos or apartments. They are guarded by doormen instead of guards. And they hold all the keys.

A very small number of high-ranking businessmen (there appear to be fewer women in the ranks of psychopaths and the upper echelons of business), chief executive officers, corporate board members, lawyers, politicians, physicians, and even scientists belong to the upper class of the psychopath community. Fearlessness, coolness under pressure, glibness, superficial charm, concentrated focus, the ability and inclination to con and manipulate others, and a willingness to backstab competitors without appearing too obvious while doing so, can all be very useful attributes in competitive occupations. Corporate psychopaths (who Karpman and Arieti would have us classify as Primary, Complex psychopaths and who are now known as "corporate" and "successful" psychopaths) manage to balance several classic features of the psychopathic personality while at the same time avoiding situations that require them to exchange their large homes for six-by-eight-foot cells. Usually, anyway.

We know more about the brains of criminal psychopaths than we do about the "snakes in suits," as Paul Babiak and Robert Hare refer to corporate psychopaths in their book about predators in the business community.[11] They are certainly not easy to study, as Cynthia Mathieu, a Professor of Business at Université du Quebec a Trois-Rivierès has found. Her Ph.D. in psychology and postdoctoral training in forensic psychology do not open boardroom doors the way requests for fMRI volunteers open prison cell doors.

"When you are a young or new professor in a business department and you're a woman, that is strike one. When that woman is a psychologist: strike two. And when that woman psychologist tells businessmen or business academics—because they can own their own businesses as well as be academics—that she is studying psychopathy: strike three."[12]

Mathieu is interested in linking psychopathic traits to leadership behavior and to the perception of leadership. The business world community, however, does not take the study of psychopaths in their midst seriously. "Not in my department, not anywhere we go," Mathieu reported. "It's very hard to present on corporate psychopathy. We've been rejected at all of the business conferences that we have applied to. I was at a conference that was mostly industrial, organizational psychologists that we applied to two weeks ago and we had to defend the existence of psychopathy. They think it's just a correlate of narcissism and they are comfortable with narcissism, while they are very uncomfortable with psychopathy."

As a psychologist, Mathieu knows there are dark personalities: "There are a lot of behaviors of great leaders that are very similar to ones that psychopaths would present."

Her business students like it when she talks about dark personalities. They tell her they like having narcissistic features; they are proud of it. "It's another world," she said.

That other world includes a fair number of people who are either successful psychopaths or who at least have a significant number of psychopathic traits. Industrial and organizational psychologist Paul Babiak, Ph.D., and his co-authors examined 203 corporate professionals who had been picked by their employers to take part in seven management-development programs. During these programs, the researchers used psychopathy evaluation tools, the PCL–R or its screening version, to get to know them better. They found that 3.9 percent of this group possessed psychopathic traits higher than those found in the rest of society.[13]

After numerous reporters misquoted their results and trumpeted the false "news" that ten percent of Wall Street Employees were psychopaths,[14] Hare, a co-author of the study, explained that wherever they got that figure, it wasn't from his scientist colleagues. He added that "The sample was not randomly selected or necessarily representative of managers or executives, or of the corporations in which they work. The approximately 4% who had a PCL–R score high enough for a research description as psychopathic cannot be generalized to the larger population of managers and executives, or to CEOs and the 'financial services industry.'"[15] Some psychologists who have worked with the business community, nevertheless, would be surprised if the actual percentage is not higher than 3.9 percent.[16]

The nature or structure of the psychopathic traits seen in this 3.9 percent appeared to be the same as that in many psychopaths you would find in your nearest prison or in your community. The presence of psychopathic traits seemed to help the business managers in terms of their in-house ratings of charisma and presentation style. They were seen as creative, strategic thinkers with good communication skills. The downside for them was the negative association of their psychopathic traits with their in-house ratings of responsibility and performance. They were not great team players, and they lacked management skills and overall accomplishments. Not surprisingly, considering all we have learned about psychopathy, "They look good, but they're not seen as being very effective so they can't necessarily do the job," Mathieu said.

Other successful individuals with many psychopath traits might choose work that offers more modest material rewards than business or finance: law enforcement, the military, or sales, for example. Whatever their economic status, when they can get away with it, these people may lie, deceive, manipulate, intimidate, and flatter to promote themselves and get what they want. As Andrea L. Glenn and her co-authors wrote, "Although the use of these tactics may have potentially serious negative social consequences, some individuals may be better able to escape detection than others."[17]

Based on their experience, Paul Babiak and Robert Hare estimate that one in ten people in the general population can be considered "soul mates" to psychopaths.[18] These are people who do not meet the criteria of psychopathy using the cutoff of the psychopathy checklist, but they nevertheless have enough psychopathic traits that they also have negative effects on those around them.

If someone with psychopathic personality traits is not undone by impulsivity, they will have a better chance of hanging out with the rest of us and their successful psychopathic soul mates than with their unsuccessful ones. In this case, they might have the inclinations of criminal psychopaths, but are smart enough or lucky enough not to get caught.

Cold-blooded versus Hot-blooded Brains

A common interpretation of "success" in the community of psychopaths is that it describes someone who does not engage in antisocial activities, or at least none serious enough to earn prison time. The people they encounter, however—co-workers, associates, friends and family—often pay a price by being used and abused. It is a difference between the cold-blooded nature of psychopathic action versus hot-blooded impulses from emotional passion. The distinction between antisocial personality disorder (ASPD) and psychopathy is highlighted in an interesting study conducted by Sarah Gregory of King's College London and her collaborators.[19] They compared the brains of 17 violent criminals with antisocial personality disorder *plus* psychopathy (the people with whom you *really* don't want to share a prison cell), to 27 violent criminals with antisocial personality disorder *without* psychopathy (well, if you have to share. . .), and to 22 non-criminals (your best bet for a roomie). The researchers made an effort to control their study by matching their subjects for age, IQ, and lifelong substance abuse histories. They also excluded anyone with a history of psychosis, bipolar disorder, or major depression.

The senior author of the study, Nigel Blackwood, described the differences between the subjects in the study in a King's College London press release: "There is a clear behavioral difference amongst those diagnosed with ASPD depending on whether or not they also have psychopathy. We describe those without psychopathy as 'hot-headed' and those with psychopathy as 'cold-hearted'."

The "cold-hearted" subjects had reduced gray matter in the part of the prefrontal cortex that is located as far to the front of the brain as you can get, right behind the forehead. They found the same thing in brain tissue situated around the edges of their temporal lobes. (See Figure 9.) Interestingly, the brains of criminals with antisocial personality disorder *without* psychopathy, the "hot-headed" group, like the brains of non-criminals, did not show this abnormality.

If reduced gray matter in these regions, resulting from fewer or smaller neurons, turns out to be a feature typical of psychopaths, it would be consistent with their behavior and with the apparent contributions of these structures in making humans capable of feeling empathy, acting morally, feeling remorse, and the type of behavior that generally makes us welcome around others.

Anatomical Disadvantages

Are successful psychopaths simply smarter than criminal psychopaths? Do they have better impulse control than less successful, cruder antisocial characters? Has their environment, upbringing, or education given them an advantage? Are their brains different? The limited amount of research that has been done suggests the answers may be Yes to these questions.

Yu Gao and Raine of the University of Pennsylvania suggested in 2010 that successful psychopaths are successful because they enjoy "intact or enhanced neurobiological functioning."[20] This advantage may explain their average or even above-average intellectual abilities. With better cognitive functioning, they find it easier to get their way without regard to the feelings of others and without getting caught or having to resort to violence. Even though they don't experience emotions exactly like most people, they are nevertheless motivated to satisfy themselves and get what they want, whether it is power, money, or sex. They often have well-developed abilities to fake feelings and manipulate others to help them achieve their goals.

If Gao and Raine are correct, unsuccessful psychopaths may end up as criminals because they were unlucky enough to be born with, or to develop, brains and nervous systems that prevent them from thinking things through and experiencing emotions like most people. These deficits could be the reason they resort to criminal, and in some cases violent, behavior. It is possible that impulsivity and a desire for thrills to offset muted emotions help undo unsuccessful psychopaths.

A few studies suggest[21] that there are indeed neuroanatomical differences between psychopaths who have had no, or only minor, run-ins with the law, compared to the psychopaths you are liable to meet in prison. For example, reduced gray matter has been reported in the prefrontal cortex of criminal psychopaths, but not in successful psychopaths. The higher-order executive functions of the frontal lobes of unsuccessful psychopaths seem to be impaired, compared to frontal-lobe function in successful psychopaths. In fact, preliminary research suggests that successful psychopaths may have better frontal-lobe function than both unsuccessful psychopaths and even many non-psychopaths.

Another difference between the two groups indicates a possible difference in the way their peripheral nervous systems work. Unsuccessful psychopaths have been shown to have reduced activity in the part of the nervous system that controls involuntary functions such as heart rate and sweating in response to events and stimuli with emotional meaning. Both of these functions, heart rate and skin conductance, are reduced in unsuccessful, but not in successful, psychopaths. As with their frontal-lobe function, successful psychopaths may enjoy an advantage over others, criminal psychopaths and non-psychopaths, in their involuntary (or what scientists call autonomic) nervous systems too.

Remember the Hippocampus

Back in 2004, Adrian Raine and his group reported that a structure in the limbic system, the hippocampus (Figure 11), differed in unsuccessful psychopaths compared to successful psychopaths.[22] Previous studies had suggested that the hippocampus did not look or work the same in institutionalized violent individuals, including psychopaths, compared to non-offenders. Raine's preliminary study was the first to make a side-by-side comparison of successful and unsuccessful psychopaths.

The researchers managed to locate 12 suitable, successful psychopaths working at temporary employment agencies who they defined as having PCL–R scores between 23 and 31. Their average was close to 28. These successful psychopaths had never been charged with crimes, although they reported breaking the law after being assured their interviews were protected by a legally binding confidentiality agreement between the researchers and subjects. This group was compared to 16 unsuccessful psychopaths who had been convicted of crimes. Their PCL–R scores averaged 31.5 and ranged from 23 to 40. The control group included 23 people with an average score of 11, ranging from 2 to 14.

The hippocampus was larger on the right side compared to the left in 94 percent of the unsuccessful psychopaths. Less than 50 percent of the successful psychopaths and non-psychopathic controls had this asymmetry.

The hippocampus is often described as the place in the brain where long-term memories are made. This association was tragically illustrated by a patient known as "HM" to several generations of neurologists and neuroscientists.

In 1953, Connecticut resident Henry Gustav Molaison involuntarily provided a famous example of just how specialized some brain tissue can appear to be.[23] Molaison was incapacitated by epileptic seizures, which had started when he was ten years old. By the time he was sixteen, the severity and frequency of his seizures made it impossible for him to live even a semblance of a normal life.

Eighteen years later, in a last-ditch effort to provide some relief from his incapacitating symptoms, surgeon William Scoville cut out small sections of Molaison's brain located beneath his temples to a depth of a little over 3 inches. Removing the medial temporal lobes including the hippocampi on both sides of Molaison's brain partially relieved his epileptic symptoms, but at a terrible price.

He was still Henry Molaison—his personality had not changed—but the surgery cost him the ability to form new memories. He could no longer remember people he had just met if they left the room and came back in. He could not remember places or anything that happened for any significant length of time after his operation. He had lost his ability to form long-term memories, although he could remember what had happened before his surgery.

Known by his initials HM, Molaison attained a type of celebrity in neuroscience circles. His name appeared in more than 11,000 journal articles. He helped convince neuroscientists that the process involved in forming long-term memories is not distributed throughout most of the brain. If it were, damaging a small part of the brain would be expected to only partially interfere with the process. Molaison's unfortunate experience identified a specific region of the brain that played a crucial role in the formation of long-term memories.

But the hippocampus, like all parts of the limbic system, is interconnected with the other key brain structures. It plays a role in more than long-term memory formation. For example, it is a key player in the processes that regulate aggression. And it plays a role in helping people learn when they should be afraid in particular situations. If the hippocampus or its connections are abnormal, it makes sense to wonder if such a deficit might not lead to impulsive behavior with antisocial consequences in unsuccessful psychopaths. Destroy the hippocampus completely and you end up with total short-term memory loss. But if you only impair its ability to participate in neural circuits underlying behavior, then you get more subtle deficits.

One explanation for the persistence of asymmetries in the brain such as these is that they are the result of developmental abnormalities. The findings do not prove this is the reason nearly all of the unsuccessful psychopaths showed signs of uneven hippocampi, but it is consistent with the suggestion that something went wrong somewhere during the development of their brains, as Raine and his colleagues contend. And this implies that this neuroanatomical abnormality might influence their behavior and personalities, specifically their criminal psychopathic behavior.

Based on the available neurobiological evidence, Yu Gao and Adrian Raine suggest that successful psychopaths have brains that function as well as or better than most people.[24] This explains how they are able to avoid prison and violence and still get what they want. Unsuccessful psychopaths appear to be hindered by abnormal brain structure and function. Their autonomic nervous systems, the neural wiring that influences their bodies' response to stress, are also abnormal. These differences could account for the deficits in thinking and emotional responsiveness that lead to more overt and ultimately self-harming, violent, and other antisocial acts. These hypotheses are consistent with what we have learned about the psychopathic brain, but all we know for certain is that success in the realm of psychopathy is defined by lack of a criminal record. And despite the charm and charisma and take-charge attitude of many successful psychopaths, they share a key feature with their criminal cousins: they are never concerned about your best interests.

Chapter Nine

Could You Become a Psychopath?

Chances are that nearly everyone with a healthy conscience and a sense of empathy will keep them. There is no need to worry about becoming a successful or unsuccessful psychopath, the prototypical type of personality associated with high scores on psychopathy inventories or evaluation tools. There is, however, a "but." Anyone can become a "pseudopsychopath." It is not the same thing as a developmental psychopath, but this neurological condition—a result of injury or disease—is just as troubling and often more tragic.

Injury to some of the same parts of the brain that are implicated in developmental psychopathy can change the way anyone views moral choices. To see how a specific brain injury can affect a person's moral judgments, test yourself with a few of the same personal moral scenarios Michael Koenigs, Ph.D., now at University of Wisconsin Department of Psychiatry, and his fellow researchers presented to some patients they worked with.[1]

What Would You Do?

Scenario 1. Imagine you are a waiter who overhears a customer you know very well declare that he is going to infect as many people with HIV as he can before he goes to prison in two days. You know he is serious and he intends to act on his threat with the many people he knows. But . . . he is highly allergic to poppy seeds. Just one will make him convulse and send him to the hospital for two days at least, and from there he would go right on to prison. Would you slip him some poppy seeds to stop him from infecting innocent people?

Scenario 2. While driving your expensive car in the country, you come across a man lying by the side of the road. His leg is severely injured and bloody, the result of a hiking accident, he explains. He asks you to help him by driving him to the local hospital. Since it is clear he might lose his leg if he doesn't receive timely medical treatment, your first impulse is to help. You realize, however, that the blood which is sure to get on your leather seats will ruin them. Would you drive off without helping the man to prevent ruining your automobile's upholstery?

Scenario 3. Using a video-and-audio satellite connection, you are negotiating with a dangerous terrorist. You know he is capable of setting off an explosion that could kill thousands of innocent people. But . . . you have his teen-aged son in your custody. You can stop the terrorist act by breaking one of his son's arms and then threatening to break the other if the terrorist does not surrender. Do you save thousands of potential victims by breaking the teenager's arm?

Scenario 4. Your cruise-ship vacation is interrupted by a fire. You and the other passengers abandon ship. The lifeboat you manage to board, like all the others, is overcrowded and close to sinking from too much weight. Rough seas begin filling the already-low-in-the-water boat with water. Inaction will result in the lifeboat sinking long before rescue is expected. If that happens, everyone will drown. But . . . one of the passengers is seriously injured and can't survive in any case, even after the rescue boats finally arrive. Throwing the mortally wounded person over the side will lighten the boat enough to prevent it sinking and save the lives of the other passengers. Would you throw the injured person out of the boat to save the others?

Three of these scenarios are classified as "high-conflict." One, Scenario 2 (about an injured leg and a potentially ruined car seat), is classified as "low-conflict." Koenigs and his colleagues presented scenarios like these to six patients whose prefrontal lobes had been damaged by tumors or aneurysms. Specifically, the patients had lesions in their ventromedial prefrontal cortices (vmPFC) (Figure 10). These lesions changed the way the patients dealt with some of the moral challenges or dilemmas Koenigs and fellow scientists presented to them.

It is important to note that the six patients had normal intellects and baseline moods. The way they made moral decisions was not influenced by an overall impairment of their ability to think or reason. The localized brain damage they experienced nevertheless severely impaired their capacity for empathy, embarrassment, and guilt. Damage to the vmPFC typically leaves patients with reduced social emotions like these, as well as with diminished compassion, all of which are linked to moral values. Patients with these lesions can have trouble controlling frustration and anger as well.

These deficits, however, do not affect how patients respond to low-conflict moral challenges like that presented in Scenario 2. They respond in the same way people without brain damage do. And they respond the same way a second control group—patients with brain damage that does not involve the vmPFC—do. Like the two control groups, patients with damaged vmPFCs reject harming anyone if no lives are at stake and they choose not to harm anyone if the stakes are petty, like damaging leather car seats. You only see a difference in their moral decision-making process when they have to get their hands dirty to save lives, such as when it is necessary to harm or kill one person to prevent more deaths. That is where the patients with damaged vmPFCs stand apart from the control groups.

Making It Personal: Two More Scenarios

Scenario 5. The trolley you are driving is out of control as it speeds toward a point where the track splits into two paths. Five workers standing with their backs toward you are on the left fork. One worker standing with his back toward you is on the right track. If you hit a switch you will divert your trolley to the right and kill the single workman there. If you do nothing, your trolley will follow the left-hand track and kill the five workers there. Would you hit the switch?

Scenario 6. This time you and a very large stranger are standing on a footbridge above a straight, single track on which an out-of-control trolley is speeding toward five workers who will soon be killed unless the trolley is stopped. You and the stranger are positioned above the tracks between the oncoming trolley and the workers. If you push the oversized stranger onto the tracks, he will die, but his body will stop the trolley before it runs down and kills the five workers. Would you save the five workers by pushing the stranger off the footbridge to his certain death?[2]

Sometimes the dilemma is not hypothetical. During World War II, Winston Churchill and members of the British Cabinet faced a moral dilemma very much like that presented by the out-of-control-trolley challenge. On September 8, 1944, the first V2 rocket, launched from Nazi-occupied Europe, struck London. Travelling faster than sound, more than 1,300 of the rockets rained down on the British capital in the following months, killing more than 2,500 Londoners. British intelligence services had the ability to feed false information to the Germans about the accuracy of the missile strikes by using captured German agents under their control. The British fed the German military inaccurate information about where the V2s were falling. The misinformation caused the German commanders to alter the paths of subsequent missile launches in hopes of improving their accuracy, not knowing that they were in fact sending their rockets off course to land outside London. This subterfuge would spare Londoners but not those living in less densely populated regions of Great Britain where the misguided missiles would fall silently from the sky, without warning, until the blasts brought destruction and death. Some cabinet members wondered "Did they have the right to play God? Did they have a right to spare Londoners by killing those in less populated regions of the country?" In the end, they went ahead with the plan. The German military was deceived by the inaccurate feedback reports, and misdirected rockets fell farther from London.[3]

Far from wartime Britain, in the laboratory, people without brain damage, patients with brain damage not affecting the vmPFC, and patients with damage to the vmPFC all tended to say they would take remote action, such as flipping the switch, which would result in one death but save the lives of five others. Patients with damaged vmPFCs, however, were nearly twice as likely to say they would push the stranger off the footbridge, to engage in hands-on killing of one person, to save five others.

This and similar studies show that patients with vmPFC damage were much more likely to make utilitarian choices when presented with moral dilemmas like that presented in Scenario 6. Such dilemmas typically make many people without brain damage squirm with discomfort, but the patients more readily decided to personally sacrifice one person to save others when presented with the hypothetical scenarios. In some cases, people with damaged vmPFCs more readily say they would kill their own infant or child in order to save the lives of other family members, other persons and themselves, compared to control groups.

We don't know how these six patients, or others with similar lesions, would behave if they were presented with the scenarios outside the laboratory, on real footbridges, above real out-of-control trolleys. We do know, however, that the vmPFC in the frontal lobes plays a role in mediating our discomfort at the prospect of harming others and in making such moral choices.

Koenigs told the *New York Times* that one patient with vmPFC damage who repeatedly indicated he would kill when faced with high-conflict decisions like that presented in Scenario 6 said "Jeez, I've turned into a killer."[4]

But the hypothetical scenarios did not cause this patient to turn into an indiscriminate hypothetical killer. He was only more likely to kill when direct action was required to save lives. Developmental psychopaths also see the decision to push the oversized man off the footbridge if they wanted to save five lives as a "no-brainer" decision. One life for five; what is the problem? One shove and the situation is resolved.

Harvard psychologist Joshua Green told the *New York Times* that "I think it's very convincing now [with the publication of this study] that there are at least two systems working when we make moral judgments. There's an emotional system that depends on this specific part of the brain [the vmPFC], and another system that performs more utilitarian cost–benefit analyses which, in these people, is clearly intact."[5]

Patients with this kind of brain injury "don't sweat" the process of making moral decisions as control subjects do. Or, more accurately, they don't show the variations in skin conductance—which reflect increased autonomic nervous system activity—the way people with intact vmPFCs do. Remember that emotion-laden challenges like deciding if you will allow five people to die or save them by personally pushing one person off a bridge, results in small increases in perspiration, which increases skin conductance. These consequences of vmPFC damage suggest that this part of the brain plays a big role in modulating moral judgments and in expecting or predicting emotional fallout from such difficult decisions.[6]

After reviewing the results of over 171 studies published over 32 years starting in 1980, Donatella Marazziti and her collaborators agree that the vmPFC might be a key processing center for the nerve circuits that produce what we interpret as a moral sense.[7] This is not the place in the brain where a little white angel sits next to a little red devil arguing about how you should act. There is no sign of angels in the vmPFC shown in Figure 10 in its ventral (toward the bottom), medial (toward the middle) position in the frontal lobe. But as you can see in Figure 7, this part of the brain is closely interconnected to all or nearly all of the brain regions that have been implicated in psychopathic behavior.[8]

Psychopathy-like

The term *pseudopsychopathy* was first used in 1975[9] to describe the personality features that appeared in some patients with damaged frontal lobes. The phrase *acquired sociopathy* was used about 10 years later to describe a patient identified as E.V.R.[10] Before he developed a tumor in the orbitofrontal region of his prefrontal cortex, E.V.R. was a successful, happily married businessman. After surgery, his personality changed. The changes severely affected his ability to successfully navigate social situations and plan for the future. Consequently, he was divorced, remarried, and divorced a second time. His poor business decisions resulted in his bankruptcy.

Other patients with similar brain damage also lost their social graces and inhibitions. They became tactless and unrestrained in their comments and showed little concern for future consequences of their actions. Prior to their frontal-lobe injuries, they showed no sign of conduct disorder in their youth or developmental psychopathy as adults.[11] But after experiencing brain damage, they could no longer plan effectively for the future. They began to behave recklessly and sometimes dangerously. They also lacked a sense of remorse.[12] They became indiscreet and impulsive.

Such personality changes can result from damage caused by injury, as well as by tumors and strokes. Hundreds of soldiers who had received head wounds during the Vietnam War were surveyed two decades after the troops of the Vietnamese People's Army captured the city of Saigon in 1975 and claimed victory. Those with damage in the frontal ventromedial region consistently scored far higher in aggression and violence than soldiers with damage in other parts of their brains. In these soldiers, the aggressive behavior was more often verbal than physical, but the results support the association between vmPFC lesions and antisocial behavior.[13]

It doesn't seem to matter when the damage occurs, either. Prefrontal-lobe injuries in two children less than 16 months of age did not impair their intelligence, memory, school work, language, or visual perception as they grew to young adulthood. The injuries did, however, affect their ability to make good decisions, control their behavior, and act acceptably in social situations. Despite their normal intellectual abilities, the early damage affecting the function of their prefrontal lobes left them with lifelong severe social behavioral problems.[14]

Some of these traits are characteristic of many developmental, successful, or unsuccessful psychopaths. Other features of pseudopsychopathy, however, distinguish it from developmental psychopathy. When violent, for example, these patients seem to act more out of frustration than in pursuit of a goal. They are more likely to strike an inanimate object than they are to hit a person during one of their sporadic violent outbursts.[15] When they use violence, developmental criminal psychopaths tend to engage in instrumental or goal-oriented aggression more than reactive aggression.

The first convincing hint that the part of the brain that houses the vmPFC, the frontal lobes, plays a significant role regulating this kind of behavior and moral decision-making processes came not from tests of moral dilemmas or fMRI scans but from 19th century medicine and a horrible workplace accident.

Neuroscience's Most Famous Patient

On Wednesday, September 13, 1848, 26-year-old Phineas Gage was at work as a railroad foreman in the Green Mountains near Cavendish, Vermont. He was a good-looking single fellow, five feet, six inches tall and respected by his men and bosses for his reliability. In addition to supervising his crew, he prepared explosive charges to blast apart the granite bedrock that stood in the way of the expanding Rutland and Burlington Railroad.

Phineas routinely used a forged metal tool called a tamping iron to pack down sand which had been poured on top of gunpowder at the bottom of narrow holes drilled into the bedrock. The compressed gunpowder was usually ignited from a safe distance, using a fuse which set off the rock-shattering blast. But around 4:30 P.M. on his last day on the job, Phineas had a horrendous workplace accident.[16]

This is what was supposed to have happened that afternoon: After an assistant poured gunpowder into the hole, Phineas would have used the narrow end of his custom-forged tamping iron to carefully poke a depression in the gunpowder to hold a fuse in place. Then the assistant would have poured sand over the gunpowder, leaving the fuse extending out of the hole. Phineas would have then used the thick end of his tamping iron to pack the sand down over the gunpowder. This helps direct more of the explosive force of the gunpowder into the rock rather than out of the hole. But for some reason on that fall day, there was no sand over the gunpowder in one hole.[17] Phineas tamped, either intentionally or accidentally. A spark sparked. The gunpowder exploded.

The tamping iron shot out of the hole. It blew through Phineas's left cheek and through the back portion of his left eye socket. It soared through the top of his head like a missile fired from a submarine. The missile was three feet, seven inches long with a diameter ranging from ¼ inch at one end to 1¼ inches at the other end.[18] The 13¾-pound iron rod-turned-missile landed about 30 feet away from where Phineas was knocked flat on his back. He never lost consciousness. After being transported in an oxcart to the Cavendish hotel where he had a room, Dr. Edward Williams arrived from a nearby village, to find a horrifically wounded Phineas, who greeted him with the words: "Well, here's work enough for you, Doctor."

Besides taking the sight from Phineas's left eye, the tamping iron took much of his left prefrontal lobe. The injury was as gruesome as it sounds. While cleaning bone fragments from the wound, Cavendish town physician John Harlow, who took over from Dr. Williams, explored the extent of the injury. He inserted one of his fingers down into the wound on the top of Phineas's skull and one of his fingers up into the wound in the cheek. His fingers touched.[19] But to everyone's surprise, including the doctor's, the patient did not die that day, or for many days after. He lived for more than a decade and made neuroscience history doing it.

It is close to impossible to get away from his story if you study neuroscience or read many "brain" books like this one, partly because it is so graphic, but more because of what it revealed about the neurobiological basis of decent and respectable human behavior and the contributions of the frontal lobes to our better natures. It demonstrated clearly and graphically to many who read about the case, from the second half of the 19th century until today, that behavior and personality are influenced by particular regions of the brain.

Although the exact details of the brain injury Phineas suffered are still debated, the path of the missile certainly led to the destruction of his left frontal lobe. He recovered with his intellect, memory, speech, perception, and motor function intact enough to survive another 11½ years. Sadly, he never recovered his pre-injury easy-going, likable personality. Instead, he became disrespectful, unpleasant, moody, and impatient. Phineas's personality changed dramatically and he became socially impaired, according to contemporary accounts.

Although Malcolm Macmillan, D.Sc., an authority on the case, claims Gage's post-injury life has sometimes been misrepresented to bolster the argument that he is a good example of pseudopsychopathy, Macmillan does acknowledge that Gage was "profoundly changed by the accident and was irreverent. . . ."[20] And we have the word of the physician who treated Phineas:

"The equilibrium or balance, so to speak, between his intellectual faculty and animal propensities, seemed to have been destroyed," physician John Harlow wrote. "He is fitful, irreverent, indulging at times in the greatest profanity (which was not previously his custom), manifesting but little deference for his fellows, impatient of restraint of advice when it conflicts with his desires, at times pertinaciously obstinate, yet capricious and vacillating, devising many plans of operation, which are no sooner arranged than they are abandoned in turn for others appearing more feasible. A child in his intellectual capacity and manifestations, he has the animal passions of a strong man."[21]

The changes in Phineas's personality prevented him from keeping his old job. He became a different person unqualified to supervise others. He died from epilepsy on Monday, May 21, 1860. The accident claimed his life in the end.

There are other ways Phineas could have acquired unpleasant personality changes. He could have experienced similar changes if his right, instead of his left, prefrontal cortex had been damaged, for example. That is what happened to a patient in the United Kingdom identified as "J. S." The trauma that destroyed his right prefrontal region including his orbitofrontal cortex left him with "acquired sociopathy," according to the researchers who examined him. "His behavior was notably aberrant and marked by high levels of aggression and a callous disregard for others."[22] Like others with similar injuries, he found it very difficult to recognize emotional expressions and to control his socially inappropriate behavior.

Damage to other brain regions implicated in psychopathy has also been linked to pseudopsychopathy or acquired sociopathy. For example, the anterior cingulate cortex, a component of the paralimbic model of psychopathy, is the region that Kent Kiehl and his colleagues say is linked to the likelihood of a criminal's reoffending. Damage to this structure resulting in epilepsy is often accompanied by psychopathic behaviors.[23]

Brain damage-induced pseudopsychopathy, or acquired sociopathy, has similarities to developmental psychopathy, but it never duplicates the condition entirely. As we've seen, the cold-blooded, goal-oriented instrumental aggression seen in some criminal psychopaths is not a characteristic of the acquired version of the disorder. Andrea Glenn and her co-authors point out that differences between the two conditions might be expected, because one presumably develops early in life and one is acquired later in life.[24]

Criminal psychopathy, or a predisposition to it, may get its start during conception and develop as the brain develops before and after birth. Acquired psychopathy is the result of a lesion inserted into an otherwise normally developed, healthy brain. Even a child who receives prefrontal-lobe damage before the age of one and a half still has a brain that developed normally in the womb and during infancy, before the injury. The criminal psychopath, by contrast, may have a brain that developed abnormally as a fetus and infant, leaving it with impaired connections and multiple sites of dysfunction.

The features of the criminal psychopath's brain that produce psychopathic behavior cannot be reproduced exactly by damaging specific, limited regions of the brain, as happens following brain damage. Psychopathy is much too complex for that to happen, but looking at unusual injuries like those suffered by Phineas and J.M. reinforces the importance of the frontal lobes in understanding the minds of psychopaths. Abnormal functioning in this and associated brain regions may be present in some people even before adulthood. In some cases, it may explain the behavior of children at risk of growing into full-fledged psychopaths.

Chapter Ten

Could Your Child Be a Budding Psychopath?

Rav's parents knew that something serious was wrong with their son.

Based on his appearance (Figure 2), there was no way to tell what Rav was capable of doing, but we know he was capable of doing some very unsettling things, if we can trust the doctor his worried and exasperated parents took him to see. It is not surprising they sought the best help they could find for their eight-year-old boy; Rav's mother and father were good people, "well-to-do," according to the respected 19th century psychiatrist they consulted, Cesare Lombroso.[1]

His parents had raised Rav in Romagna, the region in northern Italy where he was born. The region, which is located between the Apennine Mountains and the Adriatic Sea, includes the cities of Rimini, Imola, and Ravenna. Rav's home town, like other northern Italian regions was, in general, considerably better off than those in southern Italy. The rich nobles who owned much of the land in the south preferred living in Rav's birthplace and in other regions of northern Italy.[2] These rich absentee landowners hired overseers to make sure they made money from their southern property holdings. Profit interested them more than the welfare of their employees, tenants, or even the land itself. They failed to maintain the quality of the soil which, like the quality of the southerners' lives, eroded. The southern Italians suffered terribly from the neglect and exploitation, like any group of sharecroppers or unvalued tenants who worked poorly maintained land they did not own in a class-conscious culture. It wouldn't be surprising if the exploitative landowners, were they around today, would be candidates for inclusion in some corporate psychopathy surveys.

The political unification of Italy in 1871, and the new taxes that followed did nothing to ease the poverty, unemployment, poor living conditions, lack of opportunity, and lack of hope in the south. That same year, a mass migration began. In forty years, it would see four million Italians move to South and North America.

But, as far as we can determine, Rav experienced none of the hardships his fellow countrymen experienced. He was well fed and appeared healthy with thick, close-cropped hair, protruding ears, and a blithely unconcerned, perhaps slightly bemused, expression. He slouched just a bit as he sat motionless in a wooden straightback chair, hands on knees, wearing a striped shirt and a dark jacket, waiting for the photographer to tell him he could move. We don't know what he was feeling or thinking as he waited for the film to be exposed; but if he had a conscience, he would have had a lot to think about.

His expulsion from school for "the bad influence he exercised over his schoolfellows"[3] was certainly troubling but hardly an indication of criminality by itself. And his spiteful behavior toward his younger brothers and sisters might be dismissed as typical behavior of one child toward his siblings—until you hear about his attempts on more than one occasion to strangle several of them. That crossed the line from "it's just roughhousing" to "it's scary." It was also scary when the staggeringly underhanded nature of his antisocial behavior became clear.

He seemed to take pleasure in robbing nearly everyone he came into contact with and then trying to blame others for the thefts. He stole from his parents, his neighbors, and the people he did jobs for. He lied well enough to convince them for some time that others were guilty of his crimes.

At age eight, for instance, he repeatedly stole the milk set on his neighbors' doorsteps before any of them could bring the daily deliveries indoors. He couldn't drink all of it. He didn't sell it or give it away. He threw it into the trash. He evidently just wanted to steal it and create mischief. Questioned about the thefts, he convinced his parents and his neighbors that a man who worked in the neighborhood, a janitor, was responsible for the thefts. The janitor was fired. Eventually, his victims discovered Rav's deceitfulness, but not before Rav's behavior produced more damage, anger, and hurt feelings.

At age nine, he falsely accused a pawnbroker of loaning him money for a cloak. This was bad news for the pawnbroker, because pawnbrokers were forbidden by law to loan money to a minor. The pawnbroker faced arrest and likely loss of his livelihood until Rav's mother found the cloak stashed in the basement of their home.

A year later, Rav's father became the target of the boy's maliciousness and deceitfulness. Based on the boy's accusations, his father was arrested for child abuse. The bruises on the child's body looked convincing to the police until they learned that the boy was the source of the damage; the bruises were self-inflicted.

Lombroso's records indicate that Rav's family was law-abiding and honest. If we can believe them, their child was not raised among criminal role models; he didn't grow up in an environment of abuse. Rav's brothers and sisters did not impress their parents as abnormal. They did not display depravity like Rav and so did not inspire their parents to drag them to a renowned expert like Dr. Lombroso.

Today, Hollywood screenwriters might describe Rav as a "bad seed." Like Eric Harris, he came from a good home which provided no indication, hints, or clues that might account for his antisocial attitude and behavior. Like Eric's family, Rav's family were blameless for his behavior. It appears that Rav and Eric were exceptional, rare individuals who very likely were born with genetic traits that placed them on the most extreme end of the spectrum of antisocial behavior. Their robust predispositions to the disorder or personality type did not require the push of damaging environmental factors like child abuse, bad role models, or neglect to drive them from a very early age, developing what psychiatrists call conduct disorder with callous, unemotional traits.

Dr. Lombroso had a different name for Rav's condition. After hearing Rav's parents describe the boy's behavior, he decided the boy represented a typical case of "moral insanity." A modern psychiatrist would substitute "conduct" for "moral" and "disorder" for "insanity," but cases like Rav's were as familiar to Lombroso as they are to modern-day child psychiatrists and psychologists.

From the Cradle

Two years after Lombroso's death in 1909, his daughter Gina recalled: "During many years of observation, my father was able to follow innumerable cases of moral insanity in which perversity was manifested literally from the cradle, and in which the victims of this disease grew up into delinquents in no wise distinguishable from born criminals."[4]

In 2007, a group of contemporary researchers backed up Lombroso's impression with an impressive study carried out in the island nation of the Republic of Mauritius in the Indian Ocean. Psychologist Andrea Glenn, then at the University of Southern California, and her fellow researchers reported the results of a twenty-five-year-long study that started with 1,795 three-year-old Mauritians in 1972–1973.[5] The young children were observed and received a battery of tests, the results of which were carefully filed away.

Glenn and her co-authors managed to track down hundreds of these subjects 25 years after they were observed and tested. They persuaded 335 of these now-28-year-olds to answer the 60 questions on the self-report version of the Psychopathy Checklist-Revised. The results indicated that the kids who showed signs of being less inhibited, less afraid, and more inclined to seek out stimuli in a test of their startle response at age 3—a loud noise delivered through earphones—were more likely to score high on Hare's Self-Report Psychopathy scale at age 28. The results suggest that a child's ability to feel fear may be linked to the development of his or her moral sense. A child who feels fear is more likely to feel remorse after misbehaving. Not so with the subjects who weren't as fearful at age three.

Many children can misbehave in many ways and still grow up to be psychologically healthy adults. Sadly, this outcome is less likely for one group of troubled and troubling children in particular: those who lack a sense of guilt and a sense of empathy, and who demonstrate a callous disregard for, or use of, others for their own purposes. It sounds a lot like budding psychopathy. And in fact, kids with these features, which are known to child psychiatrists and researchers as callous-unemotional traits, have an increased risk of becoming adult psychopaths.

These children are a lot like Rav. They have temperaments that set them apart from their normally behaving and feeling siblings and peers. They seek thrills and may act without fear. Where other children who have trouble controlling their behavior may act violently in response to a disappointment or as a reaction to something that irritates them, callous-unemotional children engage in instrumental aggression, the cold-blooded kind that is very unnerving for adults to contemplate, let alone to witness.

The antisocial behavior of an impulsive, short-tempered child who does not obey, but who nevertheless can feel guilt and empathy, may be strongly influenced by his or her environment. Not so when there is a lack of guilt and empathy combined with a callous disregard for others. If one identical twin has callous-unemotional traits and shows antisocial behavior, the odds are excellent that the other twin will have these traits. Not surprisingly, callous-unemotional traits are highly heritable: twin studies suggest the figure is around 80 percent.[6] And as with adult psychopathy, the genetic risk for developing callous-unemotional traits may be increased by exposure to stressful or unfavorable environments.[7]

Scanning Young Brains

Based on what scientists tell us about the abnormalities they find in the brains of adult psychopaths, you might think it would be a "no-brainer" to confirm their presence in children with callous-unemotional traits. But this reasoning includes an unstated assumption, the gremlin that scientists try hard to eliminate before devoting time and money to any experiment or study. The clue to the snag is in Chapter 5, "Troubling Developments and Genes." Specifically, it is in the section about brain development.

The brains of children are actively changing and developing. We still don't know as much as we would like about the normal development of the brain, although researchers have begun systematic studies to learn more about this important topic.[8] We don't know the full extent of variations in brain structure and function in the population as a whole.[9] As challenging as it is to interpret the meaning and significance of brain scans of adults with psychopathy, it is even more challenging to draw firm conclusions from scans of children with callous-unemotional traits whose brains are growing and changing.

Despite this caution, can we learn anything useful by scanning young brains that might some day develop into the brains of old psychopaths? Some studies published so far suggest that we can. For example, a study by researchers at the National Institute of Mental Health compared brain scans of children with callous-unemotional features to those with attention deficit hyperactivity disorder and to children without behavior problems.[10] Each group consisted of a dozen children between the ages of 10 and 17. The children were asked to look at and process information about fearful, angry, or neutral facial expressions. Activity in the amygdalae in all three groups looked pretty much the same when the children considered angry or neutral expressions. When the youths with callous-unemotional traits dealt with fearful expressions, however, their amygdalae showed reduced levels of activation compared to the other two groups. The association of callous and unemotional personality traits with reduced amygdala activation to fearful faces is not inconsistent with what we see in the brains of adult psychopaths, who appear to have deficiencies processing emotional information.

A year after that study was published, researchers at King's College London confirmed the finding in seventeen boys with callous-unemotional traits compared to thirteen well-adjusted controls. The decreased activity in the amygdala suggested to the researchers that the neuronal basis of the emotional deficits seen in children with callous-unemotional traits "are already present in childhood."[11]

A second study published in 2009 by the same group in the United Kingdom presented a finding that seemed to highlight differences between childhood conduct disorder with callous and unemotional traits and adult psychopathy. A comparison of around two dozen boys with callous-unemotional conduct problems and a similar number of controls detected *increased* gray matter in some parts of the brain: the medial orbitofrontal cortex, the anterior cingulate (which has been implicated in recidivism; see Chapter 6), and the temporal lobes.[12] Yet, as we've learned, adult psychopaths have been found to have cortical *thinning* in several regions, including portions of the temporal lobes, the insula, and the prefrontal cortex, among others. Why don't children who give the impression they are developing psychopathy show the same pattern of cortical thinning? The answer probably lies in the way the brain develops. During childhood, unneeded gray matter is trimmed as the brain matures. Perhaps, as the authors suggest, youths with callous-unemotional traits experience delayed maturation of their cerebral cortices, if they ever do mature completely. If conduct disorder with callous-unemotional traits is a precursor to adult psychopathy, the flaw or flaws in brain development that affect key regions of cortex involved in empathy and morality somehow lead to less gray matter later in life.

Treating Youth and Psycho(path)therapy

Despite some similarities (and some differences that might be explained based on what we know about brain development) among fMRI studies of children with callous-unemotional traits and adult psychopaths, it would be irresponsible to equate these children with the adults they seem to resemble. Sadly, as of 2014 there were no well controlled long-term studies that showed that adult psychopaths can be effectively treated. This is not to say there will never be such a study, or that mental healthcare professionals should not try to develop therapies—but it will be a challenge. Due to the nature of criminal psychopathy, dealing with manipulative patients or prisoners who are often capable of mimicking true emotions and feelings presents challenges. In other words, therapists will have to demonstrate true change in their patients. That will require extended periods of follow-up.

Despite these challenges posed by the nature of psychopathy, Kent Kiehl is optimistic. "It is, I think, a manageable condition in the adult, and I think it is a treatable condition in youth with the current state of knowledge," Kiehl said when interviewed for *Miller-McCune* magazine.[13]

Anyone familiar with the state of psychiatry before the mid-1950s and the discovery of antipsychotic or psychotropic medications will recall that psychiatric hospitals were filled with untreatable patients, many condemned to life locked in the back wards. These hospitals virtually emptied out after the introduction of psychiatric medication, which improved the lives of many previously untreatable patients. A treatment for psychopathy could have as revolutionary an effect on forensic and clinical psychiatry. We just don't have that treatment yet, and we don't know when we will find it. Perhaps insights gained from study of the brains of psychopaths will speed progress toward this distant goal.

Children who display psychopathic traits may have an advantage over adult psychopaths. Their brains may still be plastic enough to respond to therapy more readily than adults. Treating schizophrenia as soon as its symptoms appear generally produces better results than starting treatment years after the disease has developed. We should assume that the same applies to conduct disorder with callous-unemotional traits and to psychopathy. Intensive therapy for youth might help "rewire" the brain or strengthen weak neural circuits associated with feelings of empathy, morality, and effective decision-making.

For example, Michael Caldwell at the University of Wisconsin-Madison's Mendota Juvenile Treatment Center and his collaborators followed up on potentially psychopathic youths who took part in an intensive treatment program involving very close monitoring and access to a psychiatrist, a psychologist, a social worker, and a psychiatric nurse. The program was designed to replace the young offenders' antagonistic outlooks and relationships with more conventional ones. During a two-year follow-up period, a control group of similar youths confined to a conventional juvenile correctional institution had double the risk of returning to detention for committing violent acts compared to the young people who received treatment.[14]

Such encouraging results represent good progress, but, of course, there is much room for more. Paul Frick, Ph.D., a psychologist at the University of New Orleans and a pioneer in this field, told the *New York Times Magazine* in 2012 that he is not sure what the best way is to intervene in the lives of such youth. "Before you can develop effective treatments, you need several decades of basic research just to figure out what these kids are like, and what they respond to. That's what we're doing now—but it will take a while to get real traction."[15]

Any psychologist claiming to have developed effective treatments for callous-unemotional children or adult psychopaths will have to build in safeguards to prevent being fooled. Both groups can learn to mimic emotions and be persuasive. It will be a time-consuming process to prove that a therapy works. It will be necessary to follow treated patients for years to prove that the therapy or treatment was effective, as the researchers in Wisconsin have begun to do.

Is it possible to increase empathy in a person who lacks it? Harma Meffert of the National Institute of Mental Health and Professor Christian Keysers of the University of Groningen and the Netherlands Institute for Neuroscience Social Brain Lab in Amsterdam, think it might be possible, based on the results of experiments they carried out on eighteen people with psychopathy.[16]

First, they had these prisoners, together with matching controls, watch some short film clips showing people interacting by touching each other's hands. The hand contact was either loving as indicated by a gentle squeeze or caress, pain-inducing as indicated by bending or twisting a finger, socially rejecting as indicated by pushing away, or neutral as indicated by swiping a finger across the back of the hand.

fMRI brain scans of the psychopaths watching these films revealed predictably that brain regions "involved in their own actions, emotions and sensations were less active than that of controls while they saw what happens in others," Keysers said in a press release.[17] "At first, this seems to suggest that psychopathic criminals might hurt others more easily than we do because they do not feel pain, when they see the pain of their victims."

But then the Dutch researchers asked the prisoners to try to feel empathy toward the person in the film whose hand was being subjected to loving, painful, rejecting, or neutral treatment. Surprisingly, despite their high psychopathy scores, their brain regions lit up nearly as much as those in the controls who lacked psychopathic traits. The authors suggest that psychopathy may be more a problem of a reduced inclination to feel empathy than it is an inability to feel what another person is feeling. The default mode of their personality seems to lack empathy, the authors imply, but they might be able to turn it on if and when they feel like it.

The results raise the possibility that people with psychopathy go through life unencumbered by empathy except for a certain time when they intentionally activate it, or a version of it, in order to manipulate others. Perhaps knowing just a little about how a potential victim feels makes it easier for a conning, manipulative bad guy to appear more sympathetic, more human, in the eyes of the intended victim.

The authors balance this depressing scenario with a more optimistic one. Perhaps, they suggest, it might be possible to condition or train people who normally lack empathy to turn it on automatically more often.

If neuroscientists can identify brain abnormalities in young people who begin to show signs of callous-unemotional traits and accumulate enough evidence to convincingly link them to these traits, then it would be possible that neurobiological screening could direct at-risk youth into treatment sooner rather than later for everyone's benefit. That this is even a remote possibility in the views of some neuroscience skeptics and a likelihood in the opinion of others reflects how far we have come since Rav was hauled by his frustrated parents to see psychiatrist Cesare Lombroso 125 years ago.

This Theory Is Now Modified

When he examined his new patient, Lombroso probably was not surprised by Rav's protruding ears, and he may have been suspicious of the shape of his skull too. Lombroso was convinced that physical abnormalities were markers of criminal behavior. He published five editions of his book *The Delinquent Man* (*L'uomo Delinquente*) starting in 1876 as he tried to convince the rest of the world that he was on to something. He was unsuccessful in part because his findings reflected the prejudices of his age and because he seemed to be trying to prove he was right rather than trying to challenge his own hypothesis that criminals were biologically different from non-criminals. In short, he saw what he expected and wanted to see in the faces and skulls of criminals. But Lombroso was right when he argued that biology can play a significant role in the origins of crime and antisocial behavior. Unfortunately, he was born before fMRI and other neuroscience tools were developed.

Yet even today, some critics compare the oversimplified interpretation of brain-imaging results to phrenology, the once-trendy practice of interpreting human traits and abilities based on the overall shape, bumps, and indentations of a person's skull. Phrenology was nearly, but not completely, ridiculous. It at least provided a hypothesis, something that could be measured, tested, and challenged. And don't forget that today, physical anthropologists studying brain evolution in our human ancestors rely on a scientifically valid technique for studying brain indentations. But—and this is a very important "but"—they study the indentations left on the *inside* of fossil skulls. These indentations reflect the extent of the development of different brain regions such as those associated with speech, manual dexterity, etc.

By making a latex mold of the empty space inside a fossil skull, paleoneurologists create an endocast. The inside surface of the skull is imprinted on the surface of the mold. If a prominent part of the brain or a brain blood vessel leaves an imprint on the inside of the skull, you can see it in the endocast. Of course, the mold can reveal nothing about the fine internal structure of the brain or its cells, but it can, under the right circumstances, provide direct evidence of the presence of particular brain regions in a long-deceased subject.

For example, if an endocast indicates that the brain of an early primate ancestor had a well-developed region closely associated with vision, scientists would conclude that this species had evolved a well-developed sense of sight. This conclusion would be based entirely on the impression left on the inside of the skull under which once nestled the brain tissue associated with this sense. The same would apply to other sensory systems.

The difference between phrenologists and physical anthropologists who create endocasts is that the phrenologists were on the outside, looking in, while all the interesting stuff was on the inside, pressing out. And of course phrenologists had very little understanding compared to what we know today about which parts of the brain are involved in processing different sensations and higher mental functions. The founder of phrenology, Franz Joseph Gall, working in the late 18th and early 19th centuries, deserved credit for promoting the notion that different brain functions can be associated with specific parts of the brain.

Unfortunately, he and his followers went beyond their nearly non-existent data. They did not hesitate to associate various bumps and indentations on the head to traits such as self-esteem, cautiousness, verbal memory, language, acquisitiveness, secretiveness, destructiveness, combativeness, and 29 other moral and intellectual, or mental faculties (see Figure 3, top). Unfortunately, none of the fanciful associations between mental attributes and skull bumps could be substantiated by any scientific data. As physicist Richard Feynman said about an early theory that attributed planetary motion to the force applied by angels beating their wings: "You will see that this theory is now modified."[18] Phrenology was an overenthusiastic, naïve, unscientific attempt to understand what many neuroscientists are still trying to understand: how brain structure relates to mental ability and behavior. Now, with techniques like fMRI, we have a more sophisticated tool for looking at the brain and one that may have the potential to help us prevent psychopathy from developing in the brains of susceptible youths.

Chapter Eleven

Why Do We Have to Deal with These People?

EXPLAINING CRIMINAL PSYCHOPATHS TO JURIES AND DARWINISTS

Imagine three unrelated humans living around 150,000 years ago near the southern coast of Africa. Two adults, Al and Cy, and a child stand on the edge of a ravine which blocks their progress. Rough times, including extreme drought and cold temperatures never experienced by modern humans, have reduced the population in Africa, and therefore on the planet, from thousands to hundreds.[1]

This kind of drastic reduction in the number of individuals in a species due to environmental or other misfortune is called a population bottleneck. Trimming the population of a species trims the variety of genes in the species. Not all geneticists agree when, or even if, humans faced such genetic bottlenecks in the past, but many are convinced that our species survived one or more. A brush with extinction such as this one would explain the shallowness of our present gene pool compared to those of other primates.

It would be another 149,850 years before the descendants of our three hypothetical early ancestors Al, Cy, and the kid began to suspect the existence of genes. These three, therefore, could not have thought of themselves as caretakers of a valuable, dwindling genetic treasure. And anyway, two of them are facing a more immediate, personal threat in our scenario.

Without warning, dirt, pebbles, and rocks under the child's feet slide into the narrow gorge, taking the child with them. After sliding down five feet, the child grabs onto an outcrop of rock, temporarily halting his fall. Seeing the child's precarious grip, Al shouts, drops to his stomach, and reaches farther and farther over the edge trying to grab the child's hand. Then dirt, pebbles, and rocks under Al give way. He plunges down the steep side of the gorge. The child's grip fails, and together he and Al vanish. After the rush of stone and dirt into the ravine, and after the screams subside, the landscape is quiet again, as it was before the three reached the edge. As Cy turns back to retrace the path that led to the ravine, he chuckles and shakes his head in puzzlement. "Losers," he mutters in a prehistoric language that died out long ago.

Where Do These People Come From, Anyway?

The tragedy has eliminated whatever rare genes Al and the child might have contributed to their tribe's limited gene pool. Cy's unique genes, however, including any that might predispose him and his offspring to traits of self-interest, lack of altruism, and lack of empathy, are safe for the time being, long enough for him to pass them along when he returns to the tribe. With the human species facing extinction as it did around this time, with the human gene pool shrunk by the loss of thousands of its members due to environmental change, behavior motivated by self-interest might have a survival advantage. If Al had let the child fall without risking his own life, he would have kept his own genes in the pool. If both Cy and Al had been ill-advisedly altruistic, the loss could have been even worse for our species.

If psychopathy gave some people an advantage in the struggle for survival under some conditions, psychopathy would persist in our species because psychopaths would be more likely to live long enough to reproduce and pass their genes to future generations. On another day, someone with Al's altruistic tendencies might succeed in saving someone in danger by risking his own life and so prevent the loss of a valuable member of the diminished group. Win some, lose some. By having a balance of people like Al and Cy in a group, perhaps the tribe hedges its bets.

In some cases, the lack of conscience and the inability to empathize with others make psychopaths seem almost like a subspecies of human distinct from the rest of us. Could psychopaths be Nature's way of hedging its bets if cooperation and mutual support ever become liabilities in human society? Evolutionary selective pressures can change over time. Behavioral traits are strongly influenced by genes. Some that are useful today might be less useful next month or even tomorrow. Additionally, men might experience different selection pressures than women, a fact that might contribute to the perceived relative rarity of psychopathy in females compared to males.

So far, nearly all neuroscientific investigations of psychopaths have been limited to males. While psychopathy exists in women, it appears more often and with greater severity in men, according to Rolf Wynn from the Department of Forensic Psychiatry in the University Hospital of North Norway and his colleagues. According to Wynn and his co-authors, the expression of psychopathy might differ in men and women, with women exhibiting greater emotional instability, use of verbal abuse, and manipulation of people in their social circles. Men, on the other hand, are more likely to display instrumental ("cold-blooded") violence and criminal behavior. In 2013, Kent Kiehl of the Mind Research Network received a grant from the National Institute of Mental Health for $612,158 to scan the brains of female psychopaths and conduct cognitive neuroscience studies in this understudied population. Comparing the results of male and female brains affected by psychopathy could provide further interesting insights into this poorly understood condition.

It is possible that psychopathy is an aberration that, in the big picture of human existence, provides neither an advantage nor a disadvantage in the struggle to survive. In this case it could easily persist as long as there is no evolutionary pressure to eliminate it. The net effect of psychopathy would be neither advantageous nor disadvantageous to the species as a whole. Like schizophrenia, it affects around one percent of the population. And as with schizophrenia, its effects—as costly and disturbing as they are to the many people who are directly affected by them—don't amount to much in an evolutionary sense. Nature may be able to handle a one percent incidence of psychopathy because it is, in the big picture of human evolution, not significant. Call me, unsentimental Mother Nature might say, when the figure gets a lot higher than a trifling one percent. Until then, it's not a concern. One in 17 people have one or more disorders that result in "serious functional impairment, which substantially interferes with or limits one or more major life activities," according to the National Institute of Mental Health. If the United States can function reasonably well with a one percent incidence of schizophrenia and with a six percent incidence of serious mental illness,[2] why should a measly one percent incidence of psychopathy be of much evolutionary significance? As long as the other 83 percent of the population can get by with reasonably good mental health, mental disorders, while tragic for those directly affected by them and their loved ones, are not a threat to the species on an evolutionary scale. In this view, psychopathy is just one of many minor blemishes on the face of humanity.

Some traits that characterize criminal psychopaths—extreme risk-taking, impulsiveness, callousness, conning behavior, deceitfulness, instrumental aggression, and lack of guilt, remorse, and empathy—might not seem to equip them well for thriving or surviving in some situations or environments, such as life in a law-abiding community with an efficient law-enforcement and criminal-justice system. They might, on the other hand, be very useful in other situations where an every-man-and-woman-for-themselves ethic exists, even for a limited time. In a small community where everyone interacts closely on a daily basis, psychopathy may be less tolerated. Remember what happened to Kopanuk, the alias of the real Eskimo *kunlangeta* or psychopath described in Chapter 2. He eventually was taken hunting and never returned. In New York City, London, Mexico City, Moscow, and other large urban areas he would likely have moved on after taking advantage of his victims and victimized again before his reputation caught up with him. Perhaps this might explain why psychopathy in Eskimo society was once informally estimated to have had an incidence of 1 in 500 instead of 1 in 100 as it is in the larger, more fluid societies of North America. It might have been spotted more easily and discouraged (sometimes by a shove off the ice) more efficiently in small, tight-knit societies than in large, urban landscapes filled with people who don't know each other well.

This explanation for why we have to share our world with psychopaths is related to something called evolutionary balancing theory[3] or balancing selection.[4] It assumes that psychopaths co-exist with non-psychopaths. They are, in a sense, waiting in the wings, prepared to take center stage if called upon. They are available to demonstrate their fitness by increasing their numbers when and if environmental conditions favor their unique antisocial behaviors.

In some end-of-the-world scenarios, psychopathic traits might be an advantage. Under the right (for them) or wrong (for the rest of us) conditions, psychopaths may survive better than those of us with a conscience. Criminal psychopaths have often been compared to, or described as, predators. Lacking the ability or inclination to empathize with other living things, criminal psychopaths may see them as prey. Lacking the emotional ability to relate to them, they may see them as objects. Under some extreme every-man and every-woman-for-themselves conditions, this outlook might come in handy despite our desire to wish it were not so. With an estimated seven billion-plus people on the planet, there are an estimated 30 million-plus psychopaths to draw from if conditions ever favor them more than the rest of us. And, of course, their numbers could fall if the environment or society ever rendered their distinguishing traits unfit for survival.

Might Willem Boerema, whom we met in Chapter 3, have been right when he told *Nature* magazine's Senior European Correspondent Alison Abbott "I think my high psychopath score [35 out of 40 on the Hare Psychopathy Checklist–Revised] is a talent, not a sickness?" Since Boerema was locked up at the time, the answer is no. Under other circumstances, however, he might be right.

Some well-known dystopian novels are based on this premise. Their plots rely on the emergence, or on the established presence, of psychopathic traits in their imagined societies. William Golding's *Lord of the Flies* describes the conflict between responsible, moral behavior and irresponsible, immoral behavior in a group of children isolated on an island after a plane crash. And Robert Sheckley's satirical science fiction novel *The Status Civilization*, published in 1960, describes a world populated by convicts who live in a society that rewards psychopathic behavior.

Another possibility is that psychopathy is buried, unexpressed and unsuspected, in more of us than we might like to contemplate. When conditions become right (or wrong, depending on your view) more of us develop into psychopaths when that path leads to better chances of surviving and reproducing. This is an example of what evolutionary biologists call contingent shift theory.[5]

In balancing theory, you are or you are not a psychopath. In contingent shift theory, some individuals may become psychopaths if they are exposed to environmental influences that bring psychopathy out. In this explanation, the environment influences and adjusts the settings on the scale of psychopathic traits in some individuals. A child born into a world that promotes or tolerates his or her abuse might be better off developing a coldhearted outlook that lasts long after the beatings end. And, as Dominic Murphy of the California Institute of Technology and Stephen Stich of Rutgers University suggested, some psychiatric and personality disorders described in the DSM "may turn out not to be disorders at all. The people who have these conditions don't have problems; they just cause problems!"[6]

It is very possible that psychopaths exist because both of these evolutionary explanations apply to our species. Beat Richard Kuklinski and abuse Brian Dugan when they are children and, way to go, you have helped create a pair of rare, criminal psychopaths. Raise Eric Harris, the lead Columbine shooter, in a normal home environment beside his healthy, non-criminal sibling and, through no one's fault, his psychopathic behavior develops on its own.

Loading Up on Mutations

We don't know if psychopaths existed back in Cy's time, when our species was new. We can't even be sure if someone with Cy's traits—lack of altruistic feelings and empathy—existed early in human evolution. The fact that our species survived strongly argues that cooperation among individuals in small groups of humans did exist. It is possible that psychopathy developed over time in our species. University of Pennsylvania researchers Andrea Glenn, Robert Kurzban, and Adrian Raine don't think any single evolutionary theory completely accounts for psychopathy,[7] but they do consider the possibility that mutations may have played a role in its unquestionable presence today.

Mutations are permanent changes in a gene's DNA code. We all have them, but they are not all damaging. Many are neutral. One example of a neutral mutation would be the substitution of a different amino acid in a protein's structure that does not affect its function. For example, if the protein with a neutral mutation is an enzyme that speeds up a chemical reaction, the speed of the reaction is not affected by the substitution. Mutations that gave us baldness, blue eyes (instead of the brown that humans started out with), and freckles might be considered neutral if they don't affect survival or reproductive success.

Highly disruptive mutations usually prevent a person from reaching reproductive age and so are never passed on. Those that have some drawbacks for a person—but not enough to prevent them from having children—may linger in the gene pool. Over time, they build up. Perhaps the neutral and not-so-bad mutations distinguish us from one another in good ways. They enlarge and deepen the gene pool. It is possible that some of these accumulating mutations affect behavior.[8] If so, they could contribute to the variety of different personality types and personality disorders that enrich and trouble our species. Many small changes affecting many genes that contribute to human personality and behavior picked up over our evolutionary history could have resulted in extremely altruistic and empathetic behaviors at one end of a behavioral spectrum. They could just as well have contributed to predacious, callous, unconscionable behavior at the opposite end of the spectrum.

The poster psychopaths like Ted Bundy and John Wayne Gacy, the ones even the experts use as examples to illustrate the extremes of criminal psychopathy, are stuck on the extreme end of the psychopathy spectrum. Criminal psychopathy may not have many apparent benefits in the long run for anyone affected by it, but promiscuous psychopaths may succeed in passing their genes to future generations. And psychopathic behavior that falls short of criminal is more and more considered to be a plus in many circles of modern society, including the business world, as we have seen.

Many people with psychopathic traits may lack a conscience, but they are not murdering people. Some of their personality traits like selfishness, lack of emotion, confidence, fearlessness, boldness, and persuasiveness can be advantageous if they are not self-defeating. These sub-criminal psychopaths certainly make the world unfair, and they routinely roll over and frequently crush Al's trusting descendants, but their persistence suggests they may bring something to human society. The question is: Do we want that something? Do we want winners at any cost? Do we want to be charmed and entertained even if we risk getting conned at the same time?

"Psychopaths are assertive. Psychopaths don't procrastinate. Psychopaths tend to focus on the positive. Psychopaths don't take things personally; they don't beat themselves up if things go wrong, even if they're to blame," Oxford psychologist Kevin Dutton told *Smithsonian* magazine writer Amy Crawford.[9] "And they're pretty cool under pressure. Those kinds of characteristics aren't just important in the business arena, but also in everyday life." Dutton calls these people "functional psychopaths" in his book *The Wisdom of Psychopaths: What Saints, Spies and Serial Killers Can Teach Us About Success.*[10] Robert Hare agrees: "Some psychopathic features are not necessarily a bad thing for society—in some professions they may even help. Too much empathy, for example, on the part of a police officer or a politician would interfere with the job."[11]

The key phrase is "psychopathic features." Having psychopathic features is not necessarily the same as being a successful psychopath. And it is certainly not the same as being an unsuccessful or criminal psychopath. No rational patient wants their surgeon crying in sympathy for their misfortune. They want an efficient, knowledgeable, skilled individual with a steady scalpel-holding hand who can cut cleanly and accurately into flesh and remove the bad parts. Is that ability a psychopathic feature? Or is it mental discipline and training? Or is it a combination?

Impressions, Speculations, and Conclusions

It is time for the public to distinguish between harmful psychopathic traits that bring significant discomfort or injury to others and traits that are reminiscent of psychopathy but that do not lead to harm. Not everyone with psychopathic features is a psychopath. Using the same word to describe someone capable of criminal behavior and someone who never threatens or harms anyone, or breaks the law, is confusing and illogical. Preliminary hints in the scientific literature that brain abnormalities may be absent or less apparent in successful compared to unsuccessful psychopaths support this recommendation.

Referring to someone with a few psychopathic features as a psychopath is like calling a liberal a Maoist or a conservative a fascist. Having features of "boldness," for example, which the Triarchic Model of Psychopathy defines as a connection or a series of connections linking venturesomeness, social dominance, and emotional resiliency, does not by itself make a psychopath. It is a personality feature found in psychopaths, but you can have boldness and not be a psychopath. Psychopathy is much more complex than having a few pushy or unpleasant personality traits. Being more careful with pejorative labels and making more of an effort to distinguish people with psychopathic traits from true and criminal psychopaths would go a long way to clearing up the confusion and controversy that greets anyone seeking answers in this area of abnormal psychology.

One wonders if psychiatrist Ben Karpman wasn't on to something seventy years ago when he wrote in "The Myth of the Psychopathic Personality": "With the larger number of psychopathic personality cases [secondary psychopaths] being properly put under the respective headings of the cardinal reaction types [various psychiatric and personality disorders], and the balance being put in a new group designated anethopathy, nothing remains of the original concept of psychopathic personality, for which reason it should be completely deleted from psychiatric nosology [disease classification]. The term may be left entirely for lay use."[12] Now, if we could just limit lay use of the term *psychopath* to those Karpman wanted to call anethopaths, we would be making more progress.

There is evidence to suggest the existence of distinct neurobiological differences between those who score low, medium, and high on the psychopathy checklist. Kristina Hiatt, William Schmitt, and Joseph Newman, working at the University of Wisconsin in Madison, for example, found that high-scoring psychopaths process visual clues differently from those with PCL–R scores below 28. They seem to block out distractions, as if they are blind to them, when they concentrate on a visual task.[13] Controls and those with lower PCL–R scores doing the same task find that their responses are slowed by the same distractions. Findings like this raise the possibility that psychopathy exists on a spectrum until it reaches the disturbingly high scores approaching 30, according to Kevin Dutton.[14]

Of course, many of us who are neither functional/successful nor dysfunctional/unsuccessful/criminal psychopaths regard them all as generally negative presences. Jerk is one description often applied to the overbearing, insensitive boss with significant functional psychopathic traits, for example. Other descriptions are apt but cruder. Despite our frequent irritation with the unfriendly and often-irritating behavior of people with above-average psychopathic traits, Dutton has a point: in the right dose, some of these traits may have survival advantages. If you can get away with cheating, you often will have an advantage over someone who does not cheat.

The persistence of psychopathy in our species is at least consistent with their personality traits not being a disadvantage from an evolutionary standpoint. And they may very well provide an evolutionary advantage. In this view, psychopathy is not a disorder: in many instances, it is an evolutionary adaptation. It only becomes a disorder when the traits are so extreme that they lead to victimization. The disadvantages come when anyone overdoses on these same traits.

We may have to deal with criminal psychopaths because they are outliers set apart from their more clever cousins, the functional or successful psychopaths and those with above-average psychopathic traits. This take on psychopathy is consistent with the popular idea that psychopathic traits and behavior exist on a continuum or spectrum. Some extremely empathetic and thoughtful people are on the far end of the scale. Others are in the middle of whatever psychopathic test they take. And a very few are on the extreme end. It is the degree to which they are present and how much they trouble family members, friends, acquaintances, co-workers, witnesses, and victims that determines when these traits become pathological.

There are other important questions about psychopaths that science cannot answer. This uncertainty provides readers with another opportunity to form their own opinions about the persistent questions anyone who has wondered about the presence of psychopaths in our midst has asked: Did their brains make them do it? Do they have any neurological excuse for their behavior?

From Rap Sheet to Brain Scan

Twenty-four years after Brian Dugan tried to abduct her, Opal Horton's body prepared her to escape from him one more time. In response to a completely understandable perceived threat, Opal's sympathetic nervous system stimulated the release of adrenaline into her bloodstream. This was part of her acute stress, or "fight-or-flight," response brought on by the prospect of facing her attacker once again after nearly a quarter century. The stress hormone released by her adrenal glands caused her muscles to shake as she walked to the witness stand. With the bravery of one who has survived a terrifying trauma and who is about to voluntarily relive the experience to help others, she had agreed to face the man who changed her life forever. She sat just feet from him as she testified against the criminal psychopath who killed her friend and came close to killing her.[15]

The adrenaline caused her hand to shake as she pointed to a map showing the location of the gravel road in Somonauk, Illinois where Brian Dugan had tried to abduct her. Opal, then eight years old, and her seven-year-old friend Melissa Ackerman, had been riding their bikes there on Sunday, June 2, 1985. Twenty-eight-year-old Brian drove up in his blue AMC Gremlin. He was casually dressed. His long dark hair covered most of his ears and the back of his neck. His mustache barely hinted at the Fu Manchu style of facial hair. It passed the corners of his mouth and started to extend downward but stopped short before it reached the level of his lower lip. He looked young and not particularly threatening. Seated in his car, he asked the girls for directions. Then he got out and walked toward them because, he said, he could not hear them. Opal whispered to Melissa, "We have to go."[16]

But before they could go, Brian grabbed Opal by the neck and threw her through an open window of his blue Gremlin. He threw her, Opal testified, "like a ball through a window." Brian turned toward Melissa.[17] Opal tried to open the passenger-side door but could not; the lock had been disabled. Before Brian caught her, Melissa yelled for Opal to climb through the window.[18] Opal did and fell to the ground just as Brian returned, carrying Melissa. Opal ran for her life, but Brian had a grip on Melissa which she could not escape.

Opal ran to a nearby John Deere dealership. She spotted a tractor tire and hid in it. When she peeked out, she saw her friend in Brian's car as it drove away. That was the last time she ever saw her. When the car was out of sight, Opal ran for several blocks, still trying to keep low, still trying to hide from the man who took her friend and tried to take her. She knocked on the door of one house but felt nervous asking for help from strangers. She ran to the next house, which she recognized. It belonged to a teacher she knew named Charles Hickey. "Someone took my friend," she told him.[19] Charles called the police, but Brian and his captive were gone. Blocks away, at the scene of the crime, Melissa's abandoned pink bicycle marked the site of the abduction.

An hour later, police officer James McDougall saw Brian's Gremlin at a gas station. Brian had not been identified as a suspect in the abduction, so when the officer looked in the Gremlin and saw no signs of Melissa, he let Brian go. A few hours after Brian raped and murdered the child, Brian met up with his brother Steven, who had no idea what his brother had just done. They exchanged small talk and Brian mentioned that he had purchased some new plants.[20] He gave no indication that he had committed a horrendous crime. But before the day was over, Opal—the girl who got away—had described his car to the police. Law-enforcement officers then linked her description to a car with an out-of-date vehicle sticker a local policeman had recently noted. Brian was arrested the next day as he pulled into the parking lot of the Midwest Hydraulics plant, where he worked as a machine operator.

Once in custody, he was linked to at least one recent rape and quickly became a suspect in the attack on Opal and Melissa. Two weeks later, a deputy sheriff found Melissa's body, five days after what would have been her eighth birthday. Brian had left his victim in a drainage ditch, covered by rocks. An autopsy would conclude that she had died of either suffocation or drowning. After one of Melissa's hairs was found on Brian's sleeping bag, he was charged with her murder. To avoid the death penalty, he admitted raping and killing Melissa and Donna Schnorr, a 27-year-old nurse he had attacked the year before. Brian was sentenced to two life terms. Testimony regarding these crimes, and the equally brutal rape and murder of a 10-year-old girl two years and three months before Melissa died, would bring the technology and implications of fMRI scans before a jury for the first time.

Before Brian faced a jury for the last time in his life, he had compiled a record with all of the hallmarks of the worst of the worst among criminal psychopaths. His rap sheet included signs of instrumental aggression, impulsivity, recklessness, lack of empathy, and callousness. And he had crossed the line very few psychopaths—even criminal psychopaths—cross: he became a psychopathic serial killer.

In fact, Brian's personal history includes check marks beside most of the items people associate with criminal psychopathic serial killers. Born on September 23, 1956, he may have become brain-damaged at that time, according to accounts of some family members. As an infant, he reportedly banged his head repeatedly against his crib and experienced headaches and vomiting. As he grew, he soon distinguished himself with signs of conduct disorder with callous and unemotional behavior. He fulfilled the criteria of the Homicidal Triad discussed in Chapter 7. According to FBI files obtained by the staff of the Arlington Heights, Illinois *Daily Herald*, in his youth Brian tortured animals, was a chronic bed-wetter, and set fires.[21]

His mother told the FBI that Brian had had a normal childhood spent playing baseball and reading until he began stealing at age fifteen. But Brian's siblings told a different story. While playing with matches, he and a younger brother burnt down the family's garage when Brian was eight years old. His brother Steven remembered Brian's cruelty toward pets. Brian once laughed after pouring gasoline on a cat and igniting it. According to some of her children, their mother was an alcoholic and a disciplinarian who fed hot sauce to, or whipped, Brian and his brother Steven when they behaved badly. She also made Brian sleep on dirty sheets even though he wet the bed. Once, after she found the boys playing with matches, she forced Brian and Steven to each hold a lit match until it burned their fingers. Nevertheless, Brian's siblings denied being seriously abused by their parents. His traveling salesman father was an alcoholic who died of cirrhosis of the liver when Brian was nineteen years old.

Reporters of the *Daily Herald* extracted an outline of Brian Dugan's criminal career from the files of the Illinois Department of Corrections and from court records. It does not include all of his juvenile offenses and convictions. It also leaves out the offenses he committed while he was outside his home state of Illinois,[22] but it provides more than enough information to appreciate the extreme antisocial behavior of a rare criminal psychopath like Brian:

Age 15: He was arrested for burglary.

Age 16: Brian fled Illinois after stealing $4,000 from a KFC fast food restaurant. He returned home and two months later vandalized a middle school in Aurora, Illinois. Several months later he was imprisoned for burglarizing several private schools.

Age 17: He burglarized a restaurant in Aurora. Less than a month later, he stopped and asked a 10-year-old girl named Barbara how to get to the train station. He then grabbed her and scratched her in the process. A legal technicality prevented him from being charged. Not long after, he burglarized another establishment.

Age 18: He was arrested for sniffing glue, and charged with resisting arrest and trying to kick out the window of a police car. Nearly 11 months later, he started a fire at an elementary school. The next day he threatened to kill his sister Hilary, break the lights on her car, and "chop up" her son.[23]

Age 20: Brian abducted and sexually assaulted a school teacher. She escaped and reported that he had threatened to kill her. Twelve days later, he broke into and robbed two churches.

Age 21: He burglarized a private home.

Age 22: He committed another burglary.

Age 25: He assaulted a 22-year-old clerk at a gas station. The charge was dismissed when his brother Steven, thinking Brian innocent, provided a false alibi for his brother.[24]

Age 26: He abducted, raped and bludgeoned to death 10-year-old Jeanine Nicarico. The next month he burglarized a business and assaulted a police officer, but the case was dropped.

Age 27: He claimed he assaulted, raped, and robbed a prostitute. The same year, he noticed Donna Schnorr sitting in her car waiting for a traffic light to change. He followed her, forced her off the road, and beat and raped her. He drowned her in the quarry where her body was found.

Age 28: He admitted that he tried to force a 19-year-old woman he saw walking along a highway into his car. She resisted and escaped. Twenty-two days later, he helped a 21-year-old woman start her car. He admitted that he then threatened her with a hunting knife and bound and gagged her. He drove her to a secluded spot and raped her in the back seat of the car. The woman lived. He also admitted to raping a 16-year-old girl the next day after forcing her into his car. Although threatened with a tire iron and having a belt tied around her neck, she too survived the attack. Four days later, Brian tried to abduct eight-year-old Opal Horton. During the same attack, he abducted, raped, and killed seven-year-old Melissa Ackerman.

Melissa was Brian's final victim. In 1985, when he was given two life sentences for killing her and Donna Schnorr, he also confessed to murdering Jeanine Nicarico. But he wasn't allowed to formally plead guilty to that crime until 2009. The delay between his admission of guilt and his indictment for the crime stemmed from the wrongful conviction of two others in Jeanine's murder and prosecutorial incompetence in correcting the injustice. After evidence eventually showed that those falsely accused and convicted of murdering Jeanine were in fact innocent, Brian was finally charged with her rape and murder.

That crime took place on Friday, February 25, 1983, the day Jeanine stayed home from school alone because she had the flu. Brian kicked in the door of her home with the intention of burglarizing it. Then he saw the child. The prosecutor told the jury that Jeanine struggled so hard, she left scratch marks on a wall of her home as Brian carried her out. He took her into the woods and sexually assaulted her. He told her he would wash the blood off her and drive her home. Then he crushed her skull, killing her.[25]

He pled guilty. Now he faced a trial to determine whether he would be executed or sentenced to life in prison. His lawyers hoped pictures of his fMRI brain scans would persuade the jury to spare his life.

Neurolaw

Psychopathy researcher Kent Kiehl testified for the defense at Brian's trial. He testified that Brian's psychopathy rating based on his PCL–R score was 37 out of 40.[26] That meant he had more psychopathic traits than 99.5 percent of the population. Kiehl told the jury during his more-than-four-hour testimony that Brian's psychopathic traits developed early and extended through adolescence and early adulthood, a fact borne out by the above summary of his criminal career. "In my opinion," Kiehl said, "that constitutes an emotional disturbance. I think it's a matter for the jury to determine how to interpret that data."[27] Kiehl bolstered his opinion by describing what he saw in Brian's brain scans. They indicated that he had several regions with abnormally low gray matter density, which have been associated with psychopathy in previous studies. Judge George Bakalis, however, would not allow him to show the jury Brian's fMRI brain scans with its overlaid colors showing regions of increased or decreased blood flow. The prosecutors argued the images would "confuse or mislead" the jury.[28] It is possible they suspected that such striking images of Brian's brain might be interpreted by unsophisticated jury members as more convincing proof of his abnormal mental state than the prosecuting attorney and their experts were willing to admit.

Judge Bakalis compromised. He ruled that the defense could describe the results of the brain scans but could not show them. They could only show a diagram with "X"s marking the spots where Brian's brain showed signs of abnormality.

The prosecutors countered Kiehl's opinions with the testimony of psychiatrist Jonathan Brodie. Brodie referred to the brain as a complex orchestra and said "if all we're measuring is one instrument, we're missing the sound of the entire piece."[29] The prosecutors dismissed the notion that a psychopath's impaired ability to process emotions had any legal relevance to his guilt. "His emotions have nothing to do with his choices," Illinois State's Attorney Joseph Birkett told the jury which would decide if Brian received the death penalty or an additional life sentence. "He's not forced into raping or killing or doing any of these things. He does it when he wants to. He doesn't do it when he knows he'll get caught."[30]

The jury agreed. They unanimously decided Brian should die. In 2011, however, Illinois governor Pat Quinn signed legislation abolishing the death penalty in his state. Brian's sentence was commuted to life in prison, his third. Three young, promising lives were destroyed for three life sentences that could only ever amount to one long, wasted life.

"He was cold and matter-of-fact, but never remorseful," retired Illinois state police lieutenant Ed Cisowski told the *Daily Herald*.[31] "His crimes were impulsive. He was an opportunist who was all about power and control." Officer Cisowski had interviewed Brian repeatedly and believed he would have continued killing had he not been caught. "I don't think he could stop himself," the policeman said.

That is something any good defense attorney desperate to defend the least sympathetic of defendants would latch on to. If he could not stop himself, if he was not in control, he must have diminished capacity. If he could not control himself, perhaps he should be given a break and avoid the death penalty.

Unless you have a preconceived notion about the appropriateness of neuroscience in the courtroom, your opinion might swing toward the view of the last person you hear argue the case for or against it. It makes sense that a person with brain abnormalities that prevent him from having a conscience and cause him to act impulsively without regard for future consequences should be viewed as impaired and not fully liable for his actions. After all, if a person cannot control their actions, they cannot be responsible for them. But. . . .

Then you hear that abnormal brain or not, the accused absolutely knows right from wrong, and can refrain or adjust his criminal behavior if he thinks it will likely turn out badly for him. He is "morally sane." The pro and con arguments can continue, canceling each other out in open minds considering the issue because there is no definite answer. Even psychopathy researchers are split on this issue. It depends on your opinion.

"Neuroscientists say they are capturing mental states with various types of brain-imaging techniques," Michael S. Gazzaniga, director of the Sage

Center for the Study of the Mind at the University of California in Santa Barbara told Kayt Sukel, author of a Dana Foundation briefing paper. "We say we are learning to understand the neural mechanisms of a person intending to do something. But is that really true? Can you really recreate, at one point in time, what someone's intention might have been? We can't—at least not at this time."[32] Even Robert Hare, Kent Kiehl's former mentor, questions how much brain images can reveal about the nature of psychopathy.[33]

The fact is, at this time neuroscientists understand too little about how brain structure and function regulate or influence motivation, emotion, and behavior to convincingly establish a cause-and-effect relationship between brain scans and crimes. Abnormal brain structure and activity can be correlated to criminal activity, but more basic research will be required before the correlations are widely accepted as excuses for psychopathic behavior like Brian's.

Advocates of neurolaw face a greater challenge than those who convinced the judicial system to accept the reliability and relevance of DNA evidence in criminal cases. It is relatively easy for a jury of nonscientists to imagine, if not understand the details involved in, laboratory procedures that detect the presence of molecules experts assure them are unique to an individual. All they have to do is think of DNA being like a chemical fingerprint. But some skeptics might find it harder to relate an fMRI brain scan to an intangible concept like a motivation or an intention, despite the evidence that brain abnormalities can without doubt negatively influence behavior. Often the law and juries don't accept unquestioned biological determinism unless the evidence is overwhelming. They look for responsibility, a difficult concept for science to show using brain images whose relevance is questioned by experts hired by the opposing side.

Under current law (which is likely to stay current for many years), it would be necessary to demonstrate that psychopathic criminals did not have a choice when they committed their crimes if their lawyers want to use their brain scans to keep them out of prison. This is unlikely to happen in the U.S., which tends to favor retribution for violent criminals, even in many cases for mentally ill convicts. Instead, claims of brain abnormalities are used to support requests for lighter sentences. Where, we'll see, they can be successful despite Brian's experience in court. But cortical thinning and underactive frontal lobes and amygdalae will not get anyone returned to the streets.

"As long as choice exists, difficulty in making a decision cannot be a legitimate defense for one's action," Ilana Yurkiewicz, science writer and Harvard Medical School student, wrote. "Moreover, if it were, the door would be dangerously opened for similar excuses ('living in a poor neighborhood made it harder for me to resist becoming a drug dealer,' or 'being surrounded by well-dressed friends made it harder for me to resist shoplifting'). As these excuses are not typically legitimate in court, the addition of a neural component does not make them any more legitimate."[34]

Yurkiewicz concludes that the state of a defendant's brain as indicated by a brain-scan image may not provide a sound defense for someone charged with a crime. The state of a person's brain, in her view, may reflect aggression, but "it does not pull puppet strings on the action." Behavior, she notes, results from a complex interaction of many factors involving variable brain states. Together, these states result in decisions and actions. According to this view, a desire or propensity to harm others can be balanced, even in a criminal psychopath, by a brain state that places self-preservation—not getting caught—above the risky thrill of satisfying an obscene desire. The act of violence, if you agree with this interpretation, is not the result of a brain dictating a violent act: it is the result of a decision that has been influenced by aggressive tendencies, but tendencies that are not commands.

"I think we have to remember that the neuroscience research is a really important level of analysis," psychologist Scott Lilienfeld said during a discussion of neuroscience's place in psychopathy research at the 2013 Meeting of the Society for the Scientific Study of Psychopathy.[35] Then he reminded his colleagues that it is not the only level of research. There are psychological, social, and neurological levels of research. "We know we have different levels of analysis, but we don't know how to bridge them."

fMRI brain scans, Yurkiewicz concludes, "can only tell us about proclivity, not about guilt or accountability. The use of neuroimaging in court should operate within the same legal guidelines that we currently use to define guilt. One is accountable for his criminal behavior so long as he possesses basic rational abilities, is not forced to commit the action, and is not acting under duress. The defense 'I did not do it; my brain did' is valid only if a brain scan unambiguously illustrates one of the above mitigating situations. Neuroimaging may indeed prove valuable in that it offers advanced explanation for criminal propensity. What it does not offer is justification for subsequent criminal action."[36]

Motivation, understanding, intent, responsibility, and reasons related to criminal behavior are sometimes referred to as "folk psychological" concepts. "The neuroscience won't supplant any of those folk psychological concepts. It's more likely that the neuroscience will eventually assist doctors and lawyers in determining how to apply these folk psychological concepts to a person by supplying evidence about their cognitive abilities and motivation states," the director of the Center for Neuroscience and Society at the University of Pennsylvania, Martha Farah told Kayt Sukel.[37]

Although it is unlikely for the foreseeable future that the American legal system will ever excuse rape and murder based on evidence backed up with brain scans, it has already begun adjusting itself to their introduction into the courtroom. "I have had half a dozen prominent attorneys call me and say they want to do functional imaging of their client, who is a psychopath, to try to show that his brain looks different, because prosecutors will likely take the death penalty off the table," Kent Kiehl told Michael Haederle in a 2010 story for *Miller-McCune* magazine.[38] It didn't work for Brian, but it is now common for defense attorneys to submit brain scans when they appeal death sentences.[39] An experiment conducted by researchers at the University of Utah illustrates why this may be an effective legal strategy when defending a psychopath.

You Are the Judge

Before you stands Jonathan Donahue, convicted of pistol-whipping a restaurant worker, resulting in serious injury. Although Jonathan is a hypothetical convict created for the experiment, he is based on a real person. His file indicates that he has been diagnosed by a qualified psychologist as a violent psychopath who lacks empathy. Knowing this much about him, for how many years will you send him to prison? When scores of state judges from across the U.S. answered this question, they sentenced Jonathan on average to 14 years behind bars.

Now consider a slightly different version of the same case. It differs only by having the testimony of one additional witness slipped into the record.

This version of the convict's file includes testimony by a neuroscientist who is a recognized authority on psychopathy. This expert told the court that Jonathan inherited a gene that caused his brain to develop abnormally. This developmental condition impaired his ability to process emotional information. Now, how many years would you give him? If you were like the second group of judges included in the experiment, you would give him on average one year less behind bars, a sentence of around 13 years. Most of the judges who took part in the experiment—nearly 87 percent—listed *aggravating* factors among their justifications for their sentencing decisions. But when the biologically based information was included in the convict's file, the percentage of judges who listed *mitigating* factors increased from 39 percent to 48 percent.[40]

The judges told the researchers that if Jonathan had not been labeled a psychopath, he would receive on average a sentence of nine years. Labeled a psychopath, he would on average get 15 years. "But then those who read about the biological mechanism subtracted a year, as if to say, 'This guy is really dangerous and scary, and we should treat him as such, but the biological evidence suggests that we can't hold him as responsible for the behavior,'" a co-author of the study, Associate Professor of Philosophy James Tabery, Ph.D., told the *New York Times*.[41]

We can say with near certainty that, compared to non-psychopaths, people with high psychopathy ratings show different patterns of activity in parts of their brains intimately involved in processing emotions and making and evaluating moral decisions. They have altered connections affecting these limbic systems and associated brain regions. We know that certain genes are associated with violent tendencies and that the development of psychopathy is influenced by genetics. What we have learned so far from brain-imaging studies is that the neurobiological profile of the criminal psychopath is consistent with key features of psychopathy: a lack of moral sense and a lack of empathy.

But science cannot unequivocally answer questions concerning the neurobiological basis of criminal responsibility. That remains a matter of opinion, not scientific fact. Science can only influence how questions of guilt are dealt with by our legal system.

No matter how much you or the judges were influenced by the testimony about Jonathan's hypothetical brain, one thing is certain: we will see more genetic, fMRI, and other neurobiological evidence presented as testimony in real cases despite lingering doubts over their "not ready for prime courtroom time" status. And it is the scientists who are producing this evidence who have the responsibility of educating the public, including judges and prospective jurors, about insights provided by, and limitations of, the results of their research. Neuroscientists together with jurists will have to get the timing right for introducing and accepting neurobiological evidence in the courtroom. The still-unresolved and complex relationships between brain abnormalities and legal responsibility are outside the realms of either profession alone. This is the time to watch Neurolaw move into its adolescence as the science progresses and judges and lawyers consider its practical, legal implications and usefulness. Rushing scientific results into court can be as ill-advised as rushing new treatments into medical practice. Remember the 1949 Nobel Prize winner who gave us the frontal lobotomy.

Epilogue

A Little "Big Science"

Although learning more about what is going on in the brains of criminal psychopaths would satisfy our curiosity and increase our ability to effectively deal in the courtroom, forensic hospital, and clinic with the problems they present, this type of research faces several challenges.

The field is small and underfunded. Not every lab can afford a $2 million mobile fMRI scanner. The National Institutes of Health allocated less than $2.9 million for seven grants identified with the key word "psychopath" during the fiscal year 2013. Although there are approximately as many psychopaths as there are people living with schizophrenia, the NIH allocated $270 million for schizophrenia research in 2013.[1] Schizophrenia is a devastating disease that deserves that funding and more. It is difficult, however, to justify spending more than 93 times more money on that mental illness compared to psychopathy since an estimated 15 to 25 percent of male offenders are psychopaths. The benefits for society of finding effective treatments for these individuals, as Kent Kiehl points out, could reduce the financial cost of crime by perhaps billions of dollars in direct and indirect costs. The potential psychological benefits for potential victims cannot be measured in dollars.

Since brain scans are expensive and subjects can be hard to find, researchers are sometimes forced to use subjects with psychopathy scores that are scattered across a range. Results from these subjects can be identified and analyzed separately, but it isn't an ideal way to draw conclusions about psychopaths in general if there really is a distinct separation between high-scoring and midrange psychopaths, as the results of Hiatt, Schmitt, and Newman suggest. Calling everyone in such a study "a psychopath" may be misleading. The field could also benefit from better characterization of psychopath subtypes among the subjects who agree to be studied. A significant proportion of the research in the field has been limited due to small sample sizes.

In the past, some researchers in many fields of study often behaved a little like cats; they got together when it was to their immediate, mutual benefit, but often they preferred to work alone and they sometimes clashed over territory. Scientists interested in learning more about psychopathy would benefit from a coordinated effort to agree on technical standards for assessing brain function using fMRI and other imaging technology. Establishing shared databases and brain banks of well-characterized subjects could have significant benefits. Psychology Professor Craig Neuman, Ph.D., of the University of North Texas, points out in his article "Will the Real Psychopath Please Stand Up" that the Dutch government is systematically funding research on psychopathy.[2] Such a program in the U.S. would have the potential to provide benefits that granting agencies are not yet aware of.

Kiehl is tackling the problem by compiling a database that will contain information about thousands of psychopaths including brain scans, genetic data, and case histories.[3] Coordinating and expanding this resource to accommodate and include researchers around the world may bring us much closer to answering more questions about the nature of morality than we now know to ask.

Researchers frequently collaborate on individual projects with the intention of publishing a research paper or two. Biological investigations of the psychopathic brain, like other areas of neuroscience, could benefit from adoption of a little "big science" attitude, in the sense of greater coordination and collaboration between labs around the world working to learn about the biological correlates of psychopathy.

Unfortunately, this sub-discipline of neuroscience is too small to match the emerging "big science" movements that promise to give the overall field of neuroscience a boost. Many neuroscientists have already embraced the goals of these new inter-disciplinary, multi-lab research initiatives begun in 2013, and trickle-down benefits for psychopathy researchers should follow. These initiatives include BRAIN, the U.S.-based Brain Research through Advancing Innovative Neurotechnologies program, and the Human Brain Project sponsored by the European Commission.[4] Our lack of basic information about the structure and function of the brain makes such programs crucial for future progress in neuroscience. And if the billions of dollars intended for these programs are actually allocated in the next decade, the insights gained by mapping and developing theories to explain the organization and function of the brain will pay off for all sub-disciplines of neuroscience including psychopathy research. Other game-changing programs include the Human Connectome Project (the source of Figure 6), which is making brain scans of over a thousand healthy volunteers available to research scientists, and the Psychiatric Genomics Consortium, which is doing the same with more than 100,000 of samples of genetic material obtained from patients with mental illnesses.

BRAIN started with a $100 million investment, and the Human Brain Project started with a $69 million investment. This good news comes after less-good news: the recent decline in scientific research and development funding in North America. Canadian R&D declined by more than 3 percent between 2012 and 2013, while U.S. R&D dropped by 5 percent. Over the same period, Germany, Japan, and South Korea increased funding by 5 percent, while China increased it by 15 percent.[5] It would be unfortunate for psychopathy research to remain underfunded, since it addresses one of the most important aspects of human behavior: the presence and absence of empathy, conscience, and compassion.

"The definition of psychopathy itself—what it is, what it is not—is one of the most fundamental questions for psychological science," Jennifer Skeem and her colleagues declared in 2011.[6] Continuing to uncover what happens in the brains of people with varying degrees of psychopathic traits is one way to refine this most fundamental question about human nature.

Further Reading

Columbine, by Dave Cullen (2009, Twelve, Hachette Book Group, New York). The definitive account of a school shooting and the shooters.

The Mask of Sanity: An Attempt to Clarify Some Issues About the So Called Psychopathic Personality, 5th edition, by Hervey M. Cleckley (1988, Emily S. Cleckley).

The Science of Evil: On Empathy and the Origins of Cruelty, by Simon Baron-Cohen (2011, Basic Books). The author, an expert on autism, bases his book on his research in this field. Besides autism, he discusses lack of empathy in persons with borderline personality disorder, narcissism, psychosis, and Asperger's syndrome. He devotes 30 out of 256 pages to psychopaths.

The Anatomy of Violence, the Biological Roots of Crime, by Adrian Raine (2013, Pantheon Books). A wide ranging account of biological influences on crime, with particular emphasis on the author's research and his quest to convince social scientists that biology, not just social influences, plays a key role in criminal behavior.

The Anatomy of Evil, by Michael H. Stone, M.D. (2009, Prometheus Books). The author has researched over 800 true crime accounts of murderers and other violent criminals and placed them into 22 categories based on their motivation and personality traits.

Evil Genes: Why Rome Fell, Hitler Rose, Enron Failed, and My Sister Stole My Mother's Boyfriend, by Barbara Oakley and David Sloan Wilson (2008, Prometheus Books). The author uses genetic and neurological evidence in an attempt to explain the sinister actions of her sister and those of historic figures including Adolf Hitler, Mao Zedong and Slobodan Milosevic. She concludes that borderline, antisocial and narcissistic personality disorders account for the sinister behaviors she describes.

The Psychopath: Emotion and the Brain, by James Blair, Derek Mitchell, and Karina Blair (2005, Blackwell). A more academic discussion of the authors' theories of psychopathy.

Without Conscience: The Disturbing World of the Psychopaths Among Us, by Robert D. Hare (1999, The Guilford Press). An excellent description of psychopaths and advice for dealing with them by one of the author's sources.

Snakes in Suits: When Psychopaths Go to Work, by Paul Babiak and Robert D. Hare (2006, HarperBusiness). This book concentrates on spotting and dealing with "successful" psychopaths and the damage they do in the workplace.

The Sociopath Next Door, by Martha Stout (2006, Three Rivers Press). A popular guide to psychopaths and advice for dealing with close encounters.

Dangerous Instincts: How Gut Feelings Betray Us, by Mary Ellen O'Toole, Ph.D. and Alisa Bowman (2011, Hudson Street Press). A source of useful advice for avoiding contact with exploitative and threatening individuals in day-to-day life.

Endnotes

Preface

1. Society for the Scientific Study of Psychopathy. 2013. Psychopathy: A Misunderstood Condition. http://www.psychopathysociety.org/en/. Accessed 10/25/2013.
2. Skeem, J. L., et al. 2011. Psychopathic Personality: Bridging the Gap Between Scientific Evidence and Public Policy. *Psychological Science in the Public Interest*: 12(3): 95–162.

Introduction

1. Lilienfeld, S. and Arkowitz, H. 2007. What "Psychopath" Means. *Scientific American Mind*, November 28.
2. Kiehl, K. A. and Hoffman, M. A. 2011. The Criminal Psychopath: History, Neuroscience, Treatment, and Economics. *Jurimetrics: The Journal of Law, Science & Technology*: 51(4): 355–397.
3. Skeem, J. L., et al. 2011. Psychopathic Personality: Bridging the Gap Between Scientific Evidence and Public Policy. *Psychological Science in the Public Interest*: 12(3): 95–162.
4. Sukel, K. 2013. Neuropsychiatric Disorders Share Some Genetic Risk Factors. The Dana Foundation. April 08. http://dana.org/news/features/detail.aspx?id=41810 (accessed April 11, 2013).
5. In the past decade, close to 3,650 papers concerning psychopathy were published according to the U.S. National Library of Medicine. In just the first six months of 2013, nearly 200 papers discussing psychopathy were published. 10% of them concerned brain studies.
6. Gopnik, A. 2013. How the brain really works. *The Wall Street Journal*. May 3.

Chapter One: Who Would Do Something Like This?

1. Baumann, N. 2011. Exclusive: Loughner Friend Explains Alleged Gunman's Grudge Against Giffords. *Mother Jones*. January 10. http://m.motherjones.com/politics/2011/01/jared-lee-loughner-friend-voicemail-phone-message. Accessed 5/16/2013. Tierney told CBS News the message Jared left was: "Hey, this is Jared. Um, we had some good times together. Uh, see you later."
2. Unless indicated otherwise, the sequence of events and details in this account of Loughner's actions are provided by The CNN library, Fast facts: 2011 Tucson shooting. August 7th, 2012. http://news.blogs.cnn.com/2012/08/07/fast-facts-2011-tuscon-shooting/. Accessed 3/7/2013; Bauman, Ibid.; CBS News; The NY Times, the Tucson Sentinel, and Transcripts of Interviews conducted by the Pima County, Arizona, Sheriff's Department.
3. Martinez, M. and Carter, C. J. 2013. New Details: Loughner's Parents Took Gun, Disabled Car to Keep Him Home. CNN. March 28. http://www.cnn.com/2013/03/27/justice/arizona-loughner-details. Accessed 4/3/2013.
4. Sheriff's Department of Pima County, Arizona. 2011. Statement of Stanley B. Simmons-Case 110108078. January 8,
5. Martinez, M. and Carter, C. J. Ibid.
6. Sheriff's Department of Pima County, Arizona. 2011. Statements of Randy Loughner and Amy Loughner. January 8.
7. Gassen, S. G. and Williams, T. 2013. Before Attack, Parents of Gunman Tried to Address Son's Strange Behavior. *The New York Times*. March 27.
8. Baumann. Ibid.
9. CBS News. 2013. Jared Lee Loughner grew delusional in months before Tucson rampage, police reports show. March 27, http://www.cbsnews.com/8301-201_162-57576492/jared-lee-loughner-grew-delusional-in-months-before-tucson-rampage-police-reports-show. Accessed 5/12/2013
10. Ibid.
11. Gassen, S. G. and Williams, T. Op. cit.
12. CBS News with Scott Pelley. 2013. Newly released Jared Lee Loughner files reveal chilling details. March 27. http://www.cbsnews.com/8301-18563_162-57576686/newly-released-jared-lee-loughner-files-reveal-chilling-details/. Accessed 4/3/2013.
13. Ibid.
14. Turgal, J. 2012. Jared Lee Loughner Sentenced in Arizona on Federal Charges in Tucson Shooting. The Federal Bureau of Investigation Press Release. November 08.
15. Smith, D. 2013. 'So much screaming'—Jan. 8 shooting records released. Tucson Sentinel.com. March 27. http://www.tucsonsentinel.com/local/report/032713_jan8_records/so-much-screaming-jan-8-shooting-records-released/. Accessed 4/13/2013.
16. Cullen, D. 2009. *Columbine*. Twelve, Hachette Book Group, New York. p. 63.
17. This account of the Columbine massacre is based on two sources: (1) Cullen,

Ibid. and (2) Sheriff of Jefferson County, Colorado. 2000. *The Columbine High School Shootings*, a chronological timeline of the events prepared by the Sheriff, presented by CNN.http://www.cnn.com/SPECIALS/2000/columbine.cd/Pages/NARRATIVE.Time.Line.htm

18. Sheriff, Jefferson County, Colorado. Ibid.
19. Ibid.
20. Cullen. Op. cit., p. 42.
21. U.S. Fire Administration/Technical Report Series. USFA-TR-128/April, 1999. *Special Report: Wanton Violence at Columbine High School*. p. 7.
22. Ibid.
23. Cullen. Op. cit., p. 45.
24. Ibid., p. 34.
25. Sheriff, Jefferson County, Colorado. Op. cit.
26. Ibid.
27. Cullen. Op. cit., p. 47.
28. Sheriff, Jefferson County, Colorado. Op. cit.
29. Ibid.
30. Kiehl, K. A. and Buckholtz, J. W. 2010. Inside the Mind of a Psychopath. *Scientific American Mind*. September/October. p. 22.
31. CBS News. 2013. Jared Lee Loughner grew delusional in months before Tucson rampage, police reports show. March 27. http://www.cbsnews.com/8301-201_162-57576492/jared-lee-loughner-grew-delusional-in-months-before-tucson-rampage-police-reports-show/. Accessed 5/12/2013.
32. Fast facts. Op. cit.
33. Yoon, J. H., et al. 2013. Impaired Prefrontal-Basal Ganglia Functional Connectivity and Substantia Nigra Hyperactivity in Schizophrenia. *Biological Psychiatry*. Published online 7 January. doi:10.1016/j.biopsych.2012.11.018
34. National Institute of Mental Health. 2013. Mapping Brain Circuits Provides Clues to Schizophrenia, Earlier Detection of Psychosis. *Science News*. February 26.
35. Harrison, P. J. 1998. The Neuropathology of Schizophrenia, A Critical Review of the Data and their Interpretation. *Brain*: 122(4): 593–624.
36. Torrey, E. 2011. *Schizophrenia as a Brain Disease: Studies of Individuals Who Have Never Been Treated—Backgrounder*. The Treatment Advocacy Center. http://www.treatmentadvocacycenter.org/resources/briefing-papers-and-fact-sheets/159/466. Accessed 7/3/2011.
37. Ibid.
38. Fast facts. Op. cit.
39. NPR. 2007. Can Science Help Predict Violent Behavior? *Talk of the Nation: Science Friday*. Transcript. April 20. http://m.npr.org/story/9716365 Accessed 5/2/2013.
40. Raine, A. 2013. *The Anatomy of Violence, the Biological Roots of Crime*. Pantheon, New York. p. 233.

41. Friedman, R. A. 2006. Violence and Mental Illness—How Strong is the Link? *New England Journal of Medicine*: 355(20): 2064–2066.
42. Fazel, S., et al. 2009. Schizophrenia and Violence: Systematic Review and Meta-Analysis. *PLOS Medicine*: 6(8): e1000120. doi:10.1371/journal.pmed.1000120.
43. Cloud, J. 2011. The Troubled Life of Jared Loughner. *Time*. January 15.
44. Hemphill, J. F., et al. 1994. Psychopathy and Substance Use. *Journal of Personality Disorders*: 8(3): 169–180.
45. Federal Bureau of Investigation, FBI Records: The Vault. Columbine High School Part 1 of 4. p. 38.
46. Ibid., p. 40 and Achenbach, J. and Russakoff, D. 1999. Teen Shooter's Life Paints Antisocial Portrait. *The Washington Post*. April 29. p. A1.
47. Frank Ochberg, M.D. Phone interview, May 30, 2013
48. Stenson, J. 2009. Destined as a psychopath? Experts seek clues. NBC news. April 20. http://www.nbcnews.com/id/30267075/from/ET/print/1/displaymode/1098/. Accessed 5/31/2013.
49. Cullen, D. 2004. The Depressive and the Psychopath, At Last We Know Why the Columbine Killers Did It. *Slate*. April 20.
50. Ibid.
51. Pendergast, A. 2001. "I'm Full of Hate and I Love It." Denver Westward News. December 6.
52. Ibid.
53. Interview of Mary Ellen O'Toole, PhD, June 7, 2013. Washington, D.C.
54. O'Toole and Robert Hare, both of whom attended the meeting, don't remember this exchange but acknowledged there were several meetings held to discuss the event surrounding the Columbine shootings.
55. Cullen. 2009. Op. cit., p. 247.
56. Ochberg, F. 2011. *What is a Psychopath?* Gift From Within-PTSD Resources for Survivors & Caregivers. Produced by Joyce Boaz.
57. Cullen, D. 2010. The Last Columbine Mystery. *The Daily Beast*. February 24.
58. Hare, R. D. 1993. *Without Conscience, The Disturbing World of the Psychopaths Among Us*. The Guilford Press, New York.
59. Hart, S. D., and Hare R. D. 1997. Psychopathy: Assessment and Association with Criminal Conduct. *in* Stoff DM, Breiling J. (editors). *Handbook of Antisocial Behaviour*. New York, John Wiley & Sons, Inc.

Chapter Two: *Kunlangeta*, Psychopaths, and Sociopaths: Does the Label Matter?

1. Skeem, J. L., et al. 2011. Psychopathic Personality: Bridging the Gap Between Scientific Evidence and Public Policy. *Psychological Science in the Public Interest*: 12(3): 95–162
2. Arctic people living in Canada and Greenland are referred to as Inuit. The term Eskimo is still used in Alaska, according to the Smithsonian's National Museum of Natural History.

3. Murphy, J. M. 1976. Psychiatric Labeling in Cross–Cultural Perspective. *Science*: 191:1019–1028. Since the current estimate is that approximately 1% of the population in North America are psychopaths, it is possible that the Yup'ik had a lower incidence of disorder, that they used different criteria to identify it or that the sample population was not representative.
4. Lee, N. 1993. Differential Deviance and Social Control Mechanisms Among Two Groups of Yup'ik Eskimo. *American Indian and Alaska Native Mental Health Research*. 5(2): 57–72.
5. Paukatuutit Inuit Women of Canada. 2006. *The Inuit Way, A Guide to Inuit Culture*. Canada: Paukatuutlit Inuit Women of Canada.
6. Murphy. Op. cit.
7. Ibid.
8. Tremblay, M–A. 2006. Alexander H. Leighton's and Jane Murphy's Scientific Contributions in Psychiatric Epidemiology: A Personal Appreciation. *Transcultural Psychiatry*: 43(1): 7–20.
9. Murphy. Op. cit.
10. Ibid.
11. Pollack, A. 1998. Scientists Seek a New Movie Role: Hero, Not Villain. *The New York Times*. December 01.
12. Keyes, R. 2006. *The Quote Verifier: Who Said What, Where, and When*. St. Martin's Press, New York.
13. National Institute of Mental Health. The Numbers Count: Mental Disorders in America. http://www.nimh.nih.gov/health/publications/the-numbers-count-mental-disorders-in-america/index.shtml#Schizophrenia. Accessed 3/4/2013.
14. Kiehl, K. and Hoffman, M. 2011. The Criminal Psychopath: History, Neuroscience, Treatment, and Economics in Jurimetrics. *The Journal of Law, Science & Technology*. 51(4): 355–397.
15. Hare, R. D. 1993. *Without Conscience, The Disturbing World of the Psychopaths Among Us*. The Guilford Press, New York. p. 74.
16. Kiehl, K. A. and Buckholtz, J. W. 2010. Inside the Mind of a Psychopath. *Scientific American Mind*. September/October. p. 24.
17. McEvoy, J. P. 2007. The Costs of Schizophrenia. *Journal of Clinical Psychiatry*. 68: Suppl 14: 4–7.
18. Prentky, R. A. and Knight, R. A. 1991. Identifying critical dimensions for discriminating among rapists. *Journal of Consulting and Clinical Psychology*: 59(5): 643–661.
19. Spiegel, A. 2011. *Can A Test Really Tell Who's A Psychopath?* NPR broadcast, May 26.
20. Kent Kiehl and Morris Hoffman also refer to the PCL–R as the "Gold Standard" in their 2011 article The Criminal Psychopath: History, Neuroscience, Treatment, and Economics. Ibid. It was described in the same way on a grant application prepared in Adrian Raine's lab according to the discussion of *Controversial Issues in Psychopathy Research*, he led at the 5th

Biannual Meeting of the Society for the Scientific Study of Psychopathy on June 6, 2013. Also, see S. K. Acheson's chapter "Review of the *Hare Psychopathy Checklist-Revised*, 2nd ed." in *The Sixteenth Mental Measurements Yearbook*, 2005, edited by R. A. Spies and B. S. Plake, Buros Institute of Mental Measurements, Lincoln, NE.

21. Skeem, J. L., et al. 2011. Op. cit.
22. Kosson, D. S. and Hare, R. D. 2011. *A Primer On Psychopathy*. Aftermath: Surviving Psychopathy Foundation. http://aftermath-surviving-psychopathy.org/index.php/2011/02/24/a-primer-on-psychopathy/. Accessed 3/12/2012.
23. Kiehl, K. A. and Hoffman, M. A. 2011. The Criminal Psychopath: History, Neuroscience, Treatment, and Economics. *Jurimetrics: The Journal of Law, Science & Technology*: 51(4): 355–397.
24. Spiegel. Op. cit.
25. Interview with Robert Hare. June 7, 2013, Washington, D.C.
26. Robert Hare email correspondence. July 6, 2013.
27. Hare, R. 2013. Foreword *in* Kiehl, K. A. and Sinnott-Armstrong, W. P. (editors) *Handbook on Psychopathy and Law*. New York: Oxford University Press. p. vii.
28. Porter, S., et al. 2009. Crime profiles and conditional release performance of psychopathic and non-psychopathic sexual offenders. *Legal and Criminological Psychology*: 14(1): 109–118.
29. Porter, S. Email correspondence. July 25, 2013.
30. Ibid.
31. Hart, S. D., et al. 1995. *The Hare Psychopathy Checklist: Screening Version (PCL: SV)*. Toronto, Canada: Multi-Health Systems, North Tonawanda, New York.
32. Using the lower cutoff score is common in Europe, "but it's actually not very wise," the developer of the PCL Robert Hare said. Using a score of 25 as a threshold cutoff is okay for some research purposes, "but it runs the danger of including people who have an awful lot of antisocial characteristics and behaviors, but who don't have the core features of psychopathy." Interview with Robert Hare. June 7, 2013, Washington, D.C.
33. Kosson, D. S. and Hare, R. D. Op. cit.
34. Hare, R. D. 2003. *Hare Psychopathy Checklist-Revised*. Toronto, Canada: Multi-Health Systems.
35. Williamson, S., et al. 1991. Abnormal processing of affective words by psychopaths. *Psychophysiology*. 28(3): 260–273.
36. Ibid.
37. Vronsky, P. 2004. *Serial Killers, The Method and Madness of Monsters*. New York: Berkley Books. pp. 249–258.
38. See Hare, R. D. 1993. p. 30.
39. Ramsland, K. 2003. *Dr. Robert Hare: Expert on the Psychopath*. Crime Library, Criminal Minds & Methods. http://www.trutv.com/library/crime/index.html. Accessed
40. Cleckley, H. 1988. *The Mask of Sanity: An Attempt to Clarify Some Issues About*

the So Called Psychopathic Personality, 5th edition, Augusta, Georgia: Emily S. Cleckley.

41. Book Notices. 1941. The Mask of Sanity: An Attempt to Reinterpret the So–Called Psychopathic Personality. *The Journal of the American Medical Association*. 17(6): 493.
42. Sprague, G. S. 1941. The Psychopathology of Psychopathic Personalities. *Bulletin of the New York Academy of Medicine*: 17(12): 911–921.
43. Augstein, H. S. 1996. J. C. Prichard's Concept of Moral Insanity—A Medical Theory of the Corruption of Human Nature. *Medical History*: 40(3): 311–343.
44. Lombroso-Ferrero, G. 1911. *Criminal Man According to the Classification of Cesare Lombroso*. New York: G. P. Putnam's Sons. p. 52.
45. Mason, T. 2006. An Archaeology of the Psychopath, The Medicalization of Evil *in* Mason, T. (editor). *Forensic Psychiatry, Influences of Evil*. Totowa, N.J.: Humana Press
46. Screening (1995) and Youth (2003) versions of the Psychopathy Checklist were also developed by Richard Rogers, et al. and by Hare and his colleagues, respectively.
47. Cooke, D. J. 2004. Reconstructing psychopathy: clarifying the significance of antisocial and socially deviant behavior in the diagnosis of psychopathic personality disorder. *Journal of Personality Disorders*: 18(4): 337–57.
48. Hare, R. D. and Kosson, D. S. Op. cit.
49. Raine, A. 2013. Jevon Scott Newman Award-Inaugural Paper: *Controversial Issues in Psychopathy Research*. 5th Biannual Meeting of the Society for the Scientific Study of Psychopathy. June 6.
50. Skeem, J. L., et al. 2011. Op. cit.
51. Benson, E. 2003. Intelligent Intelligence Testing. *Monitor on Psychology*: 34 (2): 48.
52. Ibid.
53. Patrick, C. J., et al. 2009. Triarchic conceptualization of psychopathy: Developmental origins of disinhibition, boldness, and meanness. *Development and Psychopathology*: 21(3): 913–938.
54. Patrick, C. 2013. R. D. Hare Lifetime Achievement Award acceptance speech. 5th Biannual Meeting of the Society for the Scientific Study of Psychopathy. June 6.
55. Cleckley, H. Op. cit., p. 80.
56. Skeem, J. L., and Cooke, D. J. 2010. Is Criminal Behavior a Central Component of Psychopathy? *Psychological Assessment*. 22(2): 433–445.
57. Carey, B. 2010. Academic Battle Delays Publication by 3 Years. *The New York Times*. June 11.
58. Dr. Skeem responded to one email on July 24, 2013 and forwarded one of her publications. She did not respond to two later emails on August 23 and 28, 2013 requesting an interview.
59. Durant, W. 1967. *The Story of Philosophy*. New York: Simon and Schuster. p. 48.

60. Cosgrove, L., et al. 2006. Financial ties between DSM-IV panel members and the pharmaceutical industry. *Psychotherapy and Psychosomatics*. 75(3): 154–60.
61. McCambridge, R. 2013. Another Wrench in the Mental Health System: DSM-5 Rejected by NIMH. *NPQ Nonprofit Quarterly*. July 7. http://www.nonprofitquarterly.org/policysocial-context/22271-another-wrench-in-the-mental-health-system-dsm-5-rejected-by-nimh.html. Accessed 7/7/2013.
62. Insel, T. 2012. Director's Blog: Transforming Diagnosis. National Institute of Mental Health. April 29, 2013. http://www.nimh.nih.gov/about/director/2013/transforming-diagnosis.shtml. Accessed. Accessed 6/4/2013.
63. Department of Justice, Office of Justice Programs. 2013. U.S. Prison Population Decline for Third Consecutive Year during 2012. http://www.ojp.usdoj.gov/newsroom/pressreleases/2013/ojppr072513.pdf. Accessed 7/28/2013.
64. Hare, R. D. and Neumann, C. S. 2006. The PCL–R Assessment of Psychopathy in *Handbook of Psychopathy*, Patrick, C. J. (editor), The Guilford Press, New York.
65. Kiehl and Hoffman. 2011. Op. cit.
66. American Psychiatric Association. 2013. *Diagnostic and Statistical Manual of Mental Disorders, Fifth Edition, DSM–5*. American Psychiatric Publishing. Washington DC.
67. Hare, R. D. 1996. Psychopathy and Antisocial Personality Disorder: A Case of Diagnostic Confusion. *Psychiatric Times*. February 01.
68. For references see Gregory, S., et al. 2012. The Antisocial Brain: Psychopathy Matters, A Structural MRI Investigation of Antisocial Male Violent Offenders. *Archives of General Psychiatry*: 69(9): 962–972.
69. Coid, J. W., et al. 2013. Gang Membership, Violence, and Psychiatric Morbidity. *The American Journal of Psychiatry*. Published online. 10.1176/appi.ajp.2013.12091188
70. Feix, J. 2006. The Handbook of Psychopathy (review). *Journal of the American Academy of Psychiatry and the Law*. 34(3): 428–430.
71. Pound, E. 1950. *The Letters of Ezra Pound, 1907–1941*. Harcourt, Brace & World, New York. p. 338.

Chapter Three: What Does Brain Imaging See?

1. Kiehl, K. A. and Buckholtz, J. W. 2010. Inside the Mind of a Psychopath. *Scientific American Mind*. 21: 22–29. September 1. Buckholtz's co-author, Kent Kiehl, attributed this account to Buckholtz. Phone interview May 21, 2013.
2. Ibid.
3. Hare, R. D. 1993. *Without Conscience, The Disturbing World of the Psychopaths Among Us*. The Guilford Press, New York. p. 125.
4. Ibid., p. 40.
5. Abbott, A. 2007. Abnormal neuroscience: Scanning psychopaths. *Nature*: 450(7172): 942–944.
6. Abbott, A. 2001. Into the mind of a killer. *Nature*: 410(6826): 296–298.

7. Abbott, 2007. Op. cit.
8. Gregory, S., et al. 2012. The Antisocial Brain: Psychopathy Matters, A Structural MRI Investigation of Antisocial Male Violent Offenders. *Archives of General Psychiatry*: 69(9): 962–972.
9. Raine, A., et al. 2000. Reduced prefrontal gray matter volume and reduced autonomic activity in antisocial personality disorder. *Archives of General Psychiatry*. 57(2): 119–127.
10. Gregory, S., et al. Op. cit.
11. Ly, M., et al. 2012. Cortical thinning in psychopathy. *American Journal of Psychiatry*. 69(7): 743–749.
12. Blair, R. J. R. 2012. Cortical Thinning and Functional Connectivity in Psychopathy. 69(7): 684–687.
13. Azevedo, F. A., et al. 2009. Equal numbers of neuronal and nonneuronal cells make the human brain an isometrically scaled-up primate brain. *Journal of Comparative Neurology*. 513(5): 532–541.
14. Field, R. D. 2011. *The Other Brain: From Dementia to Schizophrenia, How New Discoveries About the Brain are Revolutionizing Medicine and Science*. New York: Simon and Schuster.
15. Schneider, F., et al. 2000. Functional Imaging of Conditioned Aversive Emotional Responses in Antisocial Personality Disorder. *Neuropsychobiology*. 42(4): 192–20.
16. University of Oxford. 2013. A Spin Around the Brain. *Oxford Sparks*. http://www.oxfordsparks.net/about#sthash.HTLnYSrg.dpuf. Accessed 9/18/2013.
17. James Fallon email correspondence. 11/2/2013.
18. Logothetis, N. K., et al. 2001. Neurophysiological investigation of the basis of the fMRI signal. *Nature*. 412(6843): 150–157.
19. Viswanathan, A. and Freeman, R. D. 2007. Neurometabolic coupling in cerebral cortex reflects synaptic more than spiking activity. *Nature Neuroscience*. 10(10): 1308–1312.
20. Harenski, C. L., et al. 2010. Aberrant neural processing of moral violations in criminal psychopaths. *Journal of Abnormal Psychology*. 119(4): 863–874.
21. Dolan, M. C. and Fullam, R. S. 2009. Psychopathy and functional magnetic resonance imaging blood oxygenation level-dependent responses to emotional faces in violent patients with schizophrenia. *Biological Psychiatry*. 66(6): 570–577.
22. Bennett, Craig M., et al. 2009. Neural correlates of interspecies perspective taking in the post-mortem Atlantic salmon: An argument for multiple comparisons correction. Abstract. http://prefrontal.org/files/posters/Bennett-Salmon-2009.pdf. Accessed November 12, 2012.
23. Cleese, J. and Chapman, G. 1969. Dead Parrot Sketch performed on *Monty Python's Flying Circus*. Episode 8. Internet Archive Wayback Machine transcript http://web.archive.org/web/20121012135336/http://www.mtholyoke.edu/~ebarnes/python/dead-parrot.htm. Accessed 9/3/2013.
24. Craig Bennett phone interview Wednesday, September 11, 2013. Email correspondence September 13, 2013.

25. Kiehl, K. and Hoffman, M. 2011. The Criminal Psychopath: History, Neuroscience, Treatment, and Economics in Jurimetrics. *The Journal of Law, Science & Technology*. 51(4): 355–397.
26. National Coalition Against Domestic Violence. 2007. Domestic Violence Facts. July.
27. Huss, M. T. and Langhinrichsen-Rohlinga, J. 2000. Identification of the psychopathic batterer: The clinical, legal, and policy implications. *Aggression and Violent Behavior*. 5(4): 403–422.

Chapter Four: A Problem Just Behind the Forehead

1. The information about Fallon in this chapter in based on his public talks and a September 30, 2013 phone interview.
2. Hagerty, B. B. 2010. A Neuroscientist Uncovers A Dark Secret. NPR. http://www.npr.org/templates/story/story.php?storyId=127888976. Accessed 9/10/2012.
3. Naik, G. 2009. What's on Jim Fallon's Mind? A Family Secret That Has Been Murder to Figure Out. *The Wall Street Journal*. November 30.
4. Brunner, H. G., et al. 1993. Abnormal behavior associated with a point mutation in the structural gene for monoamine oxidase A. *Science*. 262(5133): 578–580,
5. McDermott, R., et al. 2009. Monoamine oxidase A gene (MAOA) predicts behavioral aggression following provocation. *Proceedings of the National Academy of Sciences*. 106(7): 2118–2123
6. Glenn, A. L. 2011. The other allele: Exploring the long allele of the serotonin transporter gene as a potential risk factor for psychopathy: A review of the parallels in findings. *Neuroscience and Biobehavioral Reviews*. 35(3): 612–620.
7. Naik. Op. cit.
8. James Fallon. Phone interview September 30, 2013.
9. Bold, K. 2010. Killer instinct. *ZotZine, UCI's Online Magazine*. 11(6): March. http://zotzine.uci.edu/v02/2010_03/fallon.php. Accessed 3/3/2013.
10. Volkow, N. D. and Tancredi, L. 1987. Neural substrates of violent behaviour. A preliminary study with positron emission tomography. *British Journal of Psychiatry*. 151(5): 668–673.
11. Goyer, P. F., et al. 1994. Positron-emission tomography and personality disorders. *Neuropsychopharmacology*. 10(1): 21–28.
12. Raine, A., et al. 1994. Selective reductions in prefrontal glucose metabolism in murderers. *Biological Psychiatry*. 36(6): 365–373.
13. Raine, A., et al. 1997. Brain Abnormalities in Murderers Indicated by Positron Emission Tomography. *Biological Psychiatry*. 42(6): 495–450.
14. U.S. Department of Justice, The Federal Bureau of Investigation. 2011. Uniform Crime Reports. Crime in the United States, 2010. Expanded Homicide Data. http://www.fbi.gov/about-us/cjis/ucr/crime-in-the-u.s/2010/crime-in-the-u.s.-2010/offenses-known-to-law-enforcement/expanded/expandhomicidemain.pdf. Accessed 11/1/2013.

15. Naik, G. Op. cit.
16. Fallon explained: "Although I'm scored always just short of the threshold for psychopathy, I uniformly score very high on factors related to pro sociality, e.g. very high on Fearless/Dominance and medium low on Impulsive/Antisociality. On the Dutton PPI modification, I score low on neuroticism, very high on extraversion, high on openness to experience, low on agreeableness, low on conscientiousness, and very high on persuasiveness. On the Hare Psychopathy Checklist, I score high on Aggressive/Narcissism but low on pathological lying (which is for losers, much more entertaining to addle people with the truth) and low on failure to accept responsibility. I score lower on Socially Deviant Lifestyle, except for scoring high on need for stimulation, poor behavioral controls, impulsivity—and I do have rather grandiose long term goals, but they often work out. Trait 3 I won't comment on . . . One fine point concerning my own behavior—my narcissism trumps other factors. For example I never cheat. I derive much more pleasure from crushing opponents in games—pristinely according to the rules." Email correspondence October 2, 2013. For a criticism of Fallon's claims, see Chamber, C. 2013. Could a brain scan diagnose you as a psychopath? *The Guardian*. November 25. http://www.theguardian.com/science/2013/nov/25/could-a-brain-scan-diagnose-you-as-a-psychopath. Accessed 11/12/2013.
17. Gu, J. and Gu, X. 2003. Induced gene expression in human brain after the split from chimpanzee. *Trends in Genetics*. 19(2): 63–65.
18. Konopka, G., et al. 2012. Human-Specific Transcriptional Networks in the Brain. *Neuron*: 75 (4): 601–617.
19. Sakia, T., et al. 2011. Differential Prefrontal White Matter Development in Chimpanzees and Humans. *Current Biology*. 21(16): 1397–1402.
20. Twomey, S. Phineas Gage: Neuroscience's Most Famous Patient. *Smithsonian* magazine. January 2010.
21. Potter, N. 2010. Inside the Mind of a Killer. *ABC News*. October 27. http://abcnews.go.com/WNT/story?id=130048&page=1
22. Hare, R. D. 1993. *Without Conscience, The Disturbing World of the Psychopaths Among Us*. The Guilford Press, New York. p. 42.
23. Cleckley, H. 1988. *The Mask of Sanity: An Attempt to Clarify Some Issues About the So Called Psychopathic Personality*, 5th edition, Augusta, Georgia: Emily S. Cleckley. p. 262.
24. Porter, S. and Porter, S. 2007. Psychopathy and Violent Crime in Hakkanen-Nyholm, H. and Nyholm, J.-O. (editors) *Psychopathy and the Law*. Chichester, West Sussex, UK: Wiley-Blackwell.
25. Raine, A., et al. 2000. Reduced Prefrontal Gray Matter Volume and Reduced Autonomic Activity in Antisocial Personality Disorder. *Archives of General Psychiatry*. 57(2): 119–127.
26. Haycock, D. A. 2001. Images of violence: What use are psychopaths' brain scans? *BioMedNet News*. April 24.
27. Newman, J. P. and Kosson, D. S. 1986. Passive Avoidance Learning in

Psychopathic and Nonpsychopathic Offenders. *Journal of Abnormal Psychology.* 95(3): 252–256.

28. Hargerty, B. B. 2010. Inside a Psychopath's Brain: The Sentencing Debate. NPR. July 30. http://www.npr.org/templates/story/story.php?storyId=128116806. Accessed 8/19/2012.
29. Harenski, C. L., et al. 2010. Aberrant neural processing of moral violations in criminal psychopaths. *Journal of Abnormal Psychology.* 119(4): 863–874.
30. Kiehl, K. A. and Hoffman, M. A. 2011. The Criminal Psychopath: History, Neuroscience, Treatment, and Economics. *Jurimetrics: The Journal of Law, Science & Technology*: 51(4): 355–397.
31. Lapierre, D., et al. 1995. Ventral frontal deficits in psychopathy: neuropsychological test findings. *Neuropsychologia.* 33(2): 139–151. Erratum in *Neuropsychologia.* 33(8): 1059.
32. Burns, J. M., et al. 2003. Right Orbitofrontal Tumor with Pedophilia Symptom and Constructional Apraxia Sign. *JAMA Neurology.* 60(3): 437–440.
33. Sedaris, D. 1998. David Sedaris talks about his OCD and reads from "Naked." *More Than a Mouthful.* http://www.therichest.org/video/david-sedaris-talks-about-his-ocd-and-reads-from-naked-1998/. Accessed 4/16/2013.
34. Sedaris, D. 1997. "A Plague of Ticks" in *Naked.* New York. Little, Brown and Company. pp. 7–22.
35. Zelkowitz, R. 2008. Why Schizophrenics Smoke. *Science Now.* October 14. http://news.sciencemag.org/2008/10/why-schizophrenics-smoke. Accessed 1/1/2013.
36. Beucke, J. C., et al. 2013. Abnormally High Degree Connectivity of the Orbitofrontal Cortex in Obsessive-Compulsive Disorder. *JAMA Psychiatry*: 70(6): 619–629.
37. James Fallon. Email correspondence October 2, 2013.
38. Houenou, J., et al. 2011. Neuroimaging-based markers of bipolar disorder: Evidence from two meta-analyses. *Journal of Affective Disorders.* 132(3): 344–355.
39. Yang, Y., et al. 2005. Volume reduction in prefrontal gray matter in unsuccessful criminal psychopaths. *Biological Psychiatry.* 15(57): 1103–1108.
40. Raine, A., et al. 2004. Hippocampal Structural Asymmetry in Unsuccessful Psychopaths. *Biological Psychiatry.* 55(2): 185–191.
41. Babiak, P. and Hare, R. D. 2006. *Snakes in Suits: When Psychopaths Go to Work.* New York: HarperCollins.

Chapter Five: Troubling Developments and Genes

1. Carlo, Philip. 2006. *The Ice Man: Confessions of a Mafia Contract Killer.* New York: St. Martin's Press. Front matter. The main source of information in this biography was Kuklinski himself. Some of his claims, such as taking part in the murders of Mafia boss Paul Castellano and Teamster boss Jimmy Hoffa, are highly questionable and unsubstantiated. These and other claims should leave

readers aware they may be reading Kuklinski's attempts to "glorify" himself more than an accurate account of his criminal history.

2. Special to the New York Times. 1970. Jersey City Man Arrested in Death of 12-Year-Old Girl. *The New York Times*. September 16.
3. Carlo. Ibid., p. 134.
4. Associated Press. 1986. Man Charged with Killing Partners in Crime. *Washington Observer-Reporter*. December 18.
5. Martin, D. 2006. Richard Kuklinski, 70, a Killer of Many People and Many Ways, Dies. *The New York Times*. March 9.
6. Monet, G. 2003. *The Iceman and the Psychiatrist*. Home Box Office (HBO) documentary. This documentary is also available in a set called *The Iceman Interviews* produced by HBO which includes two earlier interviews with Kuklinski.
7. Ibid.
8. Hare, R. D. 1993. *Without Conscience, The Disturbing World of the Psychopaths Among Us*. The Guilford Press, New York. p. 56.
9. Monet. Op. cit.
10. Caro. Op. cit., p. 22.
11. Lang, S., et al. 2002. Adult psychopathy and violent behavior in males with early neglect and abuse. *Acta Psychiatrica Scandinavica*. 106(Suppl. 412): 93–100.
12. Weiler, B. L. and Widom, C. S. 1996. Psychopathy and violent behavior in abused and neglected young adults. *Criminal Behavior and Mental Health*. 6(3): 253–257.
13. Lang. Op. cit.
14. Phone interview with Frank Ochberg, M.D. May 30, 2013.
15. Phone interview with Michael Stone, M.D. July 26, 2013.
16. Glenn, A. L., et al. 2011. Evolutionary theory and psychopathy. *Aggression and Violent Behavior*: 16 (5): 371–380.
17. Winerman, L. 2004. A Second Look at Twin Studies. *Monitor on Psychology*. 35(4): 46.
18. Larsson, H., et al. 2006. A Genetic Factor Explains Most of the Variation in the Psychopathic Personality. *Journal of Abnormal Psychology*. 115(2): 221–230.
19. Serretti, A., et al. 2013. Shared genetics among major psychiatric disorders. *The Lancet*. 381(9875): 1339–1341.
20. McGowan, P. O., et al. 2009. Epigenetic regulation of the glucocorticoid receptor in human brain associates with childhood abuse. *Nature Neuroscience*. 12(3): 342–348.
21. Simmons, D. 2008. Epigenetic Influences and Disease. *Nature Education*: 1(1).
22. Riddihough, G. and Zahn, L. M. 2010. What is Epigenetics? *Science*. 330(6004): 611.
23. Raine, A. 2010. Neurodevelopmental marker for limbic maldevelopment in antisocial personality disorder and psychopathy. *The British Journal of Psychiatry*: 197(3): 186–192.

24. Raine, A. 2013. *The Anatomy of Violence, the Biological Roots of Crime.* Pantheon, New York. pp. 121–123.
25. Gao, Y., et al. 2009. The Neurobiology of Psychopathy: A Neurodevelopmental Perspective. *Canadian Journal of Psychiatry.* 54(12): 813–823.
26. Siles, J. and Jernigan, T. L. 2010. The Basics of Brain Development. *Neuropsychological Review.* 20(4): 327–348.
27. Craig, M. C., et al. 2009. Altered connections on the road to psychopathy. *Molecular Psychiatry.* 14(10): 946–953.
28. Motzkin, J. C., et al. 2011. Reduced Prefrontal Connectivity in Psychopathy. *The Journal of Neuroscience.* 31(48): 17348–17357.
29. Sundram F., et al. 2012. White matter microstructural abnormalities in the frontal lobe of adults with antisocial personality disorder. *Cortex.* 48(2): 216–229.
30. Raine, A., et al. 2003. Corpus Callosum Abnormalities in Psychopathic Antisocial Individuals. *Archives of General Psychiatry.* 60(11): 1134–1142.
31. Colak, D., et al. 2013. Regulation of Axon Guidance by Compartmentalized Nonsense-Mediated mRNA Decay. *Cell*: 153(6): 1252–1265.
32. Gil-Sanz, C., et al. 2013. Cells Instruct Neuronal Migration by Coincidence Signaling between Secreted and Contact-Dependent Guidance Cues. *Neuron*: 79(3): 461–477.

Chapter Six: Back Again? Predicting Bad Behavior

1. Schmidt, M. S. and Goldsteine, J. 2012. Even as Violent Crime Falls, Killing of Officers Rises. *The New York Times.* April 9. According to the National Law Enforcement Officers Memorial Fund, 49 officers died from gunshot wounds in 2012, a figure below the ten-year average of 57 compiled between 2001 and 2010.
2. Rose, R. 2003. The Second Coming of Philip K. Dick. *Wired.* December.
3. Critchley, S. Philip K. Dick, Sci-Fi Philosopher, Part 1. *The New York Times.* May 20, 2012.
4. Dick, P. K. 1978. How to Build a Universe That Doesn't Fall Apart Two Days Later *in* Dick, P. K. and Sutin, L. (editors). 1995. *The Shifting Realities of Philip K. Dick, Selected Literary and Philosophical Writing.* New York: Vintage Books.
5. Porter, S., et al. 2009. Crime profiles and conditional release performance of psychopathic and non-psychopathic sexual offenders. *Legal and Criminological Psychology*: 14(1): 109–118.
6. BBC News. 2009. Psychopaths' 'early release con.' February 9. http://news.bbc.co.uk/2/hi/health/7833672.stm. Accessed 3/3/2012.
7. Hare, R. D. 1993. *Without Conscience, The Disturbing World of the Psychopaths Among Us.* The Guilford Press, New York. p. 96.
8. Hemphill, J. F., et al. 1998. Psychopathy and recidivism: A review. *Legal and Criminological Psychology*: 3(1): 139–170.
9. Vitacco, M. J., et al. 2012. Assessment in Hakkanen-Nyholm, H. and Nyholm,

J.-O. (editors). *Psychopathy and the Law*. Chichester, West Sussex, UK: Wiley-Blackwell.

10. Shaw, J. and Porter, S. 2012. Forever a Psychopath? Psychopathy and the Criminal Career Trajectory in Hakkanen-Nyholm, H. and Nyholm, J.-O. (editors). *Psychopathy and the Law*. Chichester, West Sussex, UK: Wiley-Blackwell.
11. BBC News. Op. cit.
12. Hare, R. D. 1994. This Charming Psychopath. *Psychology Today*. January1. http://www.psychologytoday.com/articles/199401/charming-psychopath. Accessed 4/12/2012.
13. Hare. 1993. Op. cit., pp. 58–59.
14. Aharoni, E., et al. 2013. Neuroprediction of Future Rearrest. *Proceedings of the National Academy of Sciences*: 110(15): 6223–6228.
15. The Mind Research Network. 2013. Brain scans might predict future criminal behavior. Press Release March 28.
16. Wood, J. 2013. Brain Scans Could Predict Future Criminal Behavior. PsychCentral. http://psychcentral.com/news/2013/03/31/brain-scans-could-predict-future-criminal-behavior/53207.html. Accessed 7 /24/2013.
17. Seabrook, J. 2008 Suffering Souls, The Search for the Roots of Psychopathy. *The New Yorker*. November 10.
18. The Mind Research Network. Op. cit.
19. The Mind Research Network. Op. cit.
20. Holroyd, C. B. and Coles, M. G. H. 2002. The neural basis of human error processing: Reinforcement learning, dopamine, and the error-related negativity. *Psychological Review*. 109(4): 679–709.
21. Ibid.
22. Glenn, A. L., et al. 2010. No Volumetric Differences in the Anterior Cingulate of Psychopathic Individuals. *Psychiatry Research: Neuroimaging*: 183(2): 140–143.
23. Christopher Patrick phone interview July 1, 2013; Email correspondence July 11 and 17, 2013.
24. Craig Bennett email correspondence September 13, 2013.
25. James Fallon phone interview September 30, 2013.
26. Kluger, J. 2013. The Evil Brain: What Lurks Inside a Killer's Mind. *Time*. May 3.
27. Kravariti, E., et al. 2009. Neurocognitive Endophenotypes for Bipolar Disorder: Evidence from Case-Control, Family and Twin Studies *in* Ritsner, M. S. (editor) *The Handbook of Neuropsychiatric Biomarkers, Endophenotypes and Gene*. Dordrecht Netherlands: Springer Science + Business Media B.V.
28. Button, K. S., et al. 2013. Power failure: why small sample size undermines the reliability of neuroscience. *Nature Reviews Neuroscience*. 14(5): 365–376.
29. Button, K. S. 2013. Unreliable neuroscience? Why power matters. *The Guardian*. April 10.
30. Button, K. S., et al. 2013. Power failure. Op. cit.

31. Editorial. 2013. Announcement: Reducing our irreproducibility. *Nature*. 496(7446): 398.
32. Neurobonkers. 2013. The Neuroscience Power Crisis: What's the fallout? Neurobonkers. http://bigthink.com/neurobonkers/the-neuroscience-power-crisis-whats-the-fallout. Accessed 5/32/2013.
33. Laurance, W. F., et al. 2013. Predicting publication success for biologists. *Bioscience*. 63(10): 817–823.
34. Editorial. Op. cit.
35. Ibid.

Chapter 7: Missing Fear and Empathy

1. Helge Hoff, et al. 2009. Evidence of Deviant Emotional Processing in Psychopathy: A fMRI Case Study. *International Journal of Neuroscience*. 119(6): 857–878.
2. Patrick, C. J., et al. 1994. Emotion in the criminal psychopath: Fear image processing. *Journal of Abnormal Psychology*. 103(3): 523–534.
3. Johns, J. H. and Quay, H. C. 1962. The effect of social reward on verbal conditioning in psychopathic and neurotic military offenders. *Journal of Consulting Psychology*. 26(3): 217–220.
4. Carozza, D. 2008. Identifying Psychopathic Fraudsters, Interview with Dr. Robert D. Hare and Dr. Paul Babiak. *Fraud Magazine*. July/August. http://www.fraud-magazine.com/article.aspx?id=404. Accessed 6/3/2013.
5. Baker, E., et al. 2013. Low Skin Conductance Activity in Infancy Predicts Aggression in Toddlers 2 Years Later. *Psychological Science*. 24(6): 1051–1056.
6. Lahey, B. B., et al. 2008. Temperament and Parenting during the First Year of Life Predict Future Child Conduct Problems. *Journal of Abnormal Child Psychology*. 36(8): 1139–1158.
7. Ryan, K. and Skrapec, C. 2008. "The Macdonald Triad: Predictor of Violence or Urban Myth?" Paper presented at the annual meeting of the American Society of Criminology Annual Meeting, St. Louis Adam's Mark, St. Louis, Missouri Nov 12, 2008.
8. Franklin, K. 2012. Homicidal Triad: Predictor of Violence or Urban Myth? in Witness, A blog about forensic psychology, *Psychology Today*. May 2. http://www.psychologytoday.com/blog/witness/201205/homicidal-triad-predictor-violence-or-urban-myth. Accessed 4/4/2013.
9. Office of the Law Revision Counsel House, U.S. 2006. *United States Code, Volume 18*. Washington, D.C.: Office of the Law Revision Counsel. p. 969.
10. Morton, R. J.(editor). 2005. Serial Murder, Multi-Disciplinary Perspectives for Investigators. Washington, D.C.: U.S. Department of Justice, Federal Bureau of Investigation.
11. Christopher Patrick phone interview July 1, 2013.
12. Park Dietz email correspondence September 30, 2013.
13. Ibid.
14. Michael Stone phone interview July 26, 2013.

15. Mary Ellen O'Toole phone interview July 28, 2013.
16. Menashe, I., et al. 2013. Co-expression profiling of autism genes in the mouse brain. *PLOS Computational Biology*. http://www.ploscompbiol.org/article/info%3Adoi%2F10.1371%2Fjournal.pcbi.1003128.
17. Hiatt, K. D., et al. 2002. Assessment of emotion and language processing in psychopathic offenders: results from a dichotic listening task. *Personality and Individual Differences*. 32(7): 1255–1268
18. Carlo, Philip. 2006. *The Ice Man: Confessions of a Mafia Contract Killer*. St. Martin's Press.
19. Pearce, J. P. 2008. MacLean, 94, Neuroscientist Who Devised 'Triune Brain' Theory, Dies. *The New York Times*. January 10.
20. Charles C. Ouimet. Phone interview May 21, 2013; Email correspondence May 22, 2013.
21. Vilensky, J. A., et al. 1982. The limbic system and human evolution. *Journal of Human Evolution*: 11(6): 447–460.
22. LeDoux, J. 2011. *Our Emotional Brains*. Copernicus Center Lecture, Kraków, Poland. http://www.youtube.com/watch?v=tjhCPhhzBqQ. Accessed 9/6/2013.
23. Greenberger, R. 2008. *The Essential Batman Encyclopedia*. New York: Random House. p. 7.
24. Kelley, D. E. and Turk, C. Attack of the Xenophobes in Listo, M. *Boston Legal* (television series). Los Angeles, CA: 20th Century Fox Television. Air date November 13, 2007.
25. LeDoux, J. 2010. The Amygdala in 5 Minutes. *Big Think*. http://bigthink.com/videos/the-amygdala-in-5-minutes. Accessed 8/2/2013.
26. Rasia-Filho, A. A., et al. 2000. Functional activities of the amygdala: an overview. *Journal of Psychiatry and Neuroscience*. 25(1): 14–23.
27. Smoller, J. 2012. *The Other Side of Normal, How Biology is Providing the Clues to Unlock the Secrets of Normal and Abnormal Behavior*. HarperCollins: New York.
28. Yang, Y., et al. 2009. Localization of deformations within the amygdala in individuals with psychopathy. *Archives of General Psychiatry*. 66(9): 986–994.
29. Blair, R. J. R. 2008. The amygdala and ventromedial prefrontal cortex: functional contributions and dysfunction in psychopathy. *Philosophical Transactions of the Royal Society of London, B, Biological Sciences*. 363(1503): 2557–2565.
30. Kiehl, K. A. 2006. A cognitive neuroscience perspective on psychopathy: Evidence for paralimbic system dysfunction. *Psychiatry Research*. 142(2-3): 107–128.
31. James Fallon. Phone interview September 30, 2013.
32. Anderson, N. E. and Kiehl, K. A. 2011. The psychopath magnetized: insights from brain imaging. *Trends in Cognitive Sciences*. 16(1): 52–60.

Chapter Eight: Successful, Unsuccessful, and Other Types of Psychopaths

1. Jaffe, I. 2011. Violence Surges at Hospital for Mentally Ill Criminals. NPR broadcast. April 08.

2. Strickland, T. 2013. A dozen Atascadero State Hospital employees hurt in attacks by patients. The Tribune. April 1. http://www.sanluisobispo.com/2013/04/01/2452734/a-dozen-atascadero-state-hospital.html#storylink=cpy
3. Jaffe, I. 2011. How Do You Hold Mentally Ill Offenders Accountable? NPR broadcast. December 21, http://www.npr.org/2011/12/21/143859695/how-do-you-hold-mentally-ill-offenders-accountable
4. Murphy, C. and Vess, J. 2003. Subtypes of Psychopathy: Proposed Differences between Narcissistic, Borderline, Sadistic, and Antisocial Psychopaths. Psychiatric Quarterly: 74 (1): 11–29.
5. Karpman, B. 1941. On the Need for Separating Psychopathy into Two Distinct Subtypes: The Symptomatic and the Idiopathic. *Journal of Criminology and Psychopathology*. 3: 112–137.
6. Interview with Robert Hare. June 7, 2013, Washington, D.C.
7. Barbenel, J. 1981. Silvano Arieti, Psychoanalyst and Writer on Schizophrenia. *The New York Times*. August 10.
8. Arieti, S. 1963. Psychopathic personality: Some views on its psychopathology and psychodynamics. *Comprehensive Psychiatry*. 4(5): 301–312.
9. Skeem, J., et al. 2007. Two subtypes of psychopathic violent offenders that parallel primary and secondary variants. *Journal of Abnormal Psychology*. 116(2): 395–409.
10. Dutton, K. 2012. *The Wisdom of Psychopaths: What Saints, Spies and Serial Killers Can Teach Us About Success*. New York: Farrar, Straus and Giroux.
11. Babiak, P. and Hare, R. D. 2006. *Snakes in Suits: When Psychopaths Go to Work*. New York: HarperBusiness.
12. Mathieu, C., et al. 2013. Corporate psychopathy and leadership. Presentation at the 5th Biennial Meeting of the Society for the Scientific Study of Psychopathy. June 6.
13. Babiak, P., et al. 2010. Corporate psychopathy: Talking the walk. *Behavioral Sciences and the Law*. 28(2): 174–193.
14. See Editor's Note. 2012. 1 In 10 Wall Street Employees Is A Psychopath, Claim Is Disputed [UPDATE]. The Huffington Post. April 23. http://www.huffingtonpost.com/2012/02/28/wall-street-psychopaths_n_1307168.html. Accessed 10/3/2013.
15. Grohol, J. M. 2012. Untrue: 1 out of Every 10 Wall Street Employees is a Psychopath. PsychCentral. http://psychcentral.com/blog/archives/2012/03/06/untrue-1-out-of-every-10-wall-street-employees-is-a-psychopath/. March 12. Accessed 3/23/2013.
16. Cangemi, J. P. & Pfohl, W. 2009. Sociopaths in high places. *Organizational Development Journal*. 27(2): 85–96.
17. Glenn, A. L., et al. 2011. Evolutionary Theory and Psychopathy. *Aggression and Violent Behavior*. 16: 371–380.
18. Babiak and Hare. Op. cit.

19. Gregory, S., et al. 2012. The Antisocial Brain: Psychopathy Matters, A Structural MRI Investigation of Antisocial Male Violent Offenders. *Archives of General Psychiatry*: 69(9): 962–972.
20. Gao, Y. and Raine, A. 2010. Successful and unsuccessful psychopaths: A neurobiological model. *Behavioral Sciences & the Law*: 28(2): 194–210. *Psychiatric Quarterly*: 74(1):
21. Sifferd, K. L. and Hirstein, W. 2013. On the Criminal Culpability of Successful and Unsuccessful Psychopaths. *Neuroethics*: 6(1): 129–140.
22. Raine, A., et al. 2004. Hippocampal Structural Asymmetry in Unsuccessful Psychopaths. *Biological Psychiatry*. 55(2): 185–191.
23. Watts, G. 2009. Henry Gustav Molaison, "HM." *The Lancet*. 373(9662): 456.
24. Gao and Raine. Op. cit.

Chapter Nine: Could You Become a Psychopath?

1. Koenigs, M., et al. 2007. Damage to the prefrontal cortex increases utilitarian moral judgments. *Nature*: 446(7138): 908–911. The scenarios in this chapter are adapted from supplementary material published with this paper. They are not identical to scenarios presented to the patients.
2. These classic problems in moral philosophy are the subject of two books: Edmonds, D. 2013. *Would You Kill the Fat Man?* Princeton, New Jersey: Princeton University Press and Cathcart, T. 2013. *The Trolley Problem: Or, Would You Throw the Fat Guy Off the Bridge?* New York: Workman Publishing.
3. Masterman, J. C. 1972. *Double-Cross System: The Incredible Story of How Nazi Spies Were Turned Into Double Agents*. New Haven: Yale University Press.
4. Carey, B. 2007. Brain Injury Said to Affect Moral Choices. *The New York Times*. March 22.
5. Ibid.
6. Marazziti, D., et al. 2013. The neurobiology of moral sense: facts or hypotheses? *Annals of General Psychiatry*: 12(6): Published online March 6.
7. Ibid.
8. Ibid.
9. Blumer, D. and Benson, D. F. 1975. Personality changes with frontal and temporal lobe lesions in Blumer, D. and Benson, D. F. (editors) *Psychiatric aspects of neurologic disease*, Vol 1. New York: Grune and Stratton. pp. 151–170.
10. Eslinger P. J. and Damasio A. R. 1985. Severe disturbance of higher cognition after bilateral frontal lobe ablation: patient EVR. *Neurology*. 35(12): 1731–1741.
11. Koenigs, M. and Tranel, D. 2006. Pseudopsychopathy: A perspective from cognitive neuroscience *in* Zald, D. and Rauch, S. (editors) *The Orbitofrontal Cortex*. New York: Oxford University Press, USA.
12. Damasio, A. R., et al. 1990. Individuals with sociopathic behavior caused by frontal damage fail to respond autonomically to social stimuli. *Behavioural Brain Research*. 41(2): 81–94.

13. Grafman, J., et al. 1996. Frontal lobe injuries, violence, and aggression: a report of the Vietnam Head Injury Study. *Neurology*. 46(5): 1231–1238.
14. Anderson, S. W., et al. 2000. Long-term sequelae of prefrontal cortex damage acquired in early childhood. *Developmental Neuropsychology*. 18(3): 281–296.
15. Blumer, D. and Benson, D. F. 2002. Pseudopsychopathy *in* Glicksohn, J. (editor) *The Neurobiology of Criminal Behavior*. Dordrech, The Netherlands: Kluwer Academic Publishers Group. pp. 158–159.
16. Details of Phineas Cage and his accident are based on the research of Malcolm Macmillan. See endnotes 9 and 11 to this chapter, on page 237. For more detailed information about this case see The Phineas Gage Information Page maintained by The University of Akron http://www.uakron.edu/gage/.
17. Fleishchman, J. 2002. *Phineas Gage, A Gruesome but True Story About Brain Science*. Boston: Houghton Mifflin Company.
18. Macmillan, M. 2002. *An Odd Kind of Fame: Stories of Phineas Gage*. Cambridge: MIT Press. p. 26.
19. Macmillan, M. 1996. Phineas Gage: A Case For All Reasons *in* Code, C., et al. (editors) *Classic Cases in Neuropsychology*. New York: Psychology Press. p. 225.
20. Ibid.
21. Harlow, J. M. 1868. Recovery from the passage of an iron bar through the head. *Publications of the Massachusetts Medical Society*. 2: 327–347.
22. Blair, R. J. R. and Cipolotti, L. 2000. Impaired social response reversal. A case of 'acquired sociopathy.' *Brain*. 123(Part 6): 1122–1141.
23. Devinsky, O., et al. 1995. Contributions of anterior cingulate cortex to behaviour. *Brain*. 118(Part 1): 279–306.
24. Glenn, A. L., et al. 2011. Evolutionary theory and psychopathy. *Aggression and Violent Behavior*: 16 (5): 371–380.

Chapter Ten: Could Your Child Be a Budding Psychopath?

1. The description of Rav is derived from the account in Lombroso-Ferrero, G. 1911. *Criminal Man According to the Classification of Cesare Lombroso*. New York: G. P. Putnam's Sons. p. 55.
2. Background information about life in Italy during the late 19th century is derived from Rapczynski, J. 1999. The Italian Immigrant Experience in America (1870-1920) in *Immigration and American Life*. Yale University: Yale-New Haven Teachers Institute, http://www.yale.edu/ynhti/ (Accessed 8/14/2013).
3. Lombroso-Ferrero, G. Op. cit., p. 54.
4. Ibid.
5. Glenn, A. L, et al. 2007. Early temperamental and psychophysiological precursors of adult psychopathic personality. *Journal of Abnormal Psychology*. 116: 508–518.
6. Viding, E. 2005. Evidence for substantial genetic risk for psychopathy in 7-year-olds. *Journal of Child Psychology and Psychiatry*. 46(6): 592–597 and Frick,

P. J. and White, F. S. 2008. Research Review: The importance of callous-unemotional traits for developmental models of aggressive and antisocial behavior. *Journal of Child Psychology and Psychiatry*. 49(4): 359–375.

7. Viding, E. 2013. Callous-Unemotional Traits in Children, Researchers Identify Link to Severe and Violent Antisocial Behavior. *Observer*. 26(8). http://www.psychologicalscience.org/index.php/publications/observer/2013/october-13/callous-unemotional-traits-in-children.html. Accessed 10/2/2013.
8. Giedd, J. N., et al. 2009. Anatomical Brain Magnetic Resonance Imaging of Typically Developing Children and Adolescents. *Journal of the American Academy of Child and Adolescent Psychiatry*. 48(5): 465–470.
9. It would be a great help to neuroscience if more people left their brains to a brain bank when they no longer needed them. Hint: Harvard Brain Tissue Resource Center, McLean Hospital, 115 Mill Street, Belmont, MA 02478. Phone: 1-800-BRAIN BANK (1-800-272-4622). Email: BTRC@mclean.harvard.edu
10. Marsh, A. A. 2008. Reduced amygdala response to fearful expressions in children and adolescents with callous-unemotional traits and disruptive behavior disorders. *American Journal of Psychiatry*. 165(6): 712–20.
11. Jones, A. P., et al. 2009. Amygdala hypoactivity to fearful faces in boys with conduct problems and callous-unemotional traits. *American Journal of Psychiatry*. 166(1): 95–102.
12. De Brito, S. A., et al. 2009. Size matters: increased grey matter in boys with conduct problems and callous-unemotional traits. *Brain*. 132(4): 843–852.
13. Haederle, M. 2010. A Mind of Crime. How brain-scanning technology is redefining criminal culpability. *Miller-McCune*. February 23.
14. Caldwell, M., et al. 2006. Treatment Response of Adolescent Offenders with Psychopathy. *Criminal Justice and Behavior*. 33(5): 571–596.
15. Kahn, J. 2012. Can You Call a 9-Year-Old a Psychopath? *The New York Times Magazine*. May 11.
16. Meffert, H., et al. Reduced spontaneous but relatively normal deliberate vicarious representations in psychopathy. *Brain*: 136(8): 2550–2562.
17. Doole, K. Brain research shows psychopathic criminals do not lack empathy, but fail to use it automatically. Press release by Oxford University Press. July 24, 2013.
18. Feynman, R., et al. 1964. *The Feynman Lectures on Physics, Vol. 1: Mainly Mechanics, Radiation, and Heat*. Reading, Massachusetts: Addison-Wesley Publishing Group. p. 7–2.

Chapter Eleven: Why Do We Have to Deal with These People? Explaining Criminal Psychopaths to Juries and Darwinists

1. Marean, C. W. 2010. When the Sea Saved Humanity. *Scientific American*. July 21.
2. Kessler, R. C., et al. 2005. Prevalence, severity, and comorbidity of twelve-month DSM-IV disorders in the National Comorbidity Survey Replication (NCS-R). *Archives of General Psychiatry*. 62(6): 617–627.

3. Ward, T. and Durrant, R. 2011. Evolutionary behavioural science and crime: Aetiological and intervention implications. *Illegal and Criminal Psychology*. 16(2): 193–210.
4. Glenn, A. L., et al. 2011. Evolutionary theory and psychopathy. *Aggression and Violent Behavior.* 16 (5): 371–380.
5. Buss, D. M. 2009. How can evolutionary psychology successfully explain personality and individual differences? *Perspectives on Psychological Science*. 4(4): 359–366.
6. Murphy, D. and Stich, S. 2000. Darwin in the Madhouse: Evolutionary Psychology and the Classification of Mental Disorders *in* Carruthers, P. and Chamberlain, A. (editors) *Evolution and the Human Mind: Modularity, Language and Meta-Cognition*.
7. Glenn, A. R., et al. Op. cit.
8. Ibid. (Also see Buss, D. M. Op. cit.)
9. Crawford, A. The Pros to Being a Psychopath. *Smithsonian*. October 29, 2012.
10. Dutton, K. 2012. *The Wisdom of Psychopaths: What Saints, Spies and Serial Killers Can Teach Us About Success*. New York: Farrar, Straus and Giroux.
11. Abbott, A. 2007. Scanning Psychopaths. *Nature*: 450: 942–944.
12. Karpman, B. 1948. The Myth of the Psychopath. *American Journal of Psychiatry*. 104(9): 523–534.
13. Hiatt, K. D., et al. 2004. Stroop Tasks Reveal Abnormal Selective Attention Among Psychopathic Offenders. *Neuropsychology*. 18(1): 50–59.
14. Dutton, K. 2012. *The Wisdom of Psychopaths: What Saints, Spies and Serial Killers Can Teach Us About Success*. New York: Farrar, Straus and Giroux. pp. 66–69.
15. Gregory, T. 2009. The Victims, Confronting Dugan Gives Them a Boost. *Chicago Tribune*. November 12. The account of Brian Dugan's crimes and material contained in FBI files relating to them are based on reporting in *Chicago Tribune*, and the *Daily Herald*.
16. Gregory, T. and Barnum, A. 2009. The girl who got away. *Chicago Tribune*. October 22.
17. Rakoczy, M. 2009. The girl who got away: Opal Horton escaped from Brian Dugan, who abducted and killed her friend. *Chicago Tribune (Triblocal Naperville)*. October 22. http://www.triblocal.com/naperville/2009/10/22/the-girl-who-got-away-opal-horton-escaped-from-brian-dugan-who-abducted-and-killed-her-friend/. Accessed 10/3/2013.
18. Barnum, A. 2009. Brian Dugan sentencing hearing: Friend of slain girl Melissa Ackerman tells of 1985 abduction. *Chicago Tribune*. October 22.
19. Gregory, T. and Barnum, A. Op. cit.
20. Gutowski, C. 2007. Inside the FBI files of Brian Dugan. *Daily Herald*. (Arlington Heights, IL). January 7.
21. Gutowski, C. 2007. Op. cit.
22. Daily Herald Staff Report. 2009. Dugan's criminal background. *Daily*

Herald. (Arlington Heights, IL). November 5. http://web.archive.org/web/20100206010412/http://dailyherald.com/story/?id=308729. Accessed 10/20/2013.

23. Gutowski, C. 2009. Strange mind of a killer: Researcher says Dugan rare psychopath. *Daily Herald*. (Arlington Heights, IL). November 6.
24. Gutowski, C. 2007. Op. cit.
25. Barnum, A. 2009. Guilty, 26 years after Jeanine Nicarico vanished from home, Brian Dugan confesses to her rape and murder. *Chicago Tribune*. July 29.
26. Gutowski, C. 2009. Op. cit.
27. Ibid.
28. Haederle, M. 2010. A Mind of Crime. How brain-scanning technology is redefining criminal culpability. *Miller-McCune*. February 23.
29. Gregory, T. 2009. Jeanine Nicarico murder case: Brian Dugan sentencing focuses on psychopathy. *Chicago Tribune*. November 8.
30. Ibid.
31. Ibid.
32. Sukel, K. 2011. Will Neuroscience Challenge the Legal Concept of Criminal Responsibility? The Dana Foundation. file:///C:/Users/Owner/Documents/Psychopathy/Will%20Neuroscience%20Challenge%20the%20Legal%20Concept%20of%20Criminal%20Responsibility%20%20-%20Dana%20Foundation.htm. Accessed 8/3/2013.
33. Interview with Robert Hare. June 7, 2013, Washington, D.C.
34. Yurkiewicz, I. 2010. "My Brain Made Me Do It:" Can Neuroimaging Undermine the Case for Criminal Punishment? *PBJ, Pen Bioethics Journal*. 6(2): 14–15.
35. Comments made during discussion of *Controversial Issues in Psychopathy Research* at the 5Th Biannual Meeting of the Society for the Scientific Study of Psychopathy, June 6, 2013.
36. Ibid.
37. Sukel, K. Op. cit.
38. Haederle, M. Op. cit.
39. Carey, B. 2012. Study of Judges Finds Evidence From Brain Scans Led to Lighter Sentences. *International New York Times*. August 16.
40. Aspinwall, L. G., et al. 2012. The Double-Edged Sword: Does Biomechanism Increase or Decrease Judges' Sentencing of Psychopaths? *Science*. 337(6096): 846–849.
41. Carey, B. Op. cit.

Epilogue: A Little "Big Science"

1. NIH, Estimates of Funding for Various Research, Condition, and Disease Categories (RCDC) http://report.nih.gov/categorical_spending.aspx. Accessed 10/23/2013.
2. Neumann, C. S. 2012. Will the Real Psychopath Please Stand Up? University

of North Texas Research Profiles. http://research.unt.edu/research-profiles/will-real-psychopath-please-stand. Accessed 11/21/2013.

3. Kiehl, K. A. and Buckholtz, J. W. 2010. Inside the Mind of a Psychopath. *Scientific American Mind.* September/October. p. 24.
4. Abbott, A. 2013. Neuroscience: Solving the brain. *Nature.* 499(7458): 272.
5. Macilwain, M. 2013. Biology Boom Goes Bust. *Cell.* 154(1): 16–19.
6. Skeem, J. L., et al. 2011. Psychopathic Personality: Bridging the Gap Between Scientific Evidence and Public Policy. *Psychological Science in the Public Interest*: 12(3): 95–162.

Figure Credits

Figure 1. Left: Hervey Cleckley: Image Provided Courtesy of the National Library of Medicine. Right: Robert Hare: Photo: Stuart McCall/North Light.

Figure 2. Lombroso-Ferrero, G. 1911. *Criminal Man According to the Classification of Cesare Lombroso*. New York: G. P. Putnam's Sons. p. 57.

Figure 3. Top: © Mcarrel | Dreamstime.com. Reprinted by permission. Bottom: With permission of Paul Wicks, Wikimedia Commons http://en.wikipedia.org/wiki/File:OFC.JPG

Figure 4. Photo courtesy of the Mind Research Network.

Figure 5. Aharoni, E. Neuroprediction of Future Rearrest. *Proceedings of the National Academy of Sciences* (PNAS). Published online before print March 27, 2013, doi: 10.1073/pnas.1219302110. Reprinted with permission of the PNAS

Figure 6. Courtesy of the Laboratory of Neuro Imaging and Martinos Center for Biomedical Imaging, Consortium of the Human Connectome Project. www.humanconnectomeproject.org.

Figure 7. Marazziti, D., et al. 2013. The neurobiology of moral sense: facts or hypotheses? *Annals of General Psychiatry*: 12(6): Published online 2013 March 6.

Figures 8, 9, 10, and 11. Courtesy of Charles C. Ouimet, Ph.D., Professor and Faculty Scholar, Department of Biomedical Sciences, College of Medicine, The Florida State University, Tallahassee, Florida.

Figure 12. Geoff B Hall. Wikimedia Commons. Creative Commons CC0 1.0 Universal Public Domain Dedication

Figure 13. Harenski, C.L., et al. (2010) Aberrant neural processing of moral violations in criminal psychopaths. *Journal of Abnormal Psychology*. 119(4): 863–874. Supplementary Material reprinted with permission of the author and the American Psychological Association.

Figure 14. Federal Bureau of Investigation, FBI Records: The Vault. Columbine High School Part 1 of 4

Acknowledgments

Marie Culver supported this work by providing resources, excellent advice and encouragement long before I had an agent and through the research and writing phases of this project. Charles Ouimet, Ph.D., spent hours preparing photographic illustrations of the human brain for this book. He also shared his expertise repeatedly over the years and commented on the manuscript. He always made time to answer numerous questions despite his heavy work load. Anna Millhauser applied her outstanding editing skills to improve much of the manuscript. Kenneth Hoffman took the time to read the work-in-progress twice and provide insightful comments and useful suggestions which improved the book. He also shared his experiences working with people in the criminal justice system which expanded my understanding of criminal and psychopathic behavior. I am grateful to them all.

Several researchers and experts in the field of psychopathy made time in their schedules to answer my questions, several on more than one occasion. These include Robert Hare, Ph.D., Kent Kiehl, Ph.D., Christopher Patrick, Ph.D., Frank Ochberg, M.D, Craig Bennett Ph.D., Michael Stone, M.D., James Fallon, Ph.D., Dr. Park Dietz and Mary Ellen O'Toole Ph.D. Dr. Fallon also offered to share his anatomical expertise. Nathan Arbuckle, Ph.D and Matthew S. Shane, Ph.D. shared information about their research. Dr. Hare kindly sponsored my application for Affiliate membership in the Society for the Scientific Study of Psychopathy. I alone am responsible for any errors in the text.

My literary agent Carrie Pestritto of the Prospect Agency is invaluable and, like my editor and Associate Publisher at Pegasus Books, Jessica Case, patient, professional, and efficient. The book's interior designer, Maria Fernandez, used her considerable skills to rescue me as deadlines approached, and copyeditor Phil Gaskill detected, corrected, and removed errors no one else saw. I was fortunate to have the help of all these people.

Finally, I appreciate the other researchers who responded to my brief queries. I also urge the few who didn't to devote a little time, at least, to explaining the nature and implications of their work to the public, particularly if they accept government grant money. Having an educated, involved public increases the chances of attaining a more supportive research environment. The negative consequences of having a wide gap between the educated and the uneducated are as dangerous as having a wide economic gap between the haves and have-nots.

Index

About the Author

Dean A. Haycock is a science and medical writer living in New York. He earned a Ph.D. in neurobiology from Brown University and a fellowship from the National Institute of Mental Health to study at The Rockefeller University. The results of his research, conducted in academia and in the pharmaceutical industry, have been published in *Brain Research*, the *Journal of Neurochemistry*, the *Journal of Biological Chemistry*, the *Journal of Medicinal Chemistry*, and the *Journal of Pharmacology and Experimental Therapeutics,* among others.

His books include *The Everything Health Guide to Adult Bipolar Disorder, Third Edition* and *The Everything Health Guide to Schizophrenia*. He also is the co-author of *Avoiding and Dealing with Complications of LASIK and Other Eye Surgeries.*

His reporting and feature articles have appeared in many newspapers and magazines including *WebMD*, *Drug Discovery and Development*, *BioWorld Today*, *BioWorld International*, *The Lancet Neurology*, *The Minneapolis Star-Tribune*, *Current Biology* and the *Annals of Internal Medicine.* In addition, he has contributed articles on a variety of topics to *The Gale Encyclopedia of Science* and *The Gale Encyclopedia of Mental Health.*

Please visit Dean on his website and Twitter at: www.DeanAHaycock.com; @Dean_A_Haycock